Praise for *That Sucked. Now What?*

"A moving read about finding the magic in messy moments and taking charge of your life."

— **Regena Thomashauer**, *New York Times* best-selling author of *Pussy* and founder of the School of Womanly Arts

"If you're someone who feels that life just isn't going your way, read this book. Dr. Neeta lays out actionable tools for overcoming obstacles and building your resiliency so you can get that extra push toward your dream."

— **Vishen Lakhiani**, *New York Times* best-selling author of *The Buddha & the Badass*

"In this moving read, Dr. Neeta combines her personal experience and lessons from helping thousands of others. She offers a well-rounded perspective on overcoming grief, loss, and hardships that's sensitive to the human experience while encouraging you to find your strength and the magic in the mess."

— **Melissa Ambrosini**, best-selling author and host of *The Melissa Ambrosini Show*

"I met Neeta once and my life changed forever. The next best thing to her being in your orbit is this book."

— **Codie Sanchez**, serial investor and entrepreneur and founder of Contrarian Thinking

"A powerful handbook for anyone rebuilding themselves after life-altering moments to fly forward."

— **Jim Kwik**, *New York Times* best-selling author of *Limitless*

"That Sucked. Now What? *is a must for anyone who feels like the world has knocked them down or derailed plans: a simple approach to create an action plan for dusting yourself off and reframing the story you're telling yourself."*

— **Lisa Nichols**, *New York Times* best-selling author of *No Matter What!* and founder of Motivating the Masses, Inc.

"If you're ready to find magic in your mess and reclaim joy during the chaotic 'life happenings' that we all go through, then this is the book for you. Dr. Neeta captures the duality of hard times to fly forward past the moments that sucked."

— **Mark Groves**, founder of Create The Love and
host of *The Mark Groves Podcast*

"In this book, Dr. Neeta offers applicable tools to foster resilience after facing adversity. It is a great read for anyone who wants to learn to move past hardships and failures and come out stronger on the other side."

— **Nawal Mustafa**, cognitive neuroscientist and
mental health expert @TheBrainCoach

"Dr. Neeta shows you how you can take your challenging moments and turn them into inspiration to fly forward."

— **Marisa Peer**, therapist, international best-selling author
of *Tell Yourself a Better Lie*, and founder of
Rapid Transformational Therapy

"Life is unpredictable and having a book like this helps you navigate moments of uncertainty with compassion, strength, and humor. Dr. Neeta has a magical gift of being able to ground and draw lessons from the messy experiences in life. This book feels like the comfort from a dear friend and years of coaching all in one."

— **Sahara Rose**, best-selling author of *Discover Your Dharma*
and host of the *Highest Self Podcast*

"Finally, a book that's clear yet FUN, relatable, and actionable. I can sit back, sift through any page, move past tough human moments with ease and grace."

— **Miki Agrawal**, best-selling author of *Do Cool Sh*t*
and founder of TUSHY and THINX

"Dr. Neeta shows you how your heartbreaks, failures, and disappointments can provide beautiful opportunities for transformation."

— **Selena Soo**, creator of Impacting Millions

"Dr. Neeta delivers an honest and refreshing look at how to take radical responsibility and align with your greatest purpose and power, in the midst of life's greatest challenges (or suckiest moments)."

— **Alyson Charles**, best-selling author of *Animal Power: 100 Animals to Energize Your Life and Awaken Your Soul* and host of *Ceremony Circle* podcast

"Dr. Neeta has an unparalleled ability to offer bite-sized and easily digestible examples of how to overcome any challenge. She shares her own lessons with candid vulnerability so you can be empowered to grab the steering wheel and move through roadblocks with ease and grace. She walks her talk and I would follow her anywhere."

— **Jenna Phillips Ballard**, co-founder of Ascension Leadership Academy and creator of I AM Her Now

"This book will teach anyone who wants to develop an unshakable belief in themselves. You will learn to work within your humanness, not despite it. Living a life with meaning is not without hard work and reflection. Only get the book if you're ready to take your life to the next level."

— **Dr. Gabrielle Lyon, D.O.**, founder of the Institute for Muscle-Centric Medicine

"Dr. Neeta has a gift for reframing the challenges we deal with and providing the kind of perspective that can turn it all around."

— **Quddus**, former MTV host and founder of The Creator Incubator

"This book reminds us that life is not the glossy images we see on social media. Dr. Neeta shows how to normalize and make sense of the sucky moments we all inevitably face, and how to experience joy through it all. That is powerful."

— **Christine Hassler**, best-selling author of *Expectation Hangover* and host of the *Over It & On with It* podcast

"That Sucked. Now What? *is the ultimate human handbook.*
Dr. Neeta Bhushan reminds us that no life is perfect,
but we can bounce back from literally anything and fly forward.
This book reminds us that there is magic in the mess,
along with so many gifts along the way."

— **Kelsey Chittick**, best-selling author of *Second Half*

"This book is a breath of fresh air! It's equal parts empathetic
and action-oriented—an outstanding guide to transform life's
inevitable breakdowns into breakthroughs."

— **Aaron Alexander**, best-selling author of *The Align Method*
and host of the *Align* podcast

"Dr. Neeta is the queen of bounceback and grit, and this book is a
testament to not only what she shares with her clients and community,
but how she truly lives her life. It's such an inspiration to read such a
raw and real book about the ups and downs of life. She captures them
in a way that's equal parts compassionate and action-oriented."

— **Emily Williams**, best-selling author of *I Heart My Life*

"Dr. Neeta empowers anyone who has ever felt like a victim to take
back control of their life. A powerful read."

— **Daniela Woerner**, host of the *Spa Marketing Made Easy* podcast

"Dr. Neeta provides simple tools rooted in your human
experience to help reinvent yourself at any stage of your life,
something that we can all use on our journey."

— **Garrain Jones**, best-selling author of *Change Your Mind,*
Change Your Life, international speaker, and host of
the top-rated *Welcome Home* podcast

"Dr. Neeta is a master of grit and resiliency with grace.
She has created the powerful and honest approach we all
need for taking radical responsibility, when life happens,
to take our power back and move forward."

— **Jessica Caver Lindholm**, founder of ToLivingFree
and best-selling author of *Spiritually Fabulous*

THAT
SUCKED.
now
what?

ALSO BY DR. NEETA BHUSHAN

*Emotional Grit: 8 Steps to Master Your Emotions,
Transform Your Thoughts & Change Your World*

The Book of Coaching

The Business Book of Coaching

THAT SUCKED.
now
what?

How to Embrace the Joy in Chaos
and Find Magic in the Mess

DR. NEETA BHUSHAN

HAY HOUSE, INC.
Carlsbad, California • New York City
London • Sydney • New Delhi

Copyright © 2023 by Neeta Bhushan

Published in the United States by: Hay House, Inc.: www.hayhouse.com®
Published in Australia by: Hay House Australia Pty. Ltd.: www.hayhouse.com.au
Published in the United Kingdom by: Hay House UK, Ltd.: www.hayhouse.co.uk
Published in India by: Hay House Publishers India: www.hayhouse.co.in

Cover design: Ajit Nawalkha and Vinita Kedia • *Interior design:* Lisa Vega
Interior illustrations: Amber Rae, @heyamberrae

Cataloging-in-Publication Data is on file at the Library of Congress

Hardcover ISBN: 978-1-4019-6865-6
E-book ISBN: 978-1-4019-6866-3
Audiobook ISBN: 978-1-4019-6867-0

10 9 8 7 6 5 4 3 2 1
1st edition, January 2023

Printed in the United States of America

For those who may not ever
have the opportunity to share or
express openly, use their voice
to be fully understood, or have
the power to be heard—
this is for you.

Contents

Introduction

When I decided to leave my first marriage for good, I didn't have a go bag.

I felt like I didn't have anything.

In fact, by the last time his fist struck my face, I barely knew who I was.

I had been keeping my shame, my guilt, my horror, my fear, *my life* a secret for so long that I had become blank. I had no idea how much that day—December 31, 2011—would change the course of my life.

In 2012, I filed for a restraining order against my abusive husband. As I walked into the courtroom, I noticed several young women confidently lined up, waiting to plead for protection. When the judge reviewed the paperwork that showed every incident of abuse—the list was so long multiple pages were stapled together—she asked, "Why are you showing me this now? Why did it take you this long?"

I replied, "My father is from India. We don't *get* divorced."

At the time, I felt humiliated. But afterward, I kept thinking about the other women waiting to see the judge. These ladies stood patiently in line, showing no outward shame or guilt about their situations. My situation wasn't unique. I wasn't alone in what I had experienced. Those women had been abused too. And each of them had found the courage, resilience, and strength to show up and defend herself. To claim her worthiness. To rise. To fly.

Inspired by that image, I decided that I needed to focus on healing. Pretty quickly, I realized I was dealing with so much more than the loss of my home and my marriage. I was dealing with a lifetime of losses, trauma, and tragedies.

When I was 10 years old, my mother was diagnosed with breast cancer, but it went into remission. When I was 14, the cancer came back. Two years later, she died, an unthinkable loss for my 16-year-old self.

When I was 17 years old, a senior on the brink of graduating, just one year out from losing my mother, my 15-year-old brother, Djay, collapsed in front of his high school from a severe asthma attack. The homecoming game was coming up, and he'd promised to meet me there. But my kid brother, my bestie, my confidant, would never make it to that game.

After the deaths of his wife and son just a year apart, my father went into a deep depression. It fell to me, the oldest child, to take care of my younger brother, Vinay, who was only 12 years old. I bit back my grief, took on one job, then another, then a third, and life got a little better.

Then my father got a diagnosis: stage 4 lung cancer. He died within 10 months.

By age 19, I was an orphan and a caregiver for my younger brother. I couldn't afford not to bounce back—it was about more than just me. Not knowing what else to do, I buried my losses and my heavy grief in working *hard* for success. Collecting high achievements, accolades, and awards was the only way I could numb the pain, to feel that I belonged somewhere and could do something—the only way to prevent the world from looking at my brother and me in pity, whispering, "There they go again, another tragedy . . ." It became my primary coping mechanism.

Like anyone else in tough circumstances, I did the best I knew how to do at the time. I did what I could to recover, to be resilient. But I desperately craved love, acceptance, that deep sense of being at home that still seemed so far off. Eventually, that pursuit led me to the doorstep of a home and into a marriage that became a prison.

But after that day in court, I had escaped. And once I finally resolved to heal and cracked open the door to my inner self, I saw a woman who had faced down so much, been through so much. I saw a little girl in need of reassurance, and a high schooler who had been saddled with too much grief and responsibility for an adult, let alone a teenager.

Yet I also saw there could still be a way forward—a new path for me. Like the women I'd seen in the courtroom, I could claim my worthiness. I could build on the resilience I'd already cultivated, that I'd spent my whole *life* cultivating, and do more than just bounce back from another life-rending setback.

I could fly forward.

In the years since, I've had a lot of identities and careers. I was a cosmetic dentist with a thriving private practice, but I left that to become an author, a researcher, a wellness nerd, a spiritual seeker, and a leadership coach. Then I became a business consultant and an angel investor, and I ended up where I am today as a serial entrepreneur and the host of a wildly successful podcast, speaking about emotional and mental health to companies, organizations, and everyday humans around the world. I teach others to embrace the imperfect, messy, chaotic, yet magically joyful moments of this human experience.

But I've also been a divorcée, a business partner, a wife, a mom, a sister, a daughter, a friend, a caretaker, a lover, a giver, a healer, a martyr, an overachiever . . . there are a million labels to describe me. And probably to describe you too.

None of us is a blank slate, and pretending we can wipe ourselves clean only leads to frustration. You're here, in this moment, as a human, with a past and a future. You were born at a particular time, come from a particular place and culture, and have worn different labels at different times.

Because you've grown. You've stretched. You've changed. You've expanded. You've evolved. You've reinvented yourself. You've had a glow-up (or two). You've code-switched. You've welcomed friends and lost them. You've lived under different roofs. You've adapted. You've expanded your thinking.

Your concept of resilience should expand too.

When I faced the question of how to heal after my divorce, I was forced to revisit almost every dimension of who I was and how I'd gotten to that place. I challenged myself to break through to yet another level of resilience. I dared to go deep and find what mattered to me. I refused to be a victim. I didn't want to just recover, to bounce back; I wanted to be *audaciously* resilient. To fly to new heights.

Yes, the early years of my life were loaded with more than their fair share of tragedy. But those years also led to a great life initiation, a big awakening, and a complete transformation that, today, seems beyond greater than I could have imagined back then.

I'm writing this book to tell you: life happens to *all of us*.

At times, you may feel like you've been punched so hard that you can't breathe.

I definitely have.

You might feel right now that the wind has been completely wiped from your lungs. When you are finally able to come up for air, you realize that you aren't dreaming. Or maybe you achieved your dreams, got those good things to happen, and then something ripped the rug out from under you, leaving you feeling traumatized all over again.

That's how the worst times of my life felt to me. But I'm not going to tell you it's going to be okay.

Because sometimes, it's totally going to suck.

Awfully, painfully suck.

Suck so hard it may take you out for a while.

It may come in different shapes and sizes, from a huge, world-rocking upset like marital infidelity to a smaller wound like a social snub from a close friend. And it really might *not* be okay. But no matter how things haven't gone to plan, no matter how the suckiness unfolded for you in those moments, your trauma is valid and real and whole. If it threw you for a loop, if it hurt you, if it knocked you on your ass—that doesn't mean you're too sensitive, or too weak, or too anything.

It means you're human.

So if these moments and feelings sound familiar, know this, my friend.

You are not broken.

You are not worthless.

You didn't fail at working hard enough or "wanting it" enough.

You are definitely not fucked up.

You are not those failures you've felt.

You are not those thoughts you think of yourself.

You are *human*.

The stuff in your life isn't perfect, but it was never meant to be.

Your human life is basically just one wild ride after another. Curveball after curveball. Surprises, shocks, and sneak attacks.

Your human life has had some (or many) sucky moments that brought you to this point on your journey.

But here's what I want you to know, truly. Wherever you are now, no matter how gut-punched or sucker-punched or knocked down you might feel at the moment, you can and will fly forward. Because that's the best—and really only—option. For all of us.

As a coach, trainer, and educator, I help people learn to embrace the *human-ness* of their lives. That there's magic in the mess and deep joy amid the wretched chaos. That they can not only make it through the tough times, but come flying out the other side more vibrant, audacious, *resilient* versions of themselves. Through the years, I've seen thousands of people pick themselves up, dust themselves off, and learn to fly forward.

In this book, I'm going to show you how. I'll share some of my clients' stories as well as my own, so you can use our journeys to inspire, shape, and discover yours. And I'll draw on my own experience of how I reflected on who I was, bounced back, and taught myself how to fly.

Today I'm a successful educator, advocate, and serial entrepreneur with leadership roles in multiple businesses. I'm the host of the popular and top-rated podcast *The Brave Table*, where I help you navigate brave moments through the different seasons in your life. I fell in love again and am married to my dream partner, co-pilot, and biggest cheerleader, Ajit Nawalkha (yes, it's true—you can find love again!), and I'm a mama to two wise little teachers, Arien and Aiyla. As the co-founder of Global Grit Institute, I teach entrepreneurs, leaders, and everyday humans how to have less burnout with mental and emotional regulation. I also support leaders and coaches on the Evercoach platform, helping them learn about utilizing our capability for grit, resilience, and emotional mastery. And as a co-founder of Dharma Coaching Institute, I help train more than 1,000 new coaches annually on becoming better versions of themselves, turning their stories into their dharma, and allowing them to transform others as spiritual life coaches.

I'm still learning and growing too—always. I know more sucky things will happen in my life. But I also know I can fly forward no matter what comes my way. And *that* is audacious resilience.

So try this for me: imagine you are capable of bouncing back from anything. Any setback, any stumble, any sucky moment.

What would your life look like?

Maybe you'd make some real progress in your career, ready to be bold, take risks, and handle sticky situations if they arise.

Maybe you'd make peace with your baby-making journey, forgive yourself and take time for you and your partner, loving your body, your vessel, and prioritizing rest and play.

Or you'd be more productive on your passion projects, letting your enthusiasm fuel you and feeling ready to handle any haters coming out of the woodwork.

Maybe you'd have a better relationship with your friends and family, not letting dramas or pettiness knock you off course. Maybe you'd make your needs crystal clear to your partner, or launch yourself back into dating, unafraid to stick to your standards and unfazed by ghosting or rejection.

You'd stop taking things personally and start taking personal responsibility instead. Your inner critic wouldn't hijack your stream of consciousness every other minute to tear you down. You wouldn't pay any mind to bad-faith comments or take every criticism to heart. You'd just brush them all off, keep going, and try again.

Sounds pretty good, right?

That's the *audaciously resilient* version of you. The you that bounces back—and then uses that momentum to fly *forward*.

The audacity of your resilience is when you step into the sucky moments with grit and grace and embrace the magic in between.

THE BOUNCE FACTOR

Now, the concept of *resilience* pops up a lot these days, but like most terms around personal growth, the more it gets repeated, the fuzzier the definition seems to get. I like to think of it as the ability to bounce back—and the reason I like to think that is because that's literally what it means. No joke.

Resilience comes from the Latin word *resilire*, "to jump back," and in its most scientific sense, it refers to the capacity for a material to recover from physical stress or strain—think of a rubber band that snaps back into place after stretching. Put another way, resilience is a measure of how much energy something can absorb without deforming and losing its fundamental shape. So when I talk about resilience as bouncing back, it's not just a cute metaphor; it's based on the actual definition of the word.

As a coach, educator, and trainer, I tend to come into people's lives right when they're facing setbacks—kind of goes with the job description. And what I've seen over and over again is that some people come out of nearly every experience—including challenges, failures, and disappointments—energized. They bounce back, in other words. But others stay stuck and can't move past the situation. They end up defeated. They don't want my guidance in tackling the situation at hand; they want a pity party, a participation trophy, or plain old revenge.

Naturally, I was curious about what was at work here. So over years of coaching people, and through in-depth research, I looked into two questions: What affects our innate ability to bounce back from setbacks? How can we achieve long-lasting positive change in our lives after we recover from setbacks?

It's true that some people bounce back more consistently than others. Research has shown that certain people do indeed have more of that natural tendency to be resilient, even as babies, and epigenetic studies point to the long-ranging effects of trauma across generations of a family. But knowing that resilience varies from person to person isn't enough for us to *do* anything about it, to know what to think or say or do when we face those sucky moments. A generic list of "what resilient people do" in the abstract isn't much help if you don't understand your *own* level of resilience. And defining resilience along a scale requires us to envision some imaginary ideal that somehow applies and appeals to everyone in the world, no matter our upbringing, personality, class, race, religion, or all of the small but influential pieces of our identity and history that make us who we are.

Looking over my clients' experiences and the body of scientific literature, it became clear to me that the idea of resilience as a matter of willpower—the standard pull-yourself-up-by-your-bootstraps mentality—is incredibly flawed.

Being a research nerd at heart (stemming from my college days as a psych major), reflecting on my own firsthand experiences of learning to integrate and heal from my own losses, and drawing on stories from my own clients, I started to map out what the individual capacity for resilience might look like. I concluded that each person's resilience, like their identity, is multidimensional. I saw that things like an individual's upbringing or their current environment could affect how they reacted to a setback as much as their emotional capacity and their self-awareness. These four components were dynamic and interrelated, and eventually, I shaped them into a single concept I call the *Bounce Factor*.

The Bounce Factor is that measure of innate resilience in each of us. It influences how easily we rebound from a given circumstance. And the more I dug into this idea, the more I saw that understanding the four components of the Bounce Factor—how they shape your mindset, condition your behavior, and influence your take on the world—could give anyone a multifaceted, holistic view of themselves and their resilience.

This is what makes the Bounce Factor different. It's personal, but it's nonjudgmental. It's not an assessment of your worth, or even your capability, nor is it a one-size-fits-all prescription to strive for a uniform standard of "good" behavior. It's a tool to explore your subconscious self and how you're subject to both internal and external influences. In my work as an educator, trainer, and coach; in my life as a perpetual, ever-evolving, work-in-progress person; and in my day-to-day as a mom raising two kids to be their best selves, I've seen firsthand that our stories, circumstances, and identities matter—and *not* in the ways people tend to assume.

Of course, just knowing your Bounce Factor doesn't mean you're not *literally* going to bounce back like a Super Ball. You're human, not rubber, after all. But you are going to absorb the energy of the thing that's just slammed into you. And then you're going to channel that momentum to *move*. To bounce back to where you were.

And bouncing back can be just the beginning.

THE FLY FORWARD FRAMEWORK

With the Bounce Factor crystallized, I turned to my second question: How we can achieve long-lasting positive change? What's happening when you don't just use the momentum of a challenge to return to your starting point, rather use it to generate your *own* forward motion? How do you progress even further than you were before the setback?

After writing my last book, *Emotional Grit: 8 Steps to Master Your Emotions, Transform Your Thoughts & Change Your World,* I realized that there's only so much change we can create while looking at the past. Though past struggles and experiences give us strength and resilience, I truly believe we need to be looking—and navigating—forward in order to fly. And, over the past few years of learning and expanding, I'd been sensing an emerging commonality—that people were following roughly the same path to personal and professional transformation.

So I looked at the data I had. I rewatched recordings of coaching sessions, read testimonials from clients whose lives had been transformed, and started to home in on the root of what I was observing. I began to identify the phases people seemed to experience and move through whenever there was a challenge or difficult situation to overcome, as well as the breakthroughs they achieved in our coaching work. Soon, I could see that those level-up moments fell into five stages: Falling, Igniting, Rising, Magnifying, and Thriving. Taken together, they make up a framework I call *Fly Forward*.

To be super simple, **Falling** is what we're all afraid of. Falling is sometimes terrifying. And, as you'll realize by reading the pages in this book, falling is inevitable. It's absolutely human! You will experience this "stage" over and over again. In anything you start for the first time. Whenever anything that you planned for doesn't happen, or if it does but not in the way you hoped! I can say with absolute certainty that falling is part of your journey.

But here's the thing: once you open yourself to accepting whatever change is brought on by the fall, you open yourself to an exponential amount of possibilities. It becomes your initiation. An awakening into your portal of your next level. Game on! For me, one major fall was when I finally woke up to the reality that my ex-husband was not going to stop being abusive toward me. My choice was to reclaim my power by getting out or stay walking on eggshells around the violence until maybe the worst ended up happening. I want to be clear: at first during a fall you often feel like a victim. You might feel helpless, ashamed, despondent, depressed. You might feel like the universe is against you or that life is happening only to you. All of that is normal. Falling sucks big time. But when you decide to accept what has happened as the reality, that can trigger the next stage.

When you're **Igniting** a desire to change, you feel motivated to do something about your present circumstances almost immediately. You're sparked, initiated for your calling, and ready for battle, knowing you can come out transformed. I like to equate this second stage to lighting a fire inside of you. Where there were ashes of negativity are now embers of positive change, and in this stage you start to spark those embers into a strong, glowing, and consistent fire. For me, my ignition took place in that courtroom when I saw the line of fellow women who had also been abused. I knew at that moment that I wasn't alone and that I desperately wanted something different, and I knew what I absolutely couldn't stand for any longer. For me, the change I desired was simply to feel physically and emotionally safe.

When you begin to stoke your inner fire, you move into the third stage, which I call **Rising**. This is where you start writing a new story on your own terms. In my life, this is where I stopped blaming myself for ending up in a relationship and marriage that was awful and traumatic. I started reclaiming my power by choosing what I wanted to believe about myself and the world. I started diving deeper and deeper into the open and painful wounds of my losses, healing the little Neeta in myself who had to grow up too early. I started crafting a vision of who I wanted to become, and got the support in books, courses, workshops, healers, and therapies to attain it. Rising up to a new version of myself was a magical consequence, and when I coach people who are in this stage there's a newfound confidence, a time of yes to exploring opportunities of growth and healing, a sense of security in oneself, and a feeling of ease that comes along with it. That's how I know a client is rising.

As you unlearn the lessons of the past that no longer serve you in this new reality and learn new ways to move forward, you start **Magnifying** and learn how to own your power. At this stage, you realize that it's safe to let go of the past and to forgive both yourself and other people. For me, I had to forgive my ex-husband, take personal responsibility for my part in romantic relationships, and heal. For others that I've coached, the forgiveness is toward parents, themselves, caretakers, childhood bullies, teachers, and even bad bosses.

In turn, that desire for change, unshackling from the past, and capacity for self-love come together to help you create a life in which you are **Thriving**. In my life, I knew this was happening when I didn't think twice about selling my successful and financially stable cosmetic dentistry practice—and all the status and money that came with it. For others, it's the moment you feel grateful for not getting the job, not marrying the guy, or for "failing" at some aspect of your life that wasn't meant for you. In this stage, magic starts happening—like meeting someone new by chance at a coffee shop, or finding a community that you wouldn't have sought out if everything went perfectly or as expected. Or it could be as simple as feeling okay being alone. Once you are through the Magnifying stage and Thriving, you know yourself better, celebrate you, and radically accept where you are as where you are supposed to be. You're in a wholly new space that is finally freeing, fulfilling, and full of pure joy.

These two key concepts—the Bounce Factor and the Fly Forward framework—are intended to help you move forward when you inevitably encounter a challenge. They'll teach you how to bounce back faster and with more grace, resilience, and grit.

This isn't always easy, but it *is* possible. Trust me; I know because I've been through it myself.

And I'm not going to sugarcoat the truth. Because—real talk, queens—life can be hard, painful, messy, and chaotic. That's what it is to be human. Pain is an integral part of our experience here. No one is exempt; no one is immune.

Yet life can also be wondrous, mysterious, beautiful, and joyous—at the *exact same time* as that mess and chaos.

You're human to break down in tears when life knocks the wind out of you, and you're just as human to find joy in the aftermath. Or even in the middle of the suck.

With this book, you'll have more tools in your toolbox to use when times get inevitably sucky, softening the blow with just a bit more compassion for yourself, and for others. My hope is that this isn't a book you read once, do the work, and then pass it on. This book is a lifer. You can pull it off your shelf every time you need to overcome a sucky human moment, a challenge, or a juicy setback—because those will come, again and again. It's totally and completely intentional that the Fly Forward framework is designed to be used over and over again. It can help you deal with what's going on right now and what will inevitably happen in the future.

In Part I, we'll take a close look at what I call the Magical Moment of Suck. We'll see how we humans tend to respond to sucky moments, and why our instinctive reactions sometimes get in the way of our resilience. We'll also lay the groundwork for some ideas that will pop up throughout the book. In Part II, we'll get to know your Bounce Factor. You'll a deeper, more nuanced understanding of your typical reactions to stress, setbacks, and challenges that will illuminate the patterns you've struggled with for years. And in Part III, we'll jump into the Fly Forward framework, and see how you can shift your perspective and take action to change your situation, your emotions, and ultimately your entire reality. When you apply the Fly Forward framework to your life, as thousands of my students and clients have, you will not only be able to relate and respond more productively to any circumstance, but also make peace with what has happened in your life and be able to create tangible action steps to move forward.

Because I know from personal experience that when we go inward, we can find or reignite our purpose, our dharma, our ultimate truth. When we are able to release our judgments and surrender to the chaos and messiness of life, we are on the journey to healing. And when you realize that life is actually happening *for* you, not *to* you, you can do more than simply bounce back.

You can look around, exhale hard, and say, "Well, that sucked."
You can stand firm, breathe in, and ask, "Now what?"
And then you can fly forward.

PART I

THE MAGICAL MOMENT OF SUCK

It's so important that you must not look at failure as a bad thing. That's where all of the beauty and magic happens. If I was afraid of what people would think of me, I would still be an English teacher.

— JAMEELA JAMIL

welcome to the
magical moment of
suck

Sometimes you just have to put on lip gloss
and pretend to be psyched.
— MINDY KALING

Ah, crap. It happened. That thing you least expected.
Had zero idea was coming.
Was never, *ever* the plan.
But it still happened.
You worked so freakin' hard. Gave it your all. Felt that twinge of burnout. The best was finally coming though. You didn't even realize your tank was empty. Yet you still kept going. Then, out of nowhere, the thing you had been working on for months, years even, just started crumbling. Slapped you right in the face.
Was it something you said?
Something you did?
Because it did *not* feel like it was in your control.
You studied hard for that test.
You paid your dues and worked late nights and weekends.
You made sure every last detail of that wedding was going to plan.
Yet it didn't go to plan.
You failed that test.
You didn't get the promised promotion.
The IVF didn't take, *again*.
You broke up with your partner.
So now what? How do you even begin to bounce back?
We all know resilience is possible. We've all seen and heard stories of people coming back from setbacks big and small. The sucky moments strike, and they dust themselves off and keep going. So

why aren't we all resilient, all the time? Why aren't we as adaptable and strong and Teflon-tough as we want to be in every situation?

Maybe your resilience shows up inconsistently, or only in low-stakes situations: a friend ghosting you for a lunch date is no big deal, but a flubbed job interview *really* hurts. Or maybe it's vice versa: you can handle the big letdowns—the scary diagnoses, the life-shattering phone calls, the plans that didn't go to plan at all—with a cool head and a can-do attitude, but a small setback can send you spiraling, and you have no idea why. What's holding us back from the audacious resilience we know is possible and see in others?

The answer is found in those magical moments of suck. In this first section, I want us to explore just what is at work within us when we experience bad things. We're going to go under the hood of our human nature and understand the inner workings of our reactions with curiosity and *without* judgment. This means you'll likely be challenging some concepts that you've learned about what it means to be resilient, mentally strong, or persistent. You're going to reframe your understanding of what it means to persevere and, in doing so, gain greater empathy for yourself *and* for others. You'll see why your less-than-resilient feelings and actions in the aftermath of a big upset aren't personal failures or character flaws; they're human nature at work. And once you embrace that, you'll be ready to work *with* your human self to fly forward instead of fighting to repress it and staying stuck in the suck.

To be clear, whatever happened to you, I'm not saying it wasn't awful. That failed test, missed opportunity, embarrassing ordeal? That complete misjudgment, broken engagement, huge loss? It sucked. It was wretched. It was awful. It was definitely *not* to plan.

But at the same time . . . when has anything *ever* gone to plan in life?

Personally, I know what it's like to plan and fail. Sometimes I feel like I've been doing it my whole life—in spectacular fashion. I bombed both college exams—the ACT and the SAT—not once but twice. Truth be told, I was not the best test taker, but I thought I could plan around that. Put in the extra work. Yet even after the Princeton Review® program, my score barely went up. But hey, at least my 3.8 GPA, extracurriculars, and my essay about both my mom *and* my brother dying during the time I was supposed to study would make up for the lousy score, right? Isn't life supposed to be fair that way?

Not exactly. In fact, not even close. Hard shit happens. And teenage Neeta wasn't actually looking for any awards for the hard shit she was going through (but if they did give those out, I'd have the equivalent of an EGOT). And grown-up Neeta isn't sharing this to brag about loss or play in the trauma Olympics. My point is simply that even though I was seasoned at tragedy early in my life, I'm still not immune to sucky moments or their effects. (Those bombed standardized tests? Just the beginning.)

So let me say it again: Things will not go to plan. Bad things happen in every human life, no matter how well you prepare yourself. You know this in your head, and you probably feel it in your heart. Because you've been there. You've lost out, screwed up, flunked, flaked, and fallen on your face. You've dropped the ball and missed the mark. You've had your hopes dashed and maybe had your heart broken. I don't need to know the specifics of your life to feel confident in saying this, because *you are human.* These are human experiences.

As a recovering perfectionist, understanding this was life changing for me. And I know it will be for you too.

So back to the resilience question. When those inevitable sucky moments arise, why do we so often find ourselves *stuck* in them? We're miserable and can't do anything but wallow. Then we start to beat ourselves up for "crying over spilled milk" or "being a drama queen" or "whining." We remind ourselves that people out there in the world have survived much worse than this: unspeakable loss, crushing disasters, violence, and cruelty. So what's *our* problem, right?

This gets at a pretty common misunderstanding of resilience. It's so easy to disqualify ourselves from "deserving" resilience. We jump to concluding that we're fundamentally flawed because we get upset instead of letting things roll off our back. We decide we're not worthy to pursue resilience on any scale because we get tripped up by "small" moments like these. But the comparison game of "Other people made it through worse, so why can't *I* deal?" is a trap that keeps us stuck in the suck. It speaks to a limited understanding of what resilience actually is.

It's easy to assume resilience is something epic and heroic—about as common in humans as the ability to win a gold medal or do differential calculus—but it isn't. Resilience isn't reserved for people suffering horrific, life-rending trauma. It may be a big-T trauma like death or violence or a little-t trauma like a friendship conflict or a work snafu. But it's still valid AF. It doesn't mean you're somehow below the threshold to qualify for resilience.

I've said it before: it means you're human.

You're absolutely human to experience the depth of those shake-up, knock-down, sometimes embarrassing, fall-on-your-face situations. You're human to feel that harsh ripping away of something you cared about or the longing for something to happen that never comes true. You're human to be mad when you miss the bus and you're human to break down in tears when you lose your job. You're human when you're hurt, stung, and damn disappointed when life doesn't follow your plans.

But you're also human when you tap into resilience. It's not a superpower, and it's not something you need to be "worthy" of. Really, resilience is a pretty everyday quality. It's as human a capacity as the capacity to feel joy, to fall in love, to aspire to greatness. You can rely on it no matter who you are or what you're going through. You can exercise it in small sucky moments and huge ones. You won't run out.

I remember a time I hustled incredibly hard on my very first internship. I was part of this huge and fancy dental office and fresh out of school. I worked days and nights. Always volunteered for weekend duty. Eagerly offered to do the odds and ends like administrative tasks or brainstorming promotions to appeal to a younger market. I thought all that hustle would secure me a full-time job *for sure*. But I never got offered a permanent position.

Ouch. That totally sucked.

Was it the worst thing that had ever happened to me? No. But did it hurt? Yes—doubly so. I was *so* disappointed that I had failed, and I was embarrassed that I couldn't "deal with it" better.

What I could have done, instead of beating myself up, instead of getting stuck in the suck, is feel what I was feeling—without judgment.

When we feel less than resilient in sucky moments, it's not because we're mere mortals and resilience is out of reach for us. Nor is it because of our specific circumstances—since sucky things happen to everyone, everywhere, and there's no "your trauma must be this big to ride" requirement. And it's definitely not because fate has resigned us to suffering. It's because of our *emotions*.

To be truly resilient, we must both feel what we're feeling truly and genuinely, *and* make a decision to act in our best interest moving forward. And that is *hard*. It's *hard* to feel your feelings and not be overtaken by them. It's possible—it's one of the most beautiful things we're capable of doing as humans—but it isn't easy or automatic. Your mind and body are programmed to survive, and survival means conserving energy as much as possible. Tapping into your resilience can take some real effort and energy—at first, anyway. So, instead, our human nature leads us to either give into the feelings of overwhelm until we're too paralyzed to act, or to squash our feelings down to nothing and take action that doesn't speak to where we really are.

In the following chapters, we'll explore exactly what this looks like. We'll see that when we resist resilience, we're actually being completely rational *and* not acting in our ultimate best interest.

Sounds impossible, right? Well, welcome to the first of many paradoxes. Embracing the duality of our experiences and the full spectrum of our emotions is a core theme of my work—and this book—and the sooner you can teach yourself to see the coexistence of opposites in your own experience, the sooner you'll be flying forward.

Speaking of paradoxes, before we dive into our reflexive barriers to resilience, I want to go back to that magical moment of suck. I'm sure you read that phrase and thought, "What is Neeta talking about? What could possibly be magical about getting fired, rejected, or dumped, or stuck in a traffic jam with my low-gas light on?"

I hear you. This isn't about finding silver linings or putting a positive spin on things. Curveball after curveball. Surprises, shocks, and sneak attacks. And every one of those moments when the sucky thing happens and the shit hits the fan—it hurts, and it freaking sucks—full stop.

But every single one of them has magic in it. Really.

Remember, you are not whatever judgmental thoughts you think of yourself. You're not doomed or hopeless. You are a human, experiencing human stuff, and doing the best you can in the face of it.

And each moment like this is a new chance to do that.

The way I see it, magic is all about *immediate transformation*. That's why it's amazing to see a rabbit come out of a hat or a whole person suddenly get sawed in half—the change is dramatic *and* it's fast. And that's why I call these incidents "magical." They're little portals that can warp-speed you to clarity and agency.

Am I saying that makes them not sucky? Again—hell no.

The magical moment of suck is both sucky *and* magical.

Yes, it's allowed to be both. In fact, it *has* to be both.

That's what makes these moments so transformational—but only if you can step outside of your reflexive reactions and see what else is possible for you to do. Every magical moment of suck is a chance to get clear with yourself and to take intentional action.

I don't know what magical moments of suck you've been through personally. But I know you've been through some of them. That's why I *also* know you picked up this book for a reason. Again, I don't know what that reason is. Maybe you're not quite sure yourself. That's okay. You don't know what you don't know. My hope for this next section is that you'll find the words and tools to make that intention inside you just a little bit clearer and brighter.

So, with that in mind, let's explore what's going on inside us when we resist resilience, and use that to understand ourselves and our actions a little better.

Chapter 1

Being Human 101

I don't know about you, but my high school schedule didn't have a class on *handling sucky moments* between Calculus and Chemistry. In fact, in my experience coaching thousands of people, very few of us were ever taught any practical human life lessons—let alone complete courses—on how to deal with overcoming obstacles, like failure, perfectionism, and just generally crappy luck.

Which, considering we know that *suck happens,* is really short-changing us as human beings.

We think of resilience in terms of what we do *after* something terrible happens to us. How we pick ourselves up and brush ourselves off, what we do next when the dust has cleared. But when we wait for that dust to settle, we miss a huge part of our chance to be resilient. Resilience starts right as the sucky moment itself is *actively unfolding.* It's what we do in the split second we're actively stumbling, not just the dazed minutes after we've smacked into the ground, that really counts.

Successfully processing the moment of suck—the emotions, the sensations, and the significance of it—is all about self-regulation. Self-regulation *in* the moment determines our reaction *after* the sucky moment, because when you can self-regulate, you can experience everything about that moment and still consciously choose to take constructive action. You fully lean into that moment and all its suckitude *without* letting those feelings, sensations, and looming sense of "what does this *mean*" call the shots. And that is the core of resilience.

So if self-regulation affects our resilience, why don't we just . . . self-regulate? Or why don't we do it *better*?

Because we simply don't know how! These aren't skills we were taught, implicitly or explicitly. We don't always know how to pilot our human body or how to manage the sensations that arise in us and make sense of them. We don't have a good sense of scale to put things in perspective. To self-regulate, we have to understand why we feel what we feel and lean into our emotions, tune into what our body needs and not overwhelm it, and step back from the present moment to see what's going on in the bigger picture so that we don't act impulsively or against our long-term best interests.

But that's easier said than done. We don't even know it's something we *should* do. So instead of regulating our emotions, we might either squash them down into nothing or get totally swept away. Instead of self-regulating our physical bodies, we overexert (or numb) ourselves. Instead of self-regulating our sense of what this moment *means,* we let our perspective zoom way too far in (or too far out) and distort what's truly going on.

All of this is a recipe for action that's less than resilient—action that doesn't help us fly forward after the challenge.

Now, if Being Human 101 *had* existed back when we were all younger, there are a few things that I would have wanted to see on the curriculum. So I want to give us a little remedial course on these self-regulation skills that put that audacious resilience in action. Handling sucky moments is all about understanding your emotions, having healthy reflexes, and shifting your perspective.

SKILL #1: UNDERSTANDING EMOTIONS

We are ruled by our emotions. How we're feeling affects our thoughts, our behaviors, our habits, and our patterns. Yet often, we barely acknowledge their existence, let alone understand them.

Now, most of us understand emotions as a concept—most of us know the difference between happy and sad, for example. We know that it's possible, and logical, for any given person to feel bummed out in one circumstance and overjoyed in another. In other words, we understand that a given emotion isn't *inherently* a part of who we are, but more a result of the circumstances of the moment.

But when we're feeling those feelings, in the heat of the moment, it's hard to stop to *apply* that understanding. That's because feelings are powerful, and they're powerful for a reason.

Emotions aren't arbitrary. Again, we know that logically, we'll feel happier opening a birthday card from our bestie than we will opening a past-due bill from the electric company. And the reason they *aren't* arbitrary is that they serve a purpose. Our emotions are engineered to motivate us to quick, decisive action. A feeling of disgust might have once signaled that we shouldn't eat that weird-looking mushroom. A feeling of anger might have amped up our body's systems to fight (or flee) for our lives. So it's easy, in the heat of the moment, to skate right past *feeling* our feelings and go straight into acting on them. That's not a character flaw or weak willpower: that's the system working as it should. That's *being human.*

Still, humans have brains to figure things out, and we're smart enough to learn from experience that when we let those intense feels overwhelm us and overtake us, it's not usually very productive. Your human brain knows enough to stop you from screaming your lungs out when you're furious with your boss—because getting fired would be harmful in the long term.

So when emotions start to creep up, what do we do instead? We dodge, deny, or even demonize them.

Dodging emotions is so common we barely even realize we're doing it. Especially in U.S. culture, we treat emotions like a formality. Outside of coaching or therapy, no one's answering the question, "Hey, how are you?" with the raw emotional truth! Subconsciously, we've all learned that this particular question isn't a genuine one. It's a question we're *expected* to dodge—so we do. We say, "Oh, I'm fine, thanks!" and get on with the conversation, because that's what it means to be polite. To be sure, it's not other people's job to shoulder all of our feelings, so not dumping our emotions on our acquaintances *is* polite. But when we tell our neighbors or our co-workers, "I'm fine," we're also telling *ourselves* we're fine. We're avoiding answering the question with any depth, just sticking to the surface of the pot to avoid stirring things up deeper down. We're dodging.

Dodging is something we learn by repeated practice and unspoken rules. But if we did receive any explicit instructions on how to cope with emotions, especially emotional overwhelm, it was likely to deny or demonize their very existence. Advice like "There's no use crying over spilled milk," denies the fundamental fact that *humans feel things*. We don't cry because it'll put the milk back in the glass. We cry because we're disappointed! And if we didn't feel disappointed when our food was taken away, we'd never be motivated to go get more. Denying emotions is just lying to yourself about the reality of what you're going through, and you can't gaslight yourself into resilience.

Similarly, hearing "man up" or "stop being so *sensitive*" or "now, now, *you're* okay" or "nobody likes a crybaby" convinces us that emotions are bad and to be avoided at all costs. While those "instructions" might help you wrestle some control over your feelings, that control comes at the cost of shaming and even gaslighting yourself. It breeds self-judgment and a sense of unworthiness. When I didn't get a full-time job offer after busting my ass at my dental internship, I was judging myself *hard* for feeling so upset. I was berating myself about it not being "professional" to be so frustrated, angry, and sad. What I failed to realize was that beating myself up for merely *feeling* something was only making it worse. If I'd thrown a hissy fit in the office and kicked over an exam chair? Sure, *that* wouldn't have been a great look. A little self-judgment would've been in order there. But just feeling those feelings, independent of any action? Nothing wrong with that at all.

We'll get more into positive, active strategies for dealing with (and acting on) emotions later. For now, the key skill is just to understand.

Understand that emotions are part of being human.

Understand that emotions are valid and they exist for a good reason.

Understand that dodging, denying, and demonizing are well-intentioned strategies, but ultimately counterproductive on the way to resilience.

Understand that you can *feel* an emotion without *becoming* that emotion. You can experience it fully *without* acting on it, and fully embody the entire spectrum of feelings in a healthy way.

And understand that emotions come up when sucky things happen. Maybe even feel grateful that they're there for you, flagging you to pay attention to what's bubbling up.

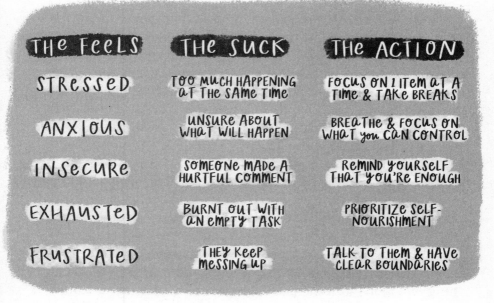

THe FeeLS	THe SUCK	THe ACTION
STReSSeD	TOO MUCH HAPPENING aT THe SAMe TIMe	FOCUS ON 1 ITeM aT A TIMe & TAKe BREAKS
ANXIOUS	UNSURe ABOUT WHaT WILL HAPPEN	BREaTHe & FOCUS ON WHaT you CaN CONTROL
INSeCURe	SOMeONe MADe A HURTFUL COMMENT	ReMIND yOURSeLF THaT yOU'Re ENOUGH
EXHAUSTeD	BURNT OUT WITH aN eMPTY TASK	PRIORITIZe SeLF-NOURISHMENT
FRUSTRATeD	THeY KeeP MeSSING UP	TALK TO THeM & HAVe CLeaR BOUNDaRIeS

Here's an example of what emotion you may feel, what the sucky moment is, and a simple action to help understand what the emotion is really telling you.

SKILL #2: HAVING HEALTHY REFLEXES

On an otherwise quiet morning, you spill coffee on a new white shirt. Next you have a flat tire. That causes you to run late, so you hustle to attend a meeting that ends up being canceled, and then your boss gives you a stern talking-to. One thing cascades into the next until you're thinking, "Why is this happening to me?" and feeling defeated. Yet you keep pushing through to the next thing on your list.

As we established earlier, sucky things happen. Sometimes that's our fault (forgetting to set our alarm and dashing out the door), and sometimes it's not (traffic, weather, or construction in our way). Just acknowledging this—bad days happen—is a big skill for exercising resilience, but it's not all there is to it. Acknowledgment alone isn't going to do the trick. After all, you could easily just say, "Yeah, bad days happen—and I'm just as cranky and tired and miserable as the last time I had one!"

Handling bad days isn't just mind over matter, because the stress can be physically exhausting. Especially when crappy things pile up in quick succession, you get tired. When you're in the thick of a crisis, when that physical stress response is activated, when those fight-or-flight hormones and cortisol are rushing through your system, when all your negative thoughts are ready to take over and push you into unhelpful familiar patterns, you don't need theories. You don't need philosophy.

Honestly, you might just need a nap.

Sometimes you need to hit the brakes, stop the action, and focus on your immediate needs. Sleep, food, some quiet time alone, five deep breaths or two sips of cool water—all of these can work wonders. The more stressed out you feel, the more overtaxed your physical systems will get. You're not a machine, remember? You're human. Slogging through a long project when you're running on empty, for example, is like trying to convince a cranky toddler to practice their letters and numbers—it's futile, and probably going to end in tears.

But knowing that you have those limits is only half the equation here. Because *when* you're feeling that tapped out, your higher-level reasoning skills are the first to start fading. In other words, as your mental and physical energy depletes from your sucky day, your body is naturally going to focus on the essential bodily processes to keep you afloat. Now is not the time to force yourself to make complicated decisions, even if they're in the name of self-care. You need to limit your options, or, even better, just have healthy, simple, no-brainer actions to fall into. Just like that cranky toddler, you don't want to be punished, but you don't want to deal with six different choices for calming down and relaxing either. You want a grown-up to make that decision. You just want that nap.

What's important for those bad-day moments is knowing *what action to take NOW,* and having that action right at your fingertips. And sometimes you may just need to practice the action of not doing, and be okay with *just being in the discomfort.* Later, we'll talk strategies for what to do once you've gotten back to that baseline, but the skill here is to cultivate reflexes, routines, and habits that will serve you well in the short *and* long term. A routine practice of self-care can work wonders (and we'll touch on that later). But there is power in merely letting yourself settle into your own physical limits. Giving yourself the gift of those "time-in" actions (as opposed to punitive "time-outs") not only soothes your body and mind, it also subtly reminds you that you can *always* do something. You don't have to be frozen like a victim.

SKILL #3: SHIFTING PERSPECTIVE

This third skill is about dealing with a bad-day moment in the context of your broader life experience. Once you've gotten comfortable understanding your emotions, and knowing what you need to do to triage them, you can move toward reframing the moment—to shifting the perspective.

In other words, it's about finding the *magic* in that *moment of suck.*

Many people get stuck in unhelpful courses of action because they're equally stuck in one perspective. They can only make sense of the facts in one particular way, usually aligned with a narrative they've been quietly, mentally reinforcing their whole life. Every slip-up and mistake becomes proof of their incompetence or unworthiness, and every achievement or big win becomes a fluke, not to be counted. These negative stories beneath the surface are just that: hidden away. They're subconscious narratives about how we're unworthy, we're hopeless, we're not good enough, we're irresponsible, we're somehow wrong and bad.

Go back to the scenario of running late for work because of the coffee spill. It's easy to cast this as confirmation of being trapped, doomed, the recipient of a million bad things tumbling down on your head over and over again. If you subconsciously subscribe to a story beneath the surface that casts you as a lost cause and total disaster of a person, it's easy to make that bad day another chip in a mosaic of a very bleak picture.

Again, these stories beneath the surface aren't necessarily something you're "letting happen" because you're weak or flawed. You're using a defense mechanism that's there to keep you safe. Your wiring wants you to "look out for number one," which means you're prone to put yourself at the center of every story—to wonder "What does this mean for *me and my survival?*" From there, it's a quick jump to conclude that any bad circumstance *could* be part of a larger, dangerous pattern, and you've got a target on your back. These doom-and-gloom scenarios with you as the star are there as your protector, an always-alert alarm system to keep you safe at all costs.

Outside the heat of the moment, though, you know these stories beneath the surface don't *quite* add up. After all, what are the odds of any one person being beyond help, doomed, condemned to misery forever? Pretty low. So skill 3 helps in letting a broader perspective shape your course of action *even as you're still reeling from the sucky moment.* When you widen your thinking, and clear out any assumptions, you can acknowledge that maybe you're not so special. You can wonder: *Is there a bigger picture here that doesn't put me in the crosshairs of bad luck?*

So let's try a perspective shift with that no-good-very-bad coffee spill morning. What if we imagined this moment as part of a different story—as the kickoff to something greater, rather than the end result of everything terrible? What if the magic in the suck gave birth to something else? We could have chosen to see this bad day as a *gift*—yes, really! By shifting our perspective, this embarrassing moment and professional stumble could be reframed as the catalyst to a better course of action, such as deciding to take the train instead of driving, which will save on gas money. It could be that aha moment of clarity that illuminates our values like a lightning bolt: a boss who chews you out for something beyond your control simply isn't someone you're willing to work with, period (cue epic, life-changing music here). It could be a chance to reflect on how we could learn and grow—after all, even at the best workplaces there will be misunderstandings, so why not start learning to navigate them now? This moment could even be a moment to feel gratitude, a chance to appreciate what you now know as a result of what happened here, and what you can do differently in the future if you choose—kinda like learning a lesson.

When you shift perspective, you don't automatically assign a negative meaning to a moment. You step just enough outside the story beneath the surface to take stock of it. You pause. You consider. You invite curiosity about the situation. And then you *choose* what to do about it.

AUDACIOUS SELF-REGULATION

Earlier, I touched on how when we resist resilience, we're actually being completely rational, even though the more resilient course of action—the one we don't usually take—is in our long-term best interest. In giving you this crash course in three skills of self-regulation, I wanted to show you why that is.

Don't worry if you're not a master of these skills just yet. All you have to know is that your audacious resilience is possible, these skills are learnable, and you've got massive potential for it in the makeup of who you are.

Emotions might have a purpose, but they're still messy. They're still chaotic. They're still overwhelming and have the power to all but knock us off our feet. But take a moment to be grateful for that power. For that sensitive, attuned system within you that lets you *experience* your life, not just watch it pass by.

Your physical body has limits. It can't push through every hardship. It can't always give you 100 percent even when you really, really need it to. But there's so much to be grateful for there as well. The systems and signals within you are pretty dang incredible, and they're worth taking care of (and giving a break now and again!).

The circumstances you're in are the result of everything that's befallen you in life so far—good and bad. The past has happened, and mistakes have been made. Embrace that truth. Yes, your story is imperfect. But you, more than anyone else, have the power to make choices to change it going forward. Your life has more of that magic in store for you, in good moments and bad. Each new screwup and stumble is a chance to brush yourself off and say, "Well, that sucked. So, now what?"

So if you've handled sucky moments by whining (or wine-ing), show yourself some kindness. That's classic, grade-A human behavior.

It's human to react to tough moments and setbacks by telling yourself the "I suck and I'm screwed" story. It's human to feel your heart pounding and head aching and jaw clenching with stress. It's human to get so swept up in anger, sadness, despair, or confusion that you can't think, let alone act.

But it's just as human to bounce back too. And it starts with self-regulation. Self-regulation is feeling the feels and then transmuting their energy into gentle, positive action. It's allowing yourself to experience the subtle waves of emotion encompassing you like the tide in the ocean, and then gradually taking action once you've drifted to shallower, calmer waters. It's being fully within your emotional, physical, and mental systems so that you can take action that's aligned with what's in your long-term best interest.

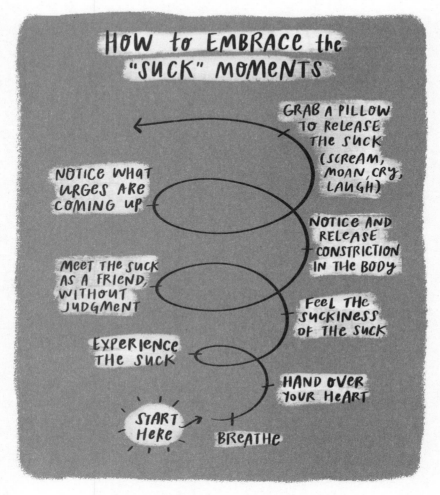

Embracing the suck is the ultimate upward spiral.

That's a massive part of what makes *audacious resilience* so, well, audacious. You're *daring* to step outside your reflexes for a second. You're daring to be both an emotional, flesh-and-blood human with a lifetime of experience behind you *and* more than merely the sum of your parts. You're daring to embrace that balance, that paradox. And that's the first step to flying forward.

*

Recap & Reflection Corner

1. What was your intention when you picked up this book? What do you hope to gain? What wisdom about yourself would you like to discover in the upcoming pages?

2. Take an inventory of all the sucky moments you've been through in life. No matter how raw, painful, traumatic, just make a list on the left side of your journal. Then, on the right side, write the words *thank you* for every sucky moment.

3. Take a moment to close your eyes. Thank yourself for everything you've gone through that led you here, to this book. Thank yourself for taking the time to get to know yourself better, to have a different perspective, to have an open heart. Place one hand on your heart, and repeat the words *thank you for this human experience*. Take three deep breaths.

* * *

Chapter 2

The Victim Mentality

Meet my client Priyanka (Pri). Pri was wicked smart, gorgeous, and totally heartbroken.

She and her long-term partner had split up a few months prior, and it had been devastating for her: she'd really thought this was The One, the person she'd spend the rest of her life with. They'd gone on vacation together, attended weddings together (ugh), and even joked around about baby names. Getting dumped had blindsided her. She was a really family-oriented person, and one of her major life goals was to get married and raise kids. The breakup felt like it had ripped that out of her hands, and in the aftermath, things had really sucked for a while.

But Pri wanted to bounce back. So, during a girls-only weekend trip with her crew, she felt brave enough to download Bumble. With her girlfriends' help, she put together her cutest photos; crafted a witty, flirty profile; and got to swiping.

And to her delight, she was getting *tons* of matches. The parade of eligible bachelors lighting up her phone made her heartbreak seem like ancient history. But there was one guy in particular who caught her eye: charming, funny, dimples, loved dogs and kids—he checked all the boxes. And when they met up for their first date, he was even better in person. Drinks turned into dinner turned into a trip back to his place, and on the subway home the next morning, Pri was totally giddy (and maybe mentally picking out baby names).

A few days later, she texted him, and they went back and forth a bit, flirting and joking.

A day after that, she texted him again, asking when they could hang out again.

A day after that, she was still left on read.

And a few days after *that,* she realized what had happened.

Pri got ghosted.

And that sucked.

So, now what?

Well, Pri chose to do what most of us would.

She threw herself a pity party. An epic one. A pity party to make the Met Gala look like a three-year-old's birthday.

She vented to a friend (or three) over text. She pulled out her tablet and went online shopping for a fancy luxe handbag she couldn't *really* afford but *totally* deserved. She poured herself some wine. She texted her friends *again* with more pleas for sympathy. She poured some *more* wine. And then she stewed.

She let all the frustration and disappointment overpower her, bathing in the feelings of her failure and soaking them in until this one-off romantic rejection had turned into so much more than just failing to keep a guy interested.

Because, come to think of it, she'd failed at a *lot* of other things. It wasn't just that her dating life was a failure; *she* was a failure. Ouch.

And then, just to prove her point to herself, she got on Instagram (as one does) and stalked her ex. Who looked super happy— *and* was engaged. Ugh.

By the time her pity party was over, Priyanka felt exhausted. And not the good kind of exhausted that comes on after a fun, energizing, unforgettable night on the town. Just *exhausted* exhausted.

PITY PARTIES ARE NO FUN

If any part of Pri's story felt familiar to you, then all I have to say is *welcome*. Pity parties are one of the classic default responses to shitty human moments. When things go wrong, we feel sorry for ourselves in a big way and take action accordingly. We've all been there.

Pity parties are such a common reaction to setbacks, challenges, and unmet expectations because they *do* make us feel better. After a big screwup or embarrassment or devastation, a pity party is a place for us to shine. It's a place where we can still be the star, not just *despite* the sucky moment in our life, but *because* of it. We can wear the brush-off, the rejection, the mistake as a badge of honor, like a sad-girl version of a bachelorette party tiara. We can nurse our bruised egos and drown our bad feelings with a glass of wine or a tub of dairy-free ice cream, and still be the center of attention.

And who's throwing this pity party? Why, the ego, of course.

Now, if I'd told Pri that she was being *egocentric* in throwing herself a pity party, she probably would've given me a blank stare, or said something like, "Neeta, were you even listening? I don't have an ego at all! I have like zero self-confidence now! Didn't you hear just how *pathetic* I am?"

So bear with me here. It's true: most people associate the word *ego* with overconfidence, self-importance, entitlement, or otherwise just thinking you're hot shit—with nothing to back it up. Being "egotistical" definitely looks like that (and we'll get to that in the next chapter). But more fundamentally, being "egocentric" doesn't necessarily mean being swaggery or full of yourself. In fact, it *can* mean the opposite: feeling pathetic or miserably unlucky.

The human ego is a powerful force that has one goal: to protect you. It's what keeps you locked into that "look out for number one" frame of mind by ensuring you devote enough energy to assessing how *you* feel right this second, *every* second. And to do this, your ego simply puts *you* at the center of the universe. That can mean being super full of yourself, *or* it can mean thinking that you are *uniquely* pathetic, *uniquely* unlucky, that you're suffering something that's an especially awful injustice.

And, as we've seen, sometimes the protective instincts and defense mechanisms we're wired with don't get us acting in our best interest. Just like all the systems that rise up in the moment of suck when you aren't self-regulating, your ego can do more long-term harm than good, even as it shields you in the short term.

So let's get back to those pity parties. We accept that these woe-is-me fests are the go-to way to recover from a sucky moment. But at the same time, it's kind of obvious that they're not the best idea. As parties go, pity parties are pretty terrible, right? Imagine if a friend said, "Hey, I'm having a party tonight, want to come? Oh, but there's no food or drinks or music or decorations or anything. Actually, we're just going to sit down, and you'll listen to me tell you all the ways everyone in my life has wronged me, and agree with me every single time. So, see you at seven?" I'm guessing you'd probably tell your friend you had other plans. Because in real life, it doesn't make sense to throw a party where the purpose is bumming yourself—and everyone around you—out.

In this chapter, we're going to look at one way the ego can throw up barriers to resilience. We'll see how it can keep us feeling trapped, helpless, and powerless instead of seeing all the choices that actually lie in front of us, and feeling empowered to seize on them.

Speaking of choices, let's take a look at Priyanka's actions to get a clearer sense of how they're counterproductive.

- She texted her friends to "vent" about her situation, but really, she just wanted to *seek validation and reassurance* from them.

- She *numbed out* with alcohol to blunt the intensity of her feelings.

- She "treated herself" to online shopping, *acting impulsively* for a short-term, feel-good fix she couldn't really afford.

- She *self-flagellated* by purposefully comparing her life and happiness to those of her ex.

Ultimately, none of these actions is going to get Priyanka any closer to what she wants: a happy, long-term relationship. The fact is, pity parties might be a "normal" way to react to tough stuff, but they're not an especially *resilient* way to react. They definitely don't help you bounce back; if anything, they keep you stuck.

So why *do* we throw ourselves these crummy parties when we have a bad day or encounter a challenge?

Because our ego is coping by falling back on one of the only methods it knows: the victim mentality.

Victimization vs. Victim Mentality

The word *victim* can be a loaded one. As a survivor of multiple traumas myself, I want to be clear: resisting the victim mentality does *not* mean ignoring, minimizing, or denying any lived experience of victimization. If you've been through any kind of trauma, violence, bullying, or emotional abuse, you deserve nothing but empathy and support. You do not need to rewrite or deflect the harm done to you in order to achieve resilience. You can be a victim, *and* you can resist the victim *mentality.*

I know this firsthand: my abusive marriage and the mentally, emotionally, spiritually, and financially draining battle to leave it certainly qualified me to identify as a victim.

The key is in how we tell the story. The facts of my experience—the fact that I've suffered—are manifestly true, but I still didn't *have* to take on a victim mentality. Don't get me wrong: I was a victim of domestic violence. I can acknowledge the real harm done to me without taking on a permanent identity defined by the abuse. I don't have to let the story in which I was the victim be the one that rules in my mindset—I can recast it to see myself as a *survivor*, and later, even as someone who is thriving.

Pushing back on the victim mentality should never be taken as a dismissal of real, valid harm done in your past. After all, it's what got you here on this journey. Congratulations for keeping that journey going.

THAT SUCKED. now what?

PLAYING THE VICTIM:
THE GAME YOU'LL NEVER WIN

Bad things always happen to me.
I can never get a partner to stay around.
Everyone who loves me treats me badly.
It never works out for me, no matter how much I try.
They just won't hire me because of who I am.

Any of these sound familiar? These aren't just the kickoffs to a bunch of pity parties. They're the victim mentality at work.

The victim mentality is what it sounds like: a mindset where we see ourselves as perpetual victims. You know how a "victor" is the person who wins? Well, a "victim" is the opposite: it's the person who loses, who gets hurt, who is defeated. The *victim mentality* is a mindset that no matter what happens to you in life, *you* are the loser. Ouch.

Depending on what our ego has learned to "watch out" for in life, we might be prone to the victim mentality as a reaction to certain kinds of stresses and setbacks, or default to it no matter what befalls us. The ultimate result, however, is the same: we're *passive*. We decide that the blame for our circumstances lies elsewhere, *anywhere* but with us. By definition, a victim can't win, so there's no point in trying. Not only no point—there's no option *to* try. For a victim, fate is sealed, defeat is constant and inescapable. Things happen *to* you. The only option left is usually some kind of wallowing, woe-is-me fest, or a pity party.

Now, as we saw with Priyanka, indulging the victim mentality—throwing a pity party—is *not* going to help us bounce back. But that doesn't mean we're acting totally illogically when we play the victim. There are some short-term, positive benefits that make the victim mentality—and choices like throwing a pity party—really attractive in the moment:

Playing the victim *seems* realistic. The victim mentality is insidious because it starts with a little grain of truth. In this case, Priyanka did fail at her goal of having an amazing first date. Failure, for a high achiever like Pri, sucks big time. She doesn't want to talk herself out of that truth—nor should she—but in dwelling on the failure, she can't step outside of it to examine it more deeply.

Playing the victim is *safe*. It means you don't have to change, because you *can't* change. If you always lose, no matter what, there's no point! You can stay in a cocoon, bury your head in the sand, and never have to break out of your shell.

Playing the victim is *fear based*. Fear is powerful, and fear is subtle. As we'll see, it's an emotion that can rule over us even when we don't *think* we're feeling afraid. The fear at work in a victim mentality paints any *other* mindset as too scary and uncertain to even consider. We may realize the victim mentality isn't healthy, but we rationalize it by declaring the alternatives as *much* worse options. Just like that, we stay stuck, tying our hands behind our backs once again.

Playing the victim *shields our ego*. This, too, is related to fear. Our ego is inherently defensive of itself. It doesn't like getting hurt. It doesn't like admitting fault or mistakes or taking responsibility (unless there's something to brag about). When we play the victim, we protect our ego from being exposed to criticism. If we're the victim—the person acted upon, instead of the victor, the one taking action—then whatever happened couldn't *possibly* be our fault, *ever*! Our ego is shouting in our ears, saying, "What was I supposed to do? I was trapped! I had no choice!" Our ego even feels victimized by the suggestion that it's anything *but* a victim!

Playing the victim is a *human response*. All of that said, you need to remember that you came to this mentality after years and years of all those stories you've told yourself swirling under the surface. There's no one person to blame over a victim mentality—not your parents, not your high school bullies, not even yourself. The stories beneath the surface that get us there are simply too enmeshed with human society and your personal history. You're only human—no more, no less. So don't double down on yourself and beat yourself up. That's not productive; that's playing by the victim mentality's rules. Remember that your feelings are something you can experience and acknowledge fully, both in and after the moment of suck. Emotions arise after a stimulus, not arbitrarily. Whatever's stirred up in you is a valid emotional response—period. Audacious resilience comes when you hold space for that emotion *and* resist your ego's defensive course of action.

Amor Fati

The good news is that being prone to a victim mentality doesn't mean you're doomed to pity parties forever. Once you have a solid sense of the influences on your personal Bounce Factor, you can move away from the victim mentality and toward its opposite: *amor fati.*

My discovery of amor fati was heartfelt and intellectual all at once. At 19, after losing my father to a nine-month battle with stage 4 lung cancer, I decided to say "fuck it," go against my aunt's and grandmother's wishes, and study abroad on my first-ever trip to Europe. I desperately needed to get away from all of the heaviness that surrounded me, and my soul desperately craved relief from that heavy, years-long load of caretaking, not to mention the trauma and pain of losing my mother, brother, and father within a span of five years. I got accepted to a summer study abroad program, arranged for my younger brother to stay with my grandmother and aunt for the summer, and hopped on a direct flight from Chicago to Rome.

I knew it would be a transition for me: I didn't speak even the tiniest bit of Italian, didn't know anyone in the program, and had never been away from home for an extended period of time. But I had also never been away from *tragedy.* Even as I was bombarded by all the other study abroad students (plus tourists) in the sweltering heat of Rome in June, I felt a glorious sense of freedom. For the first time in a decade, I had no one to answer to or take care of, no hospital visits, no knots in my stomach, no traumatic phone calls.

But meeting new people meant answering questions, and I came to dread the "So, tell me about you!" from my fellow classmates. I hated that my story involved so much heaviness for someone not even 20 years old. As freeing as the trip was, it also sent me back to stewing in my victim mentality, thinking, "Why me—why is *this* my story? Why can't I just be *normal*, and not talk about dead family members for once and be like everyone else here?"

In the midst of a whirlwind first week of class, the professor introduced us to the writings of Stoic philosopher Marcus Aurelius. This was my first exposure to Stoicism—which upheld the cardinal virtues of courage, wisdom, justice, and moderation as key to a happy and fulfilled life, and the concept of amor fati, or "love of one's fate." What I learned from class that day was that the Stoics questioned everything, and they absolutely loved their fate: no matter what arrived in life, they embraced it all the same. They saw that everything that befell them was necessary, and they didn't waste energy wishing it were different. They just *welcomed* it.

I sat there stunned, thinking of what I had been through. In the weeks that followed, I learned everything I could about Marcus Aurelius and the other ancient philosophers who managed to love their fate regardless of the cards they were dealt. The Stoics always seemed to find a silver lining to their problems, no matter how dire they were. They could ask curious, nonjudgmental questions of themselves and their circumstances. *What positive things might come about as a result of this experience, even if it's one I wouldn't have chosen? What other, even worse things might have happened here? Since I cannot change fate, what can I learn from what it drops in my path?*

I started to turn this approach to my own story, going from asking "Why me?" to "Why not me?" and seeing all the opportunities to learn, grow, and become stronger that were embedded in these hardships. Finally, one night in my dorm room, I woke up in a panicked sweat, a vivid dream clear in my mind's eye, its question ringing out: "What if there's a reason you went through all these losses before you were 19, Neeta?"

That question resonates with me to this day. It's one of the motivating factors behind my coaching and transformation programs—to show empathy and understanding to people in tough places like I was in back as a teen. It ultimately helped me fly forward to where I am today. Studying abroad was the most incredible, amazing, and deeply healing experience for me on so many levels, but learning about amor fati helped it all snap into place.

Amor fati is a powerful concept because it's in many ways the opposite of the victim mentality. It might not seem obvious at first: maybe you'd assume the opposite of the victim mentality is something like the *winner* mentality or the *kickass* mentality. But expecting to win every time (aka entitlement) can be just as counterproductive as deciding you'll always lose (and we'll get to that in the next chapter). It's still the ego taking the reins—just steering you in the opposite extreme.

Amor fati, by contrast, is a balanced, curious, and nonjudgmental way to look at your life and circumstances, one that frees you from the invisible currents of your assumptions and allows you to think for yourself. It acknowledges your ego's existence, but doesn't let it seize control.

At the same time, amor fati is more than just giving up and letting the tides of fate take you where they will. It's about loving the *choice* that fate gives you. It's about realizing that there are no *good* or *bad* things in life, just different flavors of opportunity to learn.

This gets to the two key questions at the heart of amor fati:

What can I learn from this?

What is this moment teaching me?

For my client Priyanka, being resigned to powerlessness would look like throwing that pity party for herself and dragging it out as long as she could. She could have told herself, "Well, guess that's it. I've tried enough. No one will love me and I'll die alone." (Cue dramatic music here.)

But if she could take an approach of loving her fate, she could *accept* the situation in the moment without being *resigned* to the state of things forever. Most of the work we did together centered around self-love and self-acceptance, since Pri had a pattern of seeing her own worth only through the devotion of others. Sometimes, that pattern made her feel amazing, but it would also lead her to huge disappointments. (Sound a little familiar?) But knowing that about herself let her feel that amor fati. She could ask, "Okay, what can I learn from this? Maybe I need to prep myself mentally for dating more than I thought, because it turns out dating feels like a *huge* deal. Actually, this moment is teaching me how much I need to devote and lovingly date myself. I really value people who respect me, but I need to respect me. I need to cherish who I am, and who I'm becoming, and damn, I'm fucking proud that *that's* something I care about." (A lot of this was actually in a journal entry she shared with me after the amor fati exercise.)

Do you see how she was able to accept what happened in the moment (her fate) without projecting that moment out into the rest of her life (her destiny)? That's what amor fati looks like. Priyanka didn't have to let a victim mentality freeze her in place. She could invite curiosity, openness, and even love into the situation, and start to lay the groundwork for flying forward.

EVERY MOMENT IS A CHOICE

If there's one thing I want you to take away from this chapter, it's this:

Every moment is a *powerful* choice.

You can choose to get upset at your toddler when she spills her glass of juice on the sofa or you can choose to make a mental note to shift perspective, celebrate her mistake (so she has your permission to know mistakes are okay), and yes, maybe even give her a sippy cup next time.

You can choose to think that you'll never find love when the person you're casually dating ghosts on you or you can choose to be grateful that you don't have to waste any more time on someone who's not interested.

You can choose to shut down your laptop, delete your online dating profile, and retreat under the blankets or you can choose to reflect on your new self-knowledge about what you actually need and want in a partner.

Victims are defined by their lack of choices. But it's only a perceived lack of choices. You always have a choice. You always have a choice. Even choosing not to choose is a choice!

And once you realize that you always have a choice, you free yourself from stuckness. You let your Fall be the catalyst in a chain reaction to flying forward, not the final nail in the coffin that seals your fate.

You shift from asking "Why me?" to "Why not me?"

You shift from "Why'd he ruin my night by ghosting me?!" to "Why not make tonight the night I chat up that cute stranger?"

You shift from "Why did the class I just taught have to be such a disaster?" to "Why don't I use this screwup as an example in my next class?"

You shift from defeat to possibility. And you shift into gear to fly forward.

Understanding that you're not a victim and learning you have a choice in how to react are two vital first steps toward your own expansion.

Your best self.

Your growth journey.

Your becoming.

Your next chapter.

The journal prompts that follow will help you put these ideas into practice in your own life, as you begin to develop your own sense of amor fati and move away from a victim mentality.

✳

Recap & Reflection Corner

1. Recall a time when you were the victim. What was the scenario that unfolded? Who was the pity party with? How did that time help you, and how did that time hurt you? Is there a part of you that still feels wounded? Write a letter to that wounded part of you (which could even be the little girl or little boy that got hurt). Acknowledge the trouble you went through. Acknowledge what your

ego was only trying to protect. Acknowledge your hurt. Notice what you were able to release in this letter.

2. Try incorporating *amor fati* into how you see your life and your past. Recall some of the setbacks and challenges in your life. Make a list of as many as you can recall. For example:

    A failure at work
    Something didn't go to plan
    Flunking an important exam
    A bad breakup
    A small but painful betrayal
    A period of addiction

3. Now choose one of the setbacks or challenges you listed and answer the following questions:

    - What other, even worse, things did you avoid because of what happened?

    - What did you get *after* this setback that you didn't even know you needed?

    - What positive things in your life would not have happened otherwise? For example:

        The career change for the better after your
          work mistake
        The lifelong friend you made studying for another
          try at the test
        The soulmate you met after the awful breakup
        The lightness and freedom after leaving a toxic
          friend behind
        The radical self-acceptance found in recovery from
          the addiction

    - What can you learn from this setback? Why *wouldn't* you change it, even if you could?

* * *

Chapter 3

The Entitlement Trap

No one can say my client Samuel doesn't have an inspiring story.

Samuel, his six siblings, and his mom left Vietnam as refugees. They'd been smuggled out on a boat, and traveled a long, grueling journey before arriving in the United States. Once there, their existence was better, but still right at the poverty line. Samuel grew up working hard, both supporting his family and earning top grades in school. Eventually, he graduated from high school, and then went on to college, and then medical school after that. From there, he soared to the highest heights of the American Dream: an oncology practice at a prestigious West Coast university.

But as Samuel sought coaching to achieve the next goal in his sights, he brought with him an entitled mindset.

Samuel wanted to transition from his medical practice to a career as a thought leader and influencer. He had real presence, knew how to command a room, and had a powerful radio-announcer voice, so I could absolutely see how he'd taken to presenting, speaking, and podcasting. But in our work together, he was impatient. He wanted to spread his story and gain a following like so many other public figures had, but every time I asked him some nuts-and-bolts questions—Who will your message impact the most? How do you plan on serving them? How can they learn from you? What will they learn from you?—Samuel waved them off. Or if he did answer, it was with more of a shrug. No, he didn't really know how his message would impact others. That was for them to figure out. What Samuel needed, he figured, was for the right someone to discover *him*.

"Sure, other people have to pay their dues, but I have a story," he said.

That was his response to a lot of my questions. "I *have* a *story*."

Our work together concluded, time passed, and then one day Samuel sent me a DM. He'd seen a post of mine about a prominent figure in the industry and asked if I could make an introduction.

This put me in kind of a sticky situation—though not an unfamiliar one—and I took some time to think of a diplomatic response. I was still on maternity leave at the time, mind you, and trying to keep my business running from afar while writing a book.

But Samuel didn't want to wait. After the DM, he left a few comments on some of my posts, then shot me a few e-mails, then left me a voicemail.

Finally, I responded, and broke the news as tactfully as I could that, while it was amazing that Samuel had survived so much and achieved so many things, that didn't mean event organizers were going to give him a free pass and offer him a contract to jump on stage and present.

Samuel didn't exactly get the hint: "Well, how hard can it be? I have this story, after all!"

I stared at my piles of manuscript notes, my to-do list for my team for our next big batch of content, and my constantly pinging e-mail inbox, and took a deep breath before writing back.

YOU CAN'T WIN JUST BY SHOWING UP

Samuel *did* have a story. An extraordinary one at that. But his story wasn't going to help others—wasn't going to get him to *his* goal of becoming a public figure and role model—unless he could set his entitlement to the side and start thinking about what *others* needed, not what he *deserved*.

So in one sense, his story is unique; but in another, it's not unique at all.

Maybe you didn't see *yourself* in his story the same way you did in Priyanka's, but I guarantee you that at one point, you've been in this same mindset. So have I. So has everyone—it's only human.

Every week, dozens of people like Samuel send me messages sharing their stories. These people tend to have a few things in common. First, a traumatic experience in their upbringing or current environment, whether that's a divorce, a death, a job loss, a diagnosis, being sent to prison, or some other kind of awful heartbreak. Second, an ability to work through the emotions of that experience and come out on the other side feeling fully alive and excited to share their story with others. And last, a sense of entitlement that their story is incredibly unique and that their uniqueness is that golden ticket to success.

Don't get me wrong: having big dreams is not a problem. That's what my work is all about—helping you elevate your life! It's not that Samuel's story wasn't inspiring either. What he'd been able to do in the professional and personal realms was beyond commendable and admirable; and since he was a man going through some of the toughest mental health challenges, I knew that he could make a real difference in moving an important conversation on male mental health forward.

But potential has to be nurtured and grown. In this case, Samuel needed to have an audience! If being an author and authority was his dream, he needed to work on cultivating a dedicated group of raving fans who'd be excited about his story and everything he shares. He needed to work on writing—maybe with some short-form articles or posts—and creating more videos and podcasts to see what would resonate the most with others.

In short, Samuel needed to devote his time to fully understanding *other* people, the people he desired to impact. Who would benefit from his powerful story? What did he want others to take away from his presentation? How did he see his story would transform, shift, or change others?

Samuel didn't really want to do any of that, though: "Yeah, I know technically you're supposed to have a demo reel, but don't

THAT SUCKED. now what?

you think that they'll want to have me and just figure the details out later?"

No, actually. For one thing, I've organized quite a few speaking events myself, and the odds that I'd bring in someone with no clips, no portfolio, no testimonials, and no experience to talk to a paying audience? Slim to none. For every Samuel, there's a speaker out there who has practiced, prepared, and polished their work—*and* lived through something equally inspiring. From that perspective, it's a no-brainer.

But Samuel *could* have become that practiced, prepared, and polished speaker *if* he was willing to put in time and effort. The thing holding Samuel back from achieving his dreams wasn't that his story wasn't worthwhile, or that he didn't have that one magical connection.

It was—you guessed it—his ego.

Instead of thinking about the *impact* he could have, Samuel was fixated on *fame*. Instead of how he could serve others and bring something of value to share with an audience, Samuel focused only on what was in it for him. The only benefit that he was pursuing was his own craving for recognition, for being seen as someone extra-special, on a massive scale, *without working to connect with others*. His ego was pouring his head fill of ideas, including:

- That the world owes him something
- That he'll receive opportunities others do not solely because of his unique story
- That he'll be successful without having to develop his craft
- That the rules don't apply to him
- That because of what he's been through, the rest of us should just give him a pass
- That people will give him what they know or what they sell for free

In other words, what was holding him back was entitlement.

ENTITLEMENT: BECAUSE YOU DESERVE SO MUCH BETTER

We've seen how the ego's center-of-the-universe attitude can give rise to the victim mentality and the ensuing pity parties in the face of screwups and failures. In this entitlement mindset, we'll see the ego's flip side at work. Instead of sulking and feeling sorry for ourselves as victims, we get huffy and frustrated.

We worked *hard*.

We've been through *so much*.

We gave it our all.

We *deserve* this.

We *shouldn't* have to go through this.

It may seem counterintuitive that feeling entitled and feeling victimized are two sides of the same coin. But, again, just look through the lens of the ego. Both mindsets imply that *you* are *uniquely and extremely* deserving: either deserving of pity or deserving of praise. And neither mindset considers the impact on anyone else. A victim mentality blinds us to the effort it takes *others* to tend to us in our misery, while shutting us off from the empathy we could gain from genuine connection with them. An entitlement mindset shrugs off the cost to others for us to get what we want, while ignoring the opportunity to make *their* lives a little easier.

Entitlement, I know, can be a heated subject, and can be triggering or perhaps even activating for some, but bear with me here. Ultimately, all entitlement boils down to your ego feeling *entitled not to suffer.* And that's rooted in a fear of suffering. When our ego senses we might *not* get what we want, that the big prize can only be had with *even more effort,* even more *suffering,* well, it balloons up like a spiky pufferfish. We get so fragile that one slight rejection and we become a three-year-old stomping her foot when Mom says no candy before dinner. We unleash our inner diva. We go wild AF. We want that freakin' participation trophy!

Basically, when things don't go our way, we act *entitled*.

Entitlement isn't a comfortable thing to acknowledge in ourselves. It's definitely not a comfortable thing to point out to someone else—it's hard not to feel like a grumpy old lady complaining about these kids today. But the fact is, everyone can act entitled, because the entitlement mentality can be helpful—in a short-term sense—in a few different ways:

Entitlement seems *logical*. Entitlement is a seductive mindset because it leans hard on the truth while conveniently omitting other key facts. It lets us see things selectively and cherry-pick our facts such that *we* aren't ultimately responsible. Samuel held on to the *truth* that his story was hella freakin' inspiring, while ignoring the *fact* that his ultimate goal would take more work.

Entitlement just wants things to be *fair*. And who can argue with that, right? It just feels *right* for people who've been through difficult shit to have things go easy for them afterward. Real talk, love: there's just no limit to how many sucky human moments a person faces in this beautiful lifetime. (Take it from me, the poster child.) Coming to terms with that truth is scary AF—it's audacious. Entitlement is, in its own way, safer.

Entitlement is *validating*. It's only human to want to feel secure about who we are, and asserting our uniqueness is a way to claim that sense of security. But when we insist on our uniqueness as a way to get ahead, we're weaponizing it. We're letting our entitlement drive—and letting our ego fill up the tank. Each of us is both a singular person, with gifts and talents no one else can bring to the world, *and* much, much less special than our ego wants us to believe. Again, it's a paradox—but when we can embrace it, feel validated in our *impact* on others rather than our *status* among them, we're cultivating audacious resilience.

Entitlement feels *practical*. Our ego is basically haggling for us. It's trying to strike a bargain where we get to stay unhurt and unstressed and invulnerable, but still get all of what we want in return. We don't have to "spend" our effort and risk getting nothing back. And who wouldn't want something for nothing, right? Unfortunately, the ultimate cost of *not* contributing fully, of *not* giving it our all, is never learning resilience. If we never risk anything, we never reap the rewards either.

Entitlement is *focused*. When our ego latches onto something it feels entitled to, life becomes a zero-sum game. There's only one tolerable outcome, *getting what we want,* and so we put on blinders so that nothing distracts us. But failure is *always* possible—that's just life. When we gun hard for one option and one option only, we not only risk failing, but cultivate a single-minded focus that can't even imagine a Plan B. Instead of acting out of curiosity and possibility, we forge on out of scarcity and fear—neither of which helps our resilience.

When you can accept that sucky moments happen, and suffering crops up in *everyone's* life now and again, you can start to get your ego to back off. When you offer forth your uniqueness as something that can help others, something that should be shared with no strings attached, no expectations, then you're living with authenticity. You're connecting and bringing others together. And you are resilient—because when you aren't demanding a reward, your spirit can't be crushed when no reward comes. You go from being in denial of negative feelings to being open, accepting, and curious. You transform your rigid, black-and-white mindset into one that's more flexible, nuanced—and resilient.

Privilege vs. Entitlement

If I asked you to picture someone *entitled,* what would this person look like? What's their gender, race, age, profession? Go ahead, take a few seconds to think on it.

If you pictured a man, especially a white, able-bodied man—maybe in a Patagonia fleece with a big-tech employee lanyard around his neck—you're not alone. Culturally, when we think of entitlement, we think of the groups of people who have traditionally wielded the most power and privilege. Usually the patriarchy. And on a societal level, that's certainly a problem.

But while *entitlement* and *privilege* might seem like synonyms, I do want to draw a distinction between the two. Entitlement is feeling exceptionally deserving of attention, exclusivity, and benefits. It's ego-driven and often rooted in fear. Privilege is a right or benefit enjoyed by some people and not others because of some aspect of their identity. They can be intertwined, but they're not exactly the same thing. Privilege, since it inherently shields a person from certain struggles, can easily create a fertile environment for their ego to grow unchecked and entitlement to develop—but that doesn't *always* happen. You can be privileged and entitled, or you can be privileged and not entitled, or you can be entitled, but not privileged.

Entitlement can happen to anyone. In fact, it happens to most of us. But we all have the ability to consciously step out of it and choose a resilient mindset instead.

Privilege, by contrast, is not so easily shed. A cis man can't just decide to renounce his gender privilege, for example—it's not up to him as an individual whether he has it or not. He can become conscious of his privilege, and let that inspire him to action that fosters greater equity. But privilege—gender privilege, racial privilege, class privilege, and all the rest—can only dissipate after change at a *societal* level.

Acknowledging that we all struggle with feelings of entitlement doesn't mean denying our relative privilege, or lack thereof, on any axis. It doesn't mean that our trauma, history of microaggressions, and struggles aren't real or valid. It doesn't mean we're letting systemic oppression win or colonize our thinking. And it certainly doesn't mean that we can't celebrate our stories and own our uniqueness! In fact, it's just the opposite. Recognizing your own personal entitlement is an exercise in intersectionality. It's seeing your identity, your many layers and dimensions, and your story for all its facets and spectrums rather than accepting a flat, black-and-white label. And in doing that, we're not just unpacking our own unhealthy thinking; we're building a mechanism for greater empathy for others.

Because ultimately, when it comes to our own reactions to setbacks and challenges, *other people's situations don't really matter*. It's easy to say, "What about the people who have *so much* unearned privilege?" and redirect attention away from *ourselves* and how *we* take action in our lives. In that sense, embracing our human tendency to entitlement, and the place and identity we occupy in the world, is an extension of amor fati. We can hold strong convictions that the balance of privilege in society must change *and* own the fact that we're as susceptible to entitlement as any other human.

THE MYTHS THAT KEEP US ENTITLED

We are living in an age of entitlement. We love to mythologize the lives of the successful and famous, to hear about their humble beginnings and their glamorous triumphs in one breathless paragraph. It feels inspiring to read these stories, but unfortunately, we tend to take exactly the wrong lesson from these examples. We *think* we're learning resilience from the masters, following in the footsteps of people who've made it, when in reality, we're just feeding our sense of entitlement. Let's dig into three myths that keep us from breaking out of this mentality.

Rags to Riches

Serena and Venus Williams grew up in Compton, practicing tennis amid violence, drugs, and an all-around tough environment while their father Richard worked nights to pay for their lessons. Fast forward to their pro careers, and the Williams sisters are household names, multimillionaires, and record-breaking athletes, with 30 Grand Slam titles between them. Everyone loves a good rags-to-riches story—it's hard not to. But as they're repeated, they become more "because rags, therefore riches," and that can lead us to assuming our *own* hardships guarantee us similar successes. Of course, not every girl born in Compton grew up to become a legendary athlete, and not all sports champions come from hardscrabble backgrounds. The Williams sisters didn't "earn" their success because they *only* had a rough upbringing. They earned it with hard work, dedication, and talent. Focusing on the hardships instead of hard work can give us tunnel vision.

Overnight Success

We see this one in everything from "instant" #1 hits from unknown songwriters (remember when "Gangnam Style" came out of nowhere and was suddenly, annoyingly *everywhere*?) to "unicorn" apps that suddenly dominate our phones (and rack up investor money). The idea that anyone can be shot to instant stardom just by getting in front of the right people is incredibly thrilling and seductive—especially in the age of social media. What we *forget* is that these stories get our attention because they're *not* typical. If every songwriter who tweeted out their new single shot to #1 on the charts, then the unexpected rise of "Gangnam Style" would never be newsworthy. To put it another way, if it was easy, everyone would be doing it. Overnight successes aren't *un*deserving, but they are at least somewhat lucky, and when we start chasing *luck*, we're acting out of entitlement.

Love Conquers All

It's a rom-com classic: Ryan Gosling hanging off the Ferris wheel in the *Notebook*, Shah Rukh Khan in *every single* Bollywood movie, Tom Cruise's famous words in *Jerry McGuire*: "You complete me." Boy meets girl, boy loses girl, boy wins girl back. The specifics (and genders) may change, but the moral of this story is always the same: *persistence wins out, because . . . love.* We might not take this one literally and do over-the-top romantic gestures, but we do internalize the idea that if we just want something and keep trying, it'll happen, because . . . love. That's wonderful in a movie, but less practical in real life. Unless our actions are having an *impact* that's getting us closer to our goal, just doing them over and over—and wanting that end goal so, so badly—aren't enough to get the result we want.

THE FEAR AT THE ROOT OF ENTITLEMENT

We've seen the basics of entitlement, how it can happen to all of us, how the stories we internalize create fertile ground for entitlement to spring to life. But what fuels entitlement *within* us? What emotions, habits, beliefs are feeding it?

In short: fear.

Maybe this sounds counterintuitive. But entitlement can be so tricky that way. Remember how, when we think of "entitled" people in the abstract, we tend to conjure up those obnoxious, self-absorbed, way-too-confident for their own good types with tons of societal privilege? Well, if that's "entitlement," then it's no wonder we don't see where fear comes into the mix. What could these people possibly be *fearful* of?

They fear that something is lacking.

This fear can present in a number of ways. In my first book, *Emotional Grit,* I talk about three fear cultures: the culture of aversion ("This isn't enough!"), the culture of scarcity ("There isn't enough!"), and the culture of unworthiness ("I am not enough!"). In the first culture, you do whatever it takes to avoid shame. In the second, you compete, hoard, cling to whatever you feel is scarce. In the third, you assume any and all of your efforts are doomed to failure, to never be good enough.

At the heart of the entitlement we feel is a sense of lack, a subconscious fear we are undeserving of the award, or the pay raise, or the new job title. That we need *more* and *bigger* to have anything matter at all. That we absolutely *must* outperform others or else we'll end up with nothing.

So let's remember to step back and be conscious of what entitlement really looks like. Remember that you don't have to be an all-around egotist, insanely privileged, or even especially self-confident to feel entitled. Entitlement can still seep in the cracks—for all of us—and work its way into parts of our egos we don't even recognize as ego. And that's where the lack mentality comes in. Because that scarcity—the fear that drives our entitlement to cut in line and take a shortcut—is linked to the ego.

It's the fear that if we start the process, we'll fail at the very first step, and *I can't fail, because that would make me feel unworthy.*

It's the fear that if we try the process anyway and don't like the work itself, we'll have to face quitting, and *I can't quit because that would make me feel like a loser.*

And it's the fear that if we do put in all the work, we might never get recognized for it and *that may make me feel I'm not good enough.* (Cue ripping the ego-protective Band-Aid off—ouch!)

Our entitlement wants us to move quickly so that we never have to engage with *any* of those fears of our internal lack within ourselves. We don't want to fail, quit, miss our chance, or be ignored—we don't even want to acknowledge we have those fears at all! That's part of the reason it might feel strange to realize that entitlement is so linked to our lack mentality: our ego can act like a smokescreen, hiding the true causes to protect its own sense of integrity.

We're afraid of failure.

We're afraid of being misjudged.

We're afraid we are not good enough.

We're afraid that no matter what we do, we won't belong.

We're afraid that we have to keep proving ourselves to be seen and be worthy.

We're afraid to let go.

We're afraid of being misunderstood.

We're afraid of being canceled.

We're afraid no one will see us or that we will be rejected.

We're afraid there isn't enough to go around, so we hoard, protect, and betray others to get to the top.

Even though it looks like confidence, entitlement is nothing more than a mask for these fears. It's a mindset of justification and selective truths. It cuts us off from *empathy* because it's so rooted in a fundamental sense of *lack.*

It's also, at least partially, correct.

There isn't always enough for everyone.

You aren't as special as you think you are.

Only one person can come in first.

The answer, as we've seen, is to embrace the whole truth *and* all the facts, even as they're contradictory. To make peace with the paradox. Because that's the heart of audacious resilience.

Your challenges are unique to you, but universally understandable as human experiences.

You are incredibly special, but you don't need to be special to be deserving of happiness.

You won't always come in first, but sometimes it's still worth giving it your all anyway.

Embracing that paradox is what takes you from feeling *entitled* to being *worthy.*

When we feel worthy, we see our unique gifts for what they are: not commodities to be hoarded, traded, and used up, but true *gifts,* things that exist to be given away, to be shared, to create joy and connection and positive impact on others. That kind of generosity goes against the ego, goes against our cultural myths, goes against what we *think* we need to survive.

In other words, it's audacious. It's resilient. It's magical. And it's totally beautiful.

✳

Recap & Reflection Corner

1. Reconciling and owning your entitlement and privilege can blast open the doors to portals of massive healing and leveling up. But it's most effective to explore them one at a time.

   First, define what entitlement means to you. Then dig into some ways you may have shown entitlement. (I know for sure I'm guilty of many of these shenanigans. We're all human! So don't hold back.) For example:

- Remember in your 20s when you scooted to the front of the line with friends to get into the concert or club, even though everyone else had been waiting for hours? Entitlement.

- Remember when you tried half-assing a homework assignment, and then talked back to your teacher (or silently resented them) for calling you forward? Entitlement.

- Remember when you argued with the officer to get out of a parking ticket for an expired meter, even though you were totally a full 10 minutes late to leave? Entitlement.

- Remember when you got to the airport only 30 minutes before boarding and there was a super long security line, so you asked the TSA agents if you could—pretty, pretty please—get through quicker? Entitlement.

- Remember when you hit a huge freeway slowdown right before your exit, so instead of waiting in the long line, you drove on the shoulder while cars were beeping behind you, and—phew!—lucky for you there were no cops? Entitlement.

Now consider: in what ways did your entitlement come from a place of lack?

2. Examining your privilege can provide so much empathy and compassion for others. Culturally, we've come a long way in identifying bigger privileges, like white male privilege, but there is a wide spectrum of privilege that can affect our lives: class and financial privileges, educational privileges, physical and attractiveness (beauty) privileges, to name just a few.

    Take some time to check in with your own privilege:

- Was the neighborhood you grew up in middle class or upper-middle class?
- What was the community you grew up in like? Was it diverse, supportive, transgenerational?
- Did you have both parents in your house when you were growing up?
- What sports/activities were you exposed to that gave you an advantage later on?
- What kinds of subjects/topics were you exposed to in school? How did that give you an edge up for college, entrepreneurship, or job training?
- Has your appearance or physical ability ever held you back, placed you forward, gotten you special attention, or put up a barrier for you?

3. On pages 45 and 46, I discussed the *lack mentality,* the fear-driven mindset that we are undeserving of the award, or the pay raise, or the new job title. That we need *more* and *bigger* to have anything matter at all. That we absolutely *must* outperform others or else we'll end up with nothing. How has lack mentality shown up in your life? Where does that overlap with your feelings of entitlement?

4. On page 46, I discussed the three fear cultures: the culture of aversion ("This isn't enough!"), the culture of scarcity ("There isn't enough!"), and the culture of unworthiness ("I am not enough!"). Which of the three fear cultures feels most familiar to you?

For an audio recording on making peace with privilege and entitlement, visit thatsuckednowwhat.com/resources

* * *

Chapter 4

The Chip on Your Shoulder

My client Astrid was a young freelance journalist living the girl-in-the-big-city life of her dreams. She'd loved research and reporting since she was little, and in her early 20s, she was starting to break out: placing pieces with big-name blogs and magazines, earning a steady income, mixing and mingling with other media people.

Her best friend, Blanca, was a writer too, and when she needed a roommate, Astrid was happy to move in with her. Together they survived on cheap pasta and wine while pitching publications from their respective laptops. Astrid had signed up for my nine-week Elevate Your Life course at Global Grit Institute. She knew she was yearning for support on setting boundaries and navigating interpersonal relationships—the sweet spot of the program.

But tension was gaining steam between Astrid and Blanca, and their co-working setup soon turned into competition and jealousy, including fights over mutual friends and potential boyfriends. Astrid was so anxious and stressed in her apartment that she was losing sleep. Finally, things reached a breaking point and they split up, as roommates and as friends.

At first, Astrid felt a thousand times better. She stepped up her game, pitched more, hustled harder. Her writing triumphs were exciting. She seemed to have a ton of hustle. She'd "broken out" and was doing the thing. She would show up during our live calls sharing how free she felt, how she was much more able to focus on her writing—and I even acknowledged her for boldly practicing her boundaries.

But she also developed a *new* toxic relationship—with the Internet. Specifically, with how people reacted to what she wrote. We all know "don't read the comments," but Astrid couldn't stay away. Astrid would get on one of our mindset coaching calls, yet would only ever focus on how many retweets her articles got, whether people were discussing what she'd written, and how many views she'd racked up—*especially* compared to anything Blanca wrote.

If they both published something on the same day, Astrid would constantly check Twitter to see whose article was getting more tweets. If she stumbled on a juicy story idea, she'd rush to send it out while thinking, "Ugh, Blanca had better not get on this first." And every day she told herself she needed to work harder. Be better. Get *more* people talking. Be the top story on whatever site she wrote for *no matter what.*

From the outside, and during the live program calls, Astrid was apparently crushing it. But in our private one-on-one calls, she said she still felt like she was a huge mess.

WANT SOME GUAC FOR THAT CHIP ON YOUR SHOULDER?

We've all got a chip on our shoulder about *something*. Those triggers that open up a wound still raw and fresh. Petty stuff from decades ago we can't forget. Mean-girl moments that stuck in our craw. Even genuine anger at being mistreated, lied to, or emotionally scammed. When other people let you down, it's natural—it's human—to hold some kind of grudge.

At the same time, we know this stuff is in the past. We've survived it, and we're eager to take action . . . to a point.

In Astrid's case, during our mindset coaching sessions, she would come up with a list of excuses. Take a Twitter hiatus? Not possible—she *had* to be on social media for work. Make new writer friends? She'd tried, but they'd all seemed competitive and suspicious. Try a different line of work? No way—writing was her dream, and she didn't have any other professional skills. Mentally forgive Blanca for the hurt she'd caused? Hell, no—that bitch didn't deserve forgiveness after what she'd done!

We've seen how poor self-regulation and egocentrism (in both victim and entitlement form) can block our path to resilience, but there's one more aspect to touch on that comes into every human being's life: the wounds from our past, and the inner child who carries them for us.

Now, I know reading "wounds from the past" and "inner child" might make you roll your eyes or scoff, but hear me out. These phrases are both simply referring to resilience barriers that are shaped by our personal lived experience. They're subconscious, but powerful, and can invisibly skew the paths we take in life, eventually leading us somewhere far afield from where we truly want to go. Even when we *think* we're taking action to improve ourselves and do better in life, our scars can hamper us.

Astrid was working hard on her career *and* on herself within the Elevate Your Life Program. She wasn't pity-partying or waiting for her goal on a platter. Yet she wasn't getting where she wanted to be, and a pattern started to emerge in her mindset:

- She saw her career success as a **zero-sum game** or totally **black and white.**
- She'd picked a **scapegoat** to blame for her perceived failures.
- She had **difficulty trusting** new people, whether potential friends or new professional contacts.
- She maintained **rigid boundaries** about what work she "could" do.
- She felt **resigned to her situation** because it seemed like her fate.

Astrid *thought* she had to prove herself (which was why during our live calls, she came off to the community like she was soaring ahead). She thought that her crappy feelings about her career were coming from her failure to measure up in her work (which was why she kept grinding harder and harder). She thought she'd moved on from everything and everyone that had hurt her.

But what she didn't realize was how much the wounds of her past were still there. She thought she was working to prove *herself*, but she was *actually* trying to prove someone *else* wrong.

Fact: Your dreams are *never* going to materialize if you are trying to prove someone wrong.

You can't open up to goals if you're holding on to resentment.

RESENTMENT: YOU GOTTA LET GO

Now that we've seen what the victim mindset and entitlement look like, we're going to dive into resentment. Resentment is what comes when we don't contend with the wounds of our past. It's what bubbles up when we silence the child we once were, who wasn't accepted for who she was, or who wasn't celebrated for what he could do. It's that almost *physical thing* in our way, like a bunch of rubble in the road when we're just trying to drive off on vacation.

And just like a road trip to the energizing sun and sand at the beach or the peace and quiet of the mountains, it's easy to be impatient to get to the end. When we're ready for change, we want to take the fast lane and an even faster car to get there. If there's crap in our way, we'd much rather pull a U-turn and keep moving than figure out how to go through all the mess.

In essence, we want a shortcut—a "spiritual bypass."

Astrid wanted to be a better version of herself. She was eager to get there. But—at first, at least—she didn't *really* feel like doing the work. Maybe she could understand the hard way *intellectually*, and could recite exactly what kind of growth and insights she *would* need to get there, but when it came down to taking action, there was always some excuse. She was more interested in finding ways to hit bigger numbers on Twitter rather than interrogating *why* she was caught in a scroll-refresh-scroll dopamine-hunting loop. She would rather play the game by the rules of her own resentment, even if it meant failing over and over, than do the deeper, darker, scarier internal work to let that resentment go.

Most people brush off their own internal work. They don't want to knock down all those roadblocks in their way, fill in the potholes that life has crunched into their path. They take the bypass because it's easier. They put off the "necessary steps" because they are too busy, too hopeless, too . . . fill in the blank.

But in order to go where you've never gone, you need to do things you have never done.

And that's scary!

Maybe you've heard the expression "The only way out is through," or the expression "It's the journey, not the destination." When it comes to the wounds of your past, and the inner work to contend with them, those are both exactly right. Because when you're taking *this* journey, you're not swerving around the heaps of crap that your past has piled up along the way. You're not slamming the brakes when a monumentally painful memory shows up on the horizon.

Nope—you're driving a bulldozer.

A bulldozer is technically a vehicle—it gets you from point A to point B. But the purpose of a bulldozer isn't to drive it somewhere. The purpose is to drive it *through* something. To reinvent point A and forge a new road to point B.

Bulldozers aren't fast. They aren't slick or sexy. And unless you're a construction-loving three-year-old like my son, they're probably not your vehicle of choice.

But if you want to thrive, to cultivate a greater capacity for bouncing back, you've got to bulldoze.

The allure of resentment is in how grounding and familiar it is. When we have sucky moments crop up in our lives, we don't choose actions that are unhealthy or counterproductive *because* they're unhealthy or counterproductive; we choose them because they're comforting, cozy, and because we're hurt AF! So we pack our hurtful feelings away, label them and stuff them into boxes, pile them up into little trash pyramids of memory, because at least that gives us something *solid*.

Resentment reassures us. It lets us say, "Obviously, this has nothing to do with me." It suggests that whatever's going on isn't *our* fault—there's someone else to blame. "I can't believe he cheated, again."

Resentment gives us an answer. Similarly, we get a nice, cozy sense of certainty from resentment: *this* person did *this* thing, and that's that. No confusing gray areas or complexities needed here! "She is so toxic! I trusted her as a friend for years and she just betrayed me by saying hurtful things behind my back?!"

Resentment validates our trauma. When we suffer at the hands of someone else, resentment is often the only source of validation we can get, and we cling to it as a result. Kinda like what happens when you continue overworking, even when you tell your boss you don't do weekends. So you work willingly, feeling helpless and frustrated that he can't see your worth!

Resentment is a firm foundation. In the absence of anything else, the feeling of resentment can be a backstop to keep yourself feeling grounded and, most of all, *safe*. It's why even when you want to leave that job *so* bad, you haven't even written up a résumé, because it's too hard in your mind to face the reality that in five years you haven't been acknowledged, you haven't had a raise, and it's a toxic environment. It's safer, psychologically, to instead lean in to being bitter and grumpy—an "I hate my job" type. You get a scapegoat, you take no risks, and you stay.

If you take the spiritual bypass and basically ignore your inner work, all this crap—the crap of resentment—will stay put. The heap of stuff that was blocking your way is still back there. You didn't bulldoze. If you think about the other side of all the crap you have to clear out, how can you possibly pay attention to the journey through knocking it down and crumbling it to bits?

You are giving yourself permission to take the long way, the way that's filled with clutter, chaos, and mess and the things you've boxed up so tightly you don't even remember putting them away. But in bulldozing, you create a new path and *unleash*—you rewire your brain cells, activating areas in your mind and body to release and let go of what no longer serves you.

This is the number one difference I see between clients who truly go the distance and achieve that success, and clients like Astrid who tend to stay stuck in circles, finding new and different things or people to blame, making excuse after excuse.

Successful people do the work. They dig in and get dirty. They don't spiritually bypass the stuff holding them back.

They bulldoze right through it.

It's tempting, once we've identified those chips on our shoulders, to pile them in a heap and just ignore them—or pretend they were never there in the first place. But identifying these issues is just the first step. Acknowledging your past is important, but that isn't the same as working through it. When we bulldoze, we are taking personal responsibility for our past *and* our future.

It's our responsibility to deal with what befell us in life.

It's our responsibility to embrace the body, the identity, the world we were born into.

It's our responsibility to create, plan, and direct our future successes.

It's not our *fault*. Maybe, on a soul level, we perhaps chose these experiences to learn more about ourselves in this human experience. But we still didn't cause all these things to happen. We don't choose our height or our eye color or our natural abilities, gifts, and talents.

We don't control the way others treat us—no matter if they tell us, "Look what *you* made me do!" or blame it on external circumstances.

These setbacks, these hurts: they are not our fault.

But they *are* our responsibility.

Just like we couldn't have brought such things on ourselves, we also can't vanish them away. We have to ride through them.

And how do we do that? One word: agency.

WHAT IS AGENCY?

If personal responsibility is the bulldozer, then agency is in the driver's seat.

Agency is the term used by social scientists for our ability to act independently and make our own free choices. It is the force that slams a foot on the gas and says, "Full steam ahead—this old stuff has got to go and make way for the new, because better things are on the way."

In other words, agency is action with *intention* and *independence*. It's the state of doing things for yourself, by yourself, for your own benefit, not because of any external pressures, or cultural myths, or entitled or victim mindsets. It's the feeling that *we* are the ones capable of changing what we experience in the world. When you have agency, you feel confident in not just what to do, but when to do it—or when to hold back. You're not trapped by patterns—because you've bulldozed them away.

Agency is key to thriving because agency makes us feel fulfilled. It's a virtuous circle, building up more and more the more it's exercised. In psychology, this is attributable to what's known as the *locus of control*.

Control is very important to us, as humans. Why? Humans really dislike uncertainty. Picture this: a beautifully calm day kicks off with a text from your bestie asking if you saw what so-and-so said about you online, then a call from the teacher asking for a parent-teacher conference to discuss unspecified "issues" with your kiddo, and then a weather report that can't even tell you whether to pack an umbrella or not! If you're like me, your adrenaline skyrockets and anxiety shoots through the roof just imagining all that uncertainty.

We can't even deal with the results of a test before it comes back, or the outcome of a job interview, or whether or not everyone who RSVP'd for our event will actually show their face. Discomfort is *hard*. Not being in control is *hard*. Many of the unhealthy or even destructive behaviors we engage in are driven by a deepseated need to avoid that uncertainty.

This makes sense if we look at how humans become, well, human! As babies, the world is a huge mess—new sights, sounds, and colors whirling around us all the time, with no sense of agency whatsoever. Soon, though, we learn that we have some control to make changes. We can pick up a block and let it go—it drops. We can smile or cry or make some gurgling baby noise—someone comes to see what we need. Of course, even with some kind of superparents, a baby can't get everything it needs right away, and so part of learning agency is also learning to adjust expectations, to understand that things don't always happen at the rate we want them to, or happen at all. That's how we learn patience, and even to be a tiny bit less selfish (as we learn that others have needs and drives too—often when we are greeted with a newer, tinier sibling to share the world with).

As we continue to grow, our sense of balance in the world and our own power to affect what happens firms up. Just as our kid brains absorb things like language and motor skills, so too do they internalize when control is ours, and how much of it we have. This fundamental sense of how much *we* can change things versus how much everything and everyone *around* us can change things is known as the locus of control. The word *locus* just means "place," so literally speaking, this is our understanding of where control is: within us or outside of us.

If we develop an *internal* locus of control—kinda like trusting our inner GPS wisdom—our predominant sense is that we ourselves are in the driver's seat. We are motivated to take action, try new things, and learn, because we believe that if we put our mind to something and take action, we can get closer to the success we're hoping for.

If we develop an *external* locus of control, aka getting validation outside ourselves, however, we see our fate as just that: fate. Whatever forces, chance, or luck shapes the outcome of our lives are way beyond anything we can influence. Often, we attach the control to something specific—aka, we blame something: "There's so much competition on Etsy right now, there's just no way my shop is going to get traction" or "All guys are just so picky—it's hopeless trying to date." In extreme cases of external locus of control, even things like self-care rituals and manifesting feel pointless—the gas pedal isn't just too far from our foot, it's in another parking lot entirely.

EXTERNAL V. INTERNAL LOCUS OF CONTROL

WHY DOES EVERYTHING HAPPEN TO ME?		I TAKE RESPONSIBILITY FOR MY REALITY
FATE DETERMINES YOUR DIRECTION	→	INNER GUIDANCE (GPS) DIRECTS YOU
VALIDATION COMES FROM OTHERS	→	VALIDATION COMES FROM YOU
BLAME OTHERS FOR SETBACKS	→	OWN YOUR PART WITHOUT SHAME
YOU'RE IN THE PASSENGER SEAT	→	YOU'RE IN THE DRIVER'S SEAT
VICTIM MODE: WHY ME?	→	VICTOR MODE: I'M THE DIRECTOR

Small shifts can make a huge difference in where you see control in your life.

Research has found that people with internal loci of control—namely, people with strong internal motivation—tend to be more successful: they attain higher paying jobs and rack up more achievements. They tend to be in better physical shape, experience less psychological stress, and have higher overall self-esteem. Those with external loci of control, meaning people usually motivated by outside factors, meanwhile, are more prone to mental health issues, addiction, and financial struggles.

The good news is that just because our locus of control and sense of personal agency take shape primarily when we're very young, they are by no means out of our hands when we're older. (Although, if you're heavily invested in feeling out of control, this can be hard to wrap your head around!) The important thing to know is that agency is something everyone can exercise, and it's absolutely key to achieving resilience. It wipes out the harmful and unproductive patterns that hold us back. When you exercise agency, you can't be stuck in the victim mindset, because to take action, you are by definition not frozen by circumstances. In a nutshell, it's like reclaiming your sovereignty and taking radical personal responsibility. But you also can't be working out of entitlement, because in true agency, your actions have intentions and values.

TAKING ACTION VS. HAVING AGENCY: WHEN WHAT YOU WANT ISN'T (EXACTLY) WHAT YOU NEED

Let's dive into that last point in a bit more depth, because it's an important distinction to make.

Intention and values are key to *genuine* agency.

Not all action is agency.

And not all victim mentality behavior comes from holding resentment toward a nemesis.

Like Astrid, Tori was motivated and a hard worker. But Tori's goal was one she'd come up with totally on her own, with no frenemy to compete with: she wanted to get in shape. But not just in a general way. Tori was training for a bodybuilding show, and her goal could be summed up in three words: rock-solid abs.

She hired a former fitness model to train her.

She became fanatical about her 9:30 p.m. bedtime.

She calculated her protein needs down to the gram.

It was in the midst of all this regimentation and sweat equity that she and I started our work together.

On the one hand, Tori was eager to *have* a goal. She *knew* something in her life needed to change. She was an achiever by nature, and she wanted to take action, to take personal responsibility, and move toward that better, happier life.

But on the other hand . . . well, she wasn't really feeling happier. So when we sat down for a coaching session, I asked her to walk me through her routine in detail, and then we could start to peel back the layers and look for patterns.

Well, Tori told me, first of all, she had to eat six times a day, and eat the *same thing* over and over: protein, vegetable, no carbs. She had to track her macronutrients and her micronutrients, her water intake and her sleep. Everything had to be measured and planned.

Second of all, she had to work her body *incredibly* strategically. Training for a bodybuilding competition isn't just about getting to the gym and sweating it up two or three times a week. Everything in Tori's life now revolved around the schedule of workouts and timing of food.

As she described the lifestyle, I made a casual comment about how detail-oriented she must be.

Tori laughed. "Me? Not even close."

As it turned out, and as I got to know Tori's personality, she was *not* a details person. She was this wonderful, big, broad thinker, less interested in specifics than in general concepts. A free spirit, she lived to be spontaneous and was always down for last-minute plans with friends. Plus, she *loved* trying new restaurants. She was the ultimate foodie!

Nothing about her goal—those rock-solid abs—was incompatible with her personality. But it was pretty clear that the day-to-day actions she was taking were: plate after plate of chicken and broccoli, regular weigh-ins, and early alarms are the polar opposite of spontaneous! Tori knew she was in charge of her own success. She was doing every step dutifully; she was taking action, and taking personal responsibility. But she wasn't *feeling* it, because her *actions* weren't aligned with her *values*.

To achieve our goals, we have to act. This is pretty obvious, right? Tori knew she wasn't going to get crazy fit just by sitting around on her couch. But action applied without self-knowledge isn't enough. Personal responsibility doesn't just mean *we* are the ones taking action—it means those actions should have *personal meaning* to us. Before we embark on a goal for personal growth, we need to ask ourselves, "Okay, what's the *reason* I'm doing this? How would the end result make me feel? Is that worth giving up other things that matter to me in the present?"

For Tori, eight months of a strict 9:30 bedtime and meal after monotonous meal meant she was neglecting the things that made her happy, like going out to restaurants, finding the latest places with friends, or just *not having to obey a schedule.* And because she was subconsciously searching for a firmer sense of identity, to reclaim her essential feeling of *Tori-ness,* giving up those favorite activities only made things worse—even if they got her closer to those four-pack abs.

When we feel the need to change things, improve our lives, and push for progress, we act. But that action is only true agency when it's informed by intention and driven by our values. That's what puts us in the driver's seat of that big old bulldozer.

Taking actions toward a goal when you're out to "prove someone wrong" is the opposite of acting in accordance with your values. It's *not* agency.

In order for those sacrifices to feel worth it, Tori needed to connect her new patterns of behavior to the values she's discovered in herself. When she could say on her 20th day in a row of bland chicken and broccoli, "Okay, maybe I don't love this food, but there's a reason I'm doing this, because . . ." and then fill in the blank with a values-driven statement, like "being strong and confident matters to me" or "I care about preserving my health," then her routine wasn't something she resented or felt like she was doing to prove someone wrong. She had faced her wounds and the stories of her past head-on, and in doing so could transform the actions she'd previously found frustrating and stress-inducing into something that was a choice she was making—and for good reason.

But she could also use this values-driven mindset to incorporate more of the things she loved back into her life: maybe she didn't need to *win* the bodybuilding competition—maybe another value had more priority, like spending time with friends, and she found she was willing to modify her end goal so she could bring back that core value. And she could leverage the realization of those past hurts toward a greater sense of self-awareness that she can bring out when she's evaluating any new potential goals.

When you can look hard at your goals and interrogate them with gentle but firm curiosity, when you can do that peeling back, you can tap into the ultimate sense of agency. When the process of working toward a goal, the day-to-day and step-by-step, makes you feel alive, whole, and lit up with possibility, then you're primed for success and immune to resentment, no matter what curveballs come your way in the process.

CLEARING OUT TO FLY FORWARD

We've seen how life, especially our early life, can pile chip after chip onto our shoulders. We've seen that the nature of human development leads us to learn lessons about how much control we have—or think we have—and live by those lessons almost indefinitely.

But we've also seen that when we knock those chips away, when we bulldoze the roadblocks of resentment, we clear out our path to resilience. We've seen that no matter where we've oriented our locus of control, we can still regain our sense of agency.

Clearing out doesn't mean pitching the emotional baggage of our experiences straight into the garbage. It means unpacking it. Because when we actually peer into what we've hidden from ourselves for so long, we get unprecedented insight into what we want. Acknowledging the wounds, the scars, the hurts and harms of our past, the unmet needs we felt as children and onward, might feel scarier and more vulnerable than lashing out with resentment. But unpacking that stuff, looking that inner child in the eye, *doesn't* make us weaker. It doesn't make us less resilient. In fact, giving our past selves empathy is the only way to find out what we value, what we need, and what we *want*.

When you know what you want, you are working in your power and not giving that away to someone else.

When you know what you want, and make *that* the reason you're pursuing something—whether that's starting a business, looking for The One, mastering a new skill, or saving for a home— you're so much more likely to be successful.

And when you know what you want *because* of your past, and not in spite of it, you are taking back ownership over your life— your *whole* life. You acknowledge all that's happened fully and feel gratitude and a new, exciting sense of purpose. You take responsibility for your actions (and inactions too) instead of blaming others. You no longer default to believing that anything outside of your control, whether that's other people or the past or just the situation at hand, has to be the driving force in defining what you do next.

Part 1 has covered some fundamental concepts that get in the way of our resilience: our self-regulation, the two extremes of our ego, and our past experiences. But knowing more about the inner workings of our human selves in general is just the beginning. In the next chapters, you'll build on what you've learned here and get nitty-gritty and granular. You'll understand what you—personally—are made of when times get tough.

The reality is, when life happens, no matter how much work you've done, there is a very human tendency to fall back into some of our patterns and bad habits. To melt down completely (and not self-regulate), to ask "Why me?" or insist "Me first!" (and give into the ego), or to act based on what *others* want (and let our past wounds fuel resentment and block agency). But what those patterns, those behaviors look like for each individual person will be, well, individual.

This brings us back to a fundamental question: Why do some people seem to bounce back more easily than others?

The answer lies in the Bounce Factor. Because when you're aware of your Bounce Factor—your upbringing, your environment, your emotional capacity, and your self-awareness—you'll know exactly what *you* need to be your most resilient self.

So take a moment to absorb everything you've learned here, to reflect on it, to feel good about how much work you've already done. Then get ready for Part II.

✳

Recap & Reflection Corner

1. Similar to Astrid's awakening, recall a moment where you felt that chip on your shoulder. What happened to put it there? What was the instance that brought it out again? Why did you feel you needed to prove yourself? What did that experience open up for you?

2. Think back to moments in the earlier part of your life (whatever "earlier" means to you—this could be childhood, adolescence, young adulthood, whatever formative phase is calling to you) that were painful in some way, big or small. What would you tell or give to your younger self in that moment if you could? What did your younger self need?

3. The discomfort of uncertainty can be paralyzing for some. Recall a time (could be a current event) when you felt uncertain in an aspect of your life. What did you feel like? What actions did you take as a result?

4. Describe agency. In what areas do you feel like you have agency in your life? Where could having more or stronger agency help you?

✳ ✳ ✳

Part II

THE BOUNCE FACTOR

We are complete as ourselves,
and our flaws make us unique.
Perfection is boring anyway.

— PRIYANKA CHOPRA

What Makes Us Bounce

I can't change the world,
but I can change my world.

— HASAN MINHAJ

Okay, deep breath.

We've established that life has inescapable, sucky AF moments, and that, as humans, our reactions to those moments are our best, instinctive attempts to deal with them. But we've also seen that sometimes our automatic reactions aren't the most resilient ones. We realize that, yeah, we're not doing ourselves any favors by throwing a pity party, playing the victim, or thinking we're entitled to avoid discomfort. We know that the best way to face those inescapable sucky moments is with a sense of self-regulation, a strong connection to what we want and value in life, and a tight leash for our ego.

And now that we've looked at *how* we humans tend to react to sucky things happening—to bad days, bad breakups, scary diagnoses, and earth-shattering changes—we can dig into the *why*. We're going to zoom in on what makes each of us as "bouncy" as we are, and why certain situations feel like non-issues while others leave us in a weeping puddle or a storm of rage. In short, it's time to understand the Bounce Factor.

So let's bounce.

The Bounce Factor is simple: it's how much you—or anyone—can bounce back after a sucky moment, challenge, setback, or hardship. Your Bounce Factor has four essential components:

1. your upbringing

2. your current environment

3. your emotional capacity

4. your self-awareness

These four components overlap and influence each other, and they evolve and expand as we grow and become better humans. As you might be able to tell, we've already touched on some of the concepts that are at play within the Bounce Factor in Part I: your upbringing is very closely tied with the chips on your shoulder, for example, and your ego can have a big impact on how self-aware you are. Self-regulation is a key influence on your emotional capacity, and your current environment can set off any number of triggers leading to everything from pity parties to pouting sessions.

THe BOUNCe FACTOR

Your UPBRINGING

What you can't change & can only make peace with

Your CURRENT enVIRONMeNT

The good stress that you're exposed to & can control

Your eMOTIONAL capacity

Your ability to stretch, expand, feel & grow

Your RADICAL AWAReNeSS

Your ability to integrate & align within yourself

These four core components are what make you Bounce.

Each of these components will be explained in depth, and you'll get specific, targeted exercises to reflect on what each of the four looks like for you. There's no scale or spectrum or ranking here—your Bounce Factor, and the four components that make it up, are holistic by nature. Your Bounce Factor isn't a grade or a rating to compare against others'. It's not even a metric to chart over time as you "get better at it." It's a framework for understanding how you, personally, react to those magical moments of suck.

Similarly, figuring out the makeup of your Bounce Factor does *not* mean you'll magically become your own Marvel superhero who's mega-resilient and literally bulletproof. In fact, you might experience quite the opposite—you might feel *more* vulnerable, *more* exposed, *more* subject to painful influences you thought you'd buried long ago. Some of your past may bubble up to the surface. Some of it may be juicy; some of it may be tender. *But* all of it is good—and normal. This is *human,* in fact. Because your Bounce Factor is not your fate. It's just a snapshot, a reading, a sense of how you *tend* to do in times of upheaval. It's an intertwined, holistic factor that takes its cues from nature as well as nurture.

The most important thing to understand is that while some of the facts underlying the four components of your Bounce Factor can't be changed, your reaction to them can. And, as we'll see in the fourth component, self-awareness, the stories you tell yourself about your resilience—even subconsciously—can have exponential effects downstream when you're faced with hardship.

But until you look for those stories, until you peel back and examine what's in your Bounce Factor, you'll never truly see them. They're the air that you breathe, the water you swim in. They're so subtle, they're practically invisible—but I'm here to give you a microscope. Now let's take a look.

Chapter 5

Your Upbringing

Serena was a mom of two who'd taken seven years off from her career in corporate HR to raise her kids. When she decided to immerse herself in the workforce again, all she could think about was *how much she had to prove.*

She knew she had the skills and track record to take on high-level work, but at the same time, she consistently felt that the "gap in her résumé" was holding her back from promotions and new opportunities. Serena was incredibly accomplished, to be clear, and she wasn't one to rest on her laurels. She was almost always taking one course or another on management techniques, keeping up to date on best practices, and straight-up picking up the slack for other people. Hiring her was basically bringing a triple (or even quadruple) threat on board.

When we started working together, Serena wanted to focus on hitting that next level in her work. But I suspected there was something deeper at play than just a career-centric mindset block. So I asked her a question I ask a lot of coaching clients—and I'm going to ask you the same one right now.

What was it for you like growing up?

Nope, this is not a talk therapy sesh. But there's a reason the cliché "Tell me about your childhood" comes up so often in therapy. Personally, I really love diving into the early years of life because that's when we learn to be human.

I put the upbringing component right up front for a few reasons. First of all, the upbringing component of your Bounce Factor can help you see that if you sometimes feel less than resilient, or you can't understand why some people are always able to brush things off while you feel devastated for days, it's not because you flat-out failed. It's not because you didn't try hard enough (although there's a huge role for personal responsibility—which we'll get to!). It's because much of what affects your innate resilience comes from years in the past. Those moments might be clear memories, or they might have happened so long ago you can't consciously recall them. In either case, memories of childhood struggles can be easily triggered by present-day struggles, and overtake you with an unhelpful coping response before you can even get your bearings.

Your upbringing and its influence on your Bounce Factor is also why so much one-size-fits-all advice about resilience often falls flat. Cliché advice about perseverance is *frustrating* if, for example, you grew up getting criticized for every attempt you made. At a certain point, to avoid the emotional hurt of being shouted at, you'd very logically choose to stop trying! It's why I feel for my coaching clients who say they *can't* disobey their parents. They were raised to see the cultural bonds that hold a family together as sacrosanct and the number one priority, and deviating from that feels like a massive spiritual betrayal. Combine that with "common sense" advice on how to cope and the emotional overwhelm that these triggered moments can create, and you're not likely to bounce back quickly, or maybe at all. Even worse, you might blame yourself for failing.

But you didn't fail. You were just being human.

So, with that in mind, let's *really* talk about your childhood.

Do you recall that childlike feeling of awe and wonder, that curiosity that didn't give a damn what the world thought? Remember having PB&J on your shoelaces, jumping through mud puddles, and eating your fave cereal? (Real talk, mine was Cinnamon Toast Crunch, and I never worried about the glycemic index or the effects of all that dairy—ah, childhood!)

Well, those childhood years were *the* most formative period of your life. And while it might be obvious that there are lots of things going on behind the scenes when we're kids—we're physically

Your Upbringing

growing, and acquiring language and motor skills, and so on—we're also, very crucially, learning the basics of human social life and "the way the world works." Think of being a two-year-old who has just mastered the bye-bye wave, or a six-year-old showing off their first loose tooth to mama and papa (I totally did the old "tie the tooth to the door and slam" trick to get mine out—classy!). There are so many firsts, so many new stages of development, it's no wonder that the greatest imprint into our subconscious comes within the first seven years of life.

When we're kids, there are some things we're taught explicitly—like our ABCs, counting, how to tie our shoes. But there are many more things we're taught implicitly, by observation, by positive or negative reinforcement, and even by abuse or trauma. And it's those parts of our upbringing that can have the most pull when it comes to our Bounce Factor.

Our upbringing can teach us "lessons" that were never written out for us. Our youngest years shape our sense of our own power, and are influential in whether we end up with an *internal* or *external* locus of control (as we talked about in Chapter 4). Many core self-regulation skills, like calming ourselves down or recognizing when we need to rest or have a snack, are formed when we're little. Even our sense of our ego—of our distinct *me*-ness apart from other people and things—develops early on.

It turned out that my client Serena had a lot to share about her childhood. As a kid, she learned a serious work ethic from her father, who was strict and exacting. Serena felt like this had been good for her: that he was teaching her to not give up, to always give 100 percent effort, to keep pushing for success. Clearly, she *had* learned that work ethic. But she'd also learned, implicitly, that *nothing she did was ever good enough*—not getting straight As, not winning sports trophies, nothing. The only glimmers of acknowledgment she got from her father were when she was working herself to the bone on schoolwork or extracurriculars—and even then, they were faint and fleeting.

Serena's story is a great example of how our implicit learning as kids isn't just about navigating our inner selves and the physical world. It's also social. It's about other people and how to live with them, be around them, earn their acceptance. And the first people we meet in life? Our parents.

Now, I promise this isn't just about blaming everything on Mom and Dad. It's simply that our parents, or any adults who are acting as our primary caretakers, are also the ones who are responsible for teaching us the appropriate modes of behavior, culturally, socially, and internally. Yes, our parents are supposed to keep us alive—that's job number one. But being a thriving human is about more than staying warm and having enough food. Our adult caretakers show us how to be a person in the world, and ideally, make us feel safe while doing it so that the lessons stick. They're supposed to set expectations for our external achievements and validate us every step of the way to ensure we repeat desirable behavior (and don't do anything dangerous or harmful more than once). From our parents and caretakers, we learn whose love we need to work harder for, and how to do it. We learn which parent or caretaker responds to our demands quicker, or lets us stay up later, or will sneak us treats. And we learn, of course, how to push our own boundaries along the way.

Because these "lessons" are so subtle and subconscious, however, it takes some active reflection to discover and unpack them. Often, we don't realize the depth of the effects that our parents had on us until we become parents ourselves and start to reflect on what we want to repeat—or not repeat—in our own child-rearing. My husband and I are raising two young children ourselves, and I know that Ajit's experience of growing up in a home where 23 people had to share the same space, and my own experience of losing both of my parents so early, have both been major motivators behind how we parent our kids (and for that matter, re-parent ourselves). When we were toddlers, a tantrum meant you either got the four-finger closed hand *thappad* (a slap across the face that would "knock sense some into you") or a Filipino *chinela* (flip-flop) thrown across the room at you. Now that our son Arie is that age, we've put a lot of thought into how we want to handle his behavior.

For example, I truly, madly, deeply love my son, but toddlers . . . well, they aren't known for being in super strong control of their emotions. So, as two parents deeply committed to emotional grit and emotional intelligence, my husband and I have started using an alternative system: the time-in method (created by the lovely folks at Generation Mindful). When our son starts to blow his top, we take him to a special corner we've set up with posters illustrated with faces for different emotions—happy, sad, mad, tired, and so on—and ask our tearful (or screaming) little guy if he wants to identify his emotions. Then, when he's figured out what he's feeling, we give him some options for actions to deal with that feeling. He also gets to choose how he wants to process the emotion—coloring, hugging it out with his stuffed toy, crumpling paper, or listening to music are great tools for self-regulation.

Does he still throw tantrums? Of course. He's a toddler! But he's *learning*. And this little "time-in" exercise is something we ourselves wish we could have had as kids but didn't really come to appreciate and practice until much later as adults. We spent years stuck in unproductive patterns that we could have broken much sooner if we'd just had some cartoony feelings posters. We consider ourselves very fortunate to have the time and awareness for this exercise. (And I know it all sounds very California—we're owning it. That's what happens when two coaches raise a child.) So we stand there, trying not to crack a smile as our sweet three-year-old kiddo sniffles through his tears and says, with total sincerity, "I w-wanna name my 'motions!"

The point is, even as we're doing our best with those explicit, experiential lessons about emotions, I'm sure we're far from perfect! No parent *is* perfect (which, if you're a parent yourself, or re-parenting yourself with this book, you'll understand all too well). No one is ideally equipped to teach all these lessons about emotions, struggle, disappointment, and fairness across the board. So many parents are struggling just to keep the lights on or put food on the table. Even if they had access to the ideas and materials to teach these lessons, they might not have the time or energy to do so—or vice versa.

So, even if you aren't (or aren't yet) a parent yourself, you can still take the opportunity to reflect on your parents' style of child-rearing and how it shaped you. You can think back and revisit those small moments that may have passed quickly and unobserved at the time. And in doing so, you'll start to understand how all of what you experienced in your childhood affects your Bounce Factor. Again, I want to be clear that this is *not* meant to be some cliché "blame the parents" idea, but a chance to develop a fuller understanding of the people who made us. Intentionally or not, our parents may have subjected us to criticism, neglect, invalidation, abandonment, abuse, or any combination or degree of those. We may have experienced a big upset in our lives early on, whether that was moving to a new city (or country) or losing one of our caregivers. Throw in cultural expectations for what a "well-behaved child" does, or a hardline sense of gender roles, or parents' and grandparents' own generational trauma, and it's easy to see how our upbringing can make some of those lessons about how to be human (and how to bounce back) a little bit jumbled. When you sit down and complete the reflection exercises, I encourage you to try to examine your early years with neutrality, curiosity, and acceptance—even gratitude.

There's also a big generational component to our upbringing, one that goes beyond just our immediate caretakers. We're not just products of our parents—we're products of everyone who came before us down the line, genetically and socially. In other words, it's both "nature" and "nurture."

On the nature side, our family of origin and the upbringing they expose us to is about more than just the color of our eyes or the shape of our nose. If our ancestors lived through any massive, large-scale events that shift the course of human history, like the Holocaust, slavery, wars, cultural oppressions, economic depressions, or genocides, they can actually pass on trauma symptoms through genetics. Scientists are still pinpointing the mechanism, but a growing body of research suggests that these epigenetics play a role in our resiliency. (Yes, we can learn about the generational impact our ancestors have on our own genetic makeup, and it's fascinating!) I wouldn't be surprised if the effects of a massive pandemic, political upheaval, and, at least in the U.S., many, many mass school shootings, will lead Gen Z to pass on similar trauma systems when they have children. (Although I sincerely hope that our support systems and society are better equipped for those effects in the future—the United Nations has listed mental health as one of its sustainable goals of awareness, which is a promising start.)

Even outside of hard science, looking to the lineage of our ancestors, where they come from, what world issues were happening while they were growing up, what it took to raise us, and the lens they saw the world through, can give us incredible, valuable insight on our own ability to deal with the hard shit that comes our way. I remember being absolutely fascinated when asking my maternal Filipino grandmother what it was like to come from a lineage of pageant queens. Or how her own mama had to struggle as a teenage widow with three children to raise on her own. Or how my father challenged his own father's expectations by not wanting to inherit family property after my paternal grandfather suddenly died before he was 60. These stories show me how, on both sides, I come from people who were wired to survive and thrive. And being a child of immigrants, understanding that they had to leave their homeland, struggle, and assimilate to a new land is profound, yet something often taken for granted.

On the "nurture" side, the lived experiences through different generations of our family can have meaningful effects on our upbringing as well. For one thing, child-rearing follows trends and tendencies almost as much as fashion does, and as a result, different decades of adults come through with different skill sets and hang-ups. Ajit and I know firsthand that we've made conscious choices in our parenting that are much different than those of the generation who raised us. But even well-intentioned shifts in parenting styles can have consequences. One study examined our lovely Gen Z folks as they transitioned from high school and into college, where for the first time they encountered flat-out rejection or failure without the backstop of their parents to help them out, and it found that they lacked some of the internal strength or emotional capacity to deal with situations on their own. This isn't to blame them as individual humans, of course, or their parents—the grown-ups simply wanted to shield and protect them from the big, bad, scary world (which can feel even bigger and scarier than before thanks to blazing-fast technology and constant answers at their fingertips).

In looking at her own upbringing, Serena, my coaching client who'd grown up with a demanding but emotionally distant father, was able to connect a lot of dots. She recognized that any time she had male bosses, she would work herself to the bone. After her career pause to raise kids, this tendency only got worse: she fell right back into overextending herself and then some. Even with all her training and long hours and reliable, top-notch experience, those seven years out of the workplace felt like an endless void she'd never *quite* be able to cross in order to succeed in her career. Instead of taking constructive action, she was caught in a spiral of needing to be this perfect mom, this perfect daughter, this perfect wife—the woman who does it all.

But through the lens of her Bounce Factor, and how her upbringing was affecting her resilience, Serena saw that the problem wasn't that she had a "gap in her résumé" from taking time away from the office to raise her kids. It was how she was reacting to the (neutral) reality of her years as a full-time mom. Deep down, she wanted the kind of recognition she never got from her father, and that played out over and over again.

"You have this beautiful family, you have these two amazing kids, and you're able to go get back out in the workforce!" I told her. "You're such an inspiration for so many people, including me."

The words were completely genuine—Serena is a badass, and I know so many working moms who would admire the hell out of her—but they were still hard for her to hear. She looked uncomfortable receiving praise. But she did acknowledge it.

To truly internalize those good feelings, Serena needed to strengthen her Bounce Factor. Now that we'd unearthed so much about her upbringing, she could start giving herself the space to nourish and nurture her wounds from the past. That young girl who just wanted acceptance and validation from her father. Those aching moments of failing to perform at top level. That hollowness that seemed to follow her no matter where she went in life. This was hard work, but the more grace she showed herself, the more confident she felt. She had empathy for who she was as a child, and the woman that child had grown into.

With the wounds of her past acknowledged, the next step was to put her Bounce Factor to the test. Just like a muscle, it needed to be stretched and exercised in order to really do its thing. Serena and I decided that what she needed was to take a risk—to challenge her current boss. She had to go in and ask for a pay raise (which she definitely deserved) and fewer, more flexible hours to work (which, given how capable she was, wouldn't affect her performance at all). Her upbringing had left her with the mindset that sticking her neck out and making "demands" would lead to rejection and failure. That she'd be fired, and no other corporation would hire her because of that "gap in her résumé."

To counter that mindset, I encouraged Serena to put together a fresh résumé and CV, complete with all her new trainings and qualifications, and listing *all* the duties she'd taken on at her current employer, and send it out widely. And to Serena's surprise, she got not only interviews, but offers: jobs with better pay and flexible hours, because she'd made it clear from the get-go that those were nonnegotiable.

Serena was finally able to sit back and be expansive about herself. In writing up those job applications and taking those interviews, she was saying: *This is who I am. This is what my value is, and this is what I need. Take it or leave it.* She wasn't reacting out of fear or trying to do what she thought others wanted. She was claiming her agency in a big way. In letting herself look beyond what she *thought* was the issue (her "professional shortcomings") and into her upbringing, Serena was able to pinpoint where her Bounce Factor needed beefing up. The result? Job offers in hand that gave her what she was worth and what she desired, but also that stronger, more flexible Bounce Factor to carry forward into any of life's sucky moments down the road.

BOUNCE FACTOR DEEP DIVE: QUESTIONS TO PONDER ABOUT YOUR UPBRINGING

So, how were you raised? How were you taught, or shown by example, to think of certain situations happening in your life? What was valued and praised and cherished in your family's eco-system? What was punished, shamed, or simply not talked about?

Where do you fall in the birth order? Are you the oldest? The youngest? An only child? Somewhere in between? If you were the oldest, perhaps your parents were more strict with you and didn't let you do a lot of things, while they softened up by the time your little siblings got to that same age. If you were the youngest or an only child, maybe you were given free rein to do as you pleased, or got a lot of attention as the baby of the family.

And then think about gender roles. If you were raised female, and especially if you were raised by immigrant parents, then maybe you were shielded from the "real world." Or maybe you were given a lot of responsibility in taking care of your younger siblings, or your family members, or the home. If you were raised male, maybe you were burdened with expectations of toughness and success, or punished for showing your emotions. Maybe you were expected to act as the "man of the house" when your family situation shifted.

Some of this is very heavy stuff. But at the same time, it's fascinating, because as we come to understand our Bounce Factor holistically, we see how it begins with our ancestral lineage and goes all the way to the care and education our parents imparted in raising us. We'll see how we can change and shift the influence of our upbringing so that we acknowledge our past while still compensating for areas where we want to cultivate more resilience. As adults, we're relying on our Bounce Factor almost every day— because we can't just throw a tantrum when things don't turn out how we wished (or we *can*, but it's definitely not a resilient way to face problems). And as we dig into our past and peel back what was really going on in our younger years, we'll come to understand some of the reasons why we're still so held back, why we don't want to take risks, or why we play small.

Deep Roots of the Family Tree: When Generational Trauma Holds Us Back

My family has wanderlust in its genes. My paternal grandfather was a diplomat and traveled all across the globe for work. I always knew I wanted a similar kind of life, one that took me to exciting places to see incredible things.

When I applied for a study abroad program in Italy, that wanderlust was a major factor. But I also *needed* that trip after so much darkness and heaviness and responsibility in my young life. So I was stunned when my *Bhua* (which means "dad's sister" in Hindi), who'd been a mother figure to me for so long, put her foot down. "No, you're not going to go."

I was stunned. I pleaded my case, about how this experience would be good for dental school (which was only half-true), and how I had to go to stay competitive, but she wouldn't hear it.

It made no sense to me—at first. But I reflected on our family, on the trauma that was deep-rooted, and the sense started to appear.

My diplomat grandfather passed away when my aunt was a teenager—around the same age I was at the time when I lost my father. She had been studying at an elite boarding school at his insistence, but flew home to Delhi immediately for the funeral rites. Yet when the time came to return to boarding school, my grandmother stood in her way.

"No," she'd said. "You're not going to go."

Now, my aunt had basically grown up at her boarding school. She'd been there since she was 10 years old, living her life, making friends, knowing her classmates better than she knew members of her own family. My grandfather, who'd been so adamant that she attend, never visited, but sent the occasional lavish gift, like a Swiss watch, for good grades. And now that it was time to return, my strict grandmother wouldn't budge.

My aunt was furious, confused, hurt: first she was shipped off to boarding school, then she couldn't go back? The only conclusion she could draw was that her mother hated women. For the rest of her young adulthood, she thought women must work harder, that nothing would ever be good enough, that no amount of achievement would ever make you worthy of what you wanted.

All those years later, when my aunt and I stood toe to toe over my study abroad trip to Italy, I realized how this exact situation brought all of the feels surging back for her. My aunt had wanted to travel, too—first back to boarding school, the place where she felt comfortable, but eventually to get away, to leave India and perhaps come to the States, where her brother, my dad, had gone. But her mother, who'd been deprived of education and experience herself, who'd stayed home and worked hard raising six children, imposed that same deprivation on my aunt. And then, in turn, here we were, two generations of women in the same family, reenacting the same type of generational conflict once again—rooted in upbringing and the gender role obligations for women in our family.

In the end, I did get to Italy, and as soon as I smelled the European air, it was an incredible rush, an incredible moment of breakthrough, of *yes*. What I got in that moment was the freedom that I needed. And I needed that empowering sense of sovereignty for myself—not just from my own trauma and experiences, but because of the compounded needs of the generations of women in my family before me.

This is just one example of how generational trauma—past wounds in our family history—can affect us, and our Bounce Factor, in the present day. Ultimately, confronting generational trauma is an act of understanding, of knowing what befell the people who shaped your life and your world, and using that to power you forward toward thriving. For me, moving forward wasn't about casting blame on my aunt, my grandmother, or my grandfather. It was realizing that the roadblocks in my way weren't roadblocks at all, but the crumbling remains of safety barriers, thrown up in haste by people just trying to keep going in their own lives. Clearing those was transformational not just in terms of my one trip to Italy, but how I saw my own life.

✳

Recap & Reflection Corner

1. Take a few moments to think about your own childhood and upbringing. Get to re-know your parents, and ask them questions about their childhood—over a meal or over Facetime. Ask them what was it like to grow up with your grandparents, aunts and uncles, and great-grandparents. What were some of the struggles they faced? Poverty, wars, the Holocaust, oppression, enslavement, racism, gender discrimination? Or perhaps family expectations? How did it contribute to your parents raising you?

2. Now, with your childhood, what were you exposed to? Did your caretaker try to constantly control your emotional outbursts? Or were you allowed to cry, fall apart, and make mistakes?

3. How did your family deal with sucky life moments?

4. Make a list of expressions of emotion that were allowed and not allowed. Did people in your family scream and yell? Act violently? Avoid and deny? What were the consequences for expressing yourself in a "forbidden" way? What patterns do you see?

5. What did your parents value? Education, success, good grades, kindness, independence? How did they view failure?

6. Look at all your responses and consider this: How did your upbringing affect what you value in your life today?

✳   ✳   ✳

Chapter 6

Your Current Environment

On the outside, my client Cruz seemed unstoppable. Growing up in Las Vegas, he had lived on the streets on and off because his parents were into drugs. He grew up fast—and survived—because he's intelligent and charismatic and, frankly, he just hustled like crazy. He worked hard to avoid the kinds of tragic fates he saw claim his friends and loved ones. He has suffered, seen violence, and felt pain, and experienced some of the most psychologically difficult moments a human being can encounter. There is no denying it: Cruz had been through some real shit.

When we started working together, Cruz wanted to be a coach and a motivational speaker. He wanted to be famous, but something was holding him back. It wasn't that he lacked ability; I saw the potential in him on our very first call together. It wasn't that he wasn't a hard worker either. It was that, in the world of coaches and seminars and weekend motivational summits, he was totally out of his element. This was a totally new environment for him. Yet, at the same time, it was also *particularly* triggering for him—it jabbed his Bounce Factor right in its weak spot.

Our environment matters. The spaces and things that surround us affect our resilience and decision-making on a daily basis. We can see this on a very simple level with things like habit-building: keep the sugary snacks out of sight (or out of the house) and you're more likely to opt for something nourishing. Set your running shoes by the door (or buy some running shoes in the first place) and you're more likely to go out for a jog. Move the TV out of the bedroom and you'll have an easier time falling asleep.

But our environment comprises more than just stuff. The people we spend time with, whether they are family, friends, co-workers, or even the folks on our block and in our town, make up that environment too. The habits and behaviors that result from that part of our environment can have an effect on our Bounce Factor in much the same way our upbringing can. If our social group's idea of a fun get-together is watching football games at the local sports bar, we're probably not going to suggest a Sunday afternoon group hike. If our religious community frowns on cohabitating with a partner before marriage, we're probably not going to sign a lease with our long-term partner until there's a ring on our finger. Of course, neither climbing a mountain trail nor sharing a living space with a partner are inherently dangerous or harmful decisions—plenty of people do these things and survive to tell the tale—but in the right *environment,* they can seem *socially* dangerous.

So, to avoid that social stress, that risk of being shunned or lonely or not accepted, we play small. And in doing so, we weaken our Bounce Factor.

Cruz is a great example of how environment can profoundly change our Bounce Factor. On the streets, Cruz had been through the wringer, faced down intense threats, and rolled with the (literal) punches. But in the world of Ted Talks and small-group seminars, he was *completely* out of his element, and his Bounce Factor plummeted. Each new rejection hit harder and harder. And for a "tough guy" like Cruz, the prospect of looking weak wasn't just a fear—it was an existential threat. In the hardscrabble environment that he was most accustomed to, you could keep other people's judgment at bay with threats and intimidation. Look badass and scary enough and no one would mess with you. And if they did? Well, you could make good on that threat. The culture of violence was, in a way, self-protection from criticism.

Taken out of that environment, stripped of the tools and situations he was used to, Cruz found it much harder to bounce back. For Cruz, it was uncomfortable to be turned down when he pitched himself for an event. On a Zoom call or in an interview, the "thanks but no thanks" from the organizers immediately triggered a stress response—pounding pulse, fluttering stomach, sweaty palms. So, to avoid that discomfort, Cruz simply looked for shortcuts. He made excuses. And soon, like Samuel in Chapter 3, he retreated into the entitlement trap. Rather than work alongside his feelings of stress and nervousness, Cruz let his ego take the reins and started casting blame externally, angry that no one saw how important his story was.

The environment of Cruz's new career was almost tailor-made to wear out his Bounce Factor. And given how powerful our current environment can be on how we react to a sucky moment, it might seem like the solution is to optimize the space around us to keep ourselves as comfortable as we can be. But that's not in the best interest of our resilience. For one thing, addressing the problem *outside* of ourselves—even if it's rooted in our current environment—doesn't have any long-term positive effects on our Bounce Factor. For another thing, social stress, like the rejection that Cruz felt, is part of life—at least, it is when you're looking to grow and achieve your goals. So building up our Bounce Factor here isn't about making the environment more tolerable for us. It's about teaching ourselves to recognize the kinds of environments that can trigger us *and* learning to tolerate the stress that results.

This is where the concept of "positive stressful states" comes in. A positive stressful state is essentially the opposite of a comfort zone. It's an environment that demands you work, rather than relax. It's *stress-inducing*.

And stress can be good for you.

You see, stress in the physiological and psychological sense isn't always a negative. It's a force that signals to your body, mind, or spirit that it's time to *work*. Stress on a muscle, as in weightlifting or cardio, pushes that muscle to its limits and, with the proper rest and nutrition, allows it to rebuild stronger, more flexible, and more resilient. When we don't get ourselves into positive stressful states routinely enough, our Bounce Factor gets out of shape. And when our Bounce Factor's out of shape, and sucky moments inevitably happen, it's that much easier to overextend ourselves, get hurt, and retreat. Imagine rolling right off a comfortable, cushy couch and trying to run a marathon in your slippers and PJs— you're going to pull a muscle, right? That's what's happening psychologically when, for example, a sheltered high-school student enters college or their first real job and encounters definitive rejection—no retakes, no undoing, no calls from their parents to bail them out. *Ouch.* It really hurts! They're just not used to bouncing back from something like that. Their environment, up until that point, has been shielding them from handling those kinds of challenges, and they have not been exposed to that kind of environment (thank you, Mom and Dad).

Just like a satisfying gym session, a positive stressful state doesn't wipe you out or work you to exhaustion. It's about making micro-leaps of resilience moment to moment. It's about doing something new or different, even if it's just a little bit. Why? Because when your brain encounters novelty, it makes new neural connections—even if that new experience isn't something you like at first! The stimulus of something new slowly releases dopamine, the neurotransmitter responsible for motivation and creativity. By finding those mini moments of newness and challenge, we can pump up our Bounce Factor considerably over time, *and* we help get our creative brains in the zone.

Even better, our environment is the aspect of our Bounce Factor that we're most immediately and directly in control of in our day-to-day lives. Your upbringing is something you can work to understand, accept, and find new angles on, but it's not something you can *change*. It's part of you—your roots—and one to be appreciated fully and wholly in order to get into the next aspects of your Bounce Factor. The past may be the past. But your current environment is totally under your control: your present, moment-to-moment, instantaneous control. Your evolution begins the moment you realize shaking up your current environment is vital to managing the inevitable sucky moments in your life. Failing to examine and evaluate our environment is just leaving so much of the power of our Bounce Factor (and, ultimately, our resilience) on the table.

So how could we shift that environment so that every day we're making new strides, stretching ourselves, expanding ourselves?

Let me share an example. When I signed up for my first triathlon, I was not the best swimmer—at *all*. I wasn't so terrified of the cycling or the run, because I'd done both of those before and felt super comfortable on a bike or in a 5K. But the swim was terrifying. *Terrifying*. If the bike and road race were my comfort zone, the pool was my stressful state. And let me tell you, it did *not* feel positive. At the beginning, I was so bad at swimming that I could only swim from one side of the pool to the other—as in, one lap—before I felt so winded that I could not keep my breath.

The triathlon swim was much longer than one lap, obviously. And I'd still have to bike and run afterward. I really wanted to get to *that* part of the race—the part where I felt more comfortable. And to do that, I'd have to get better at swimming.

So I got a coach, one who would help me with my challenge.

And I trained every single day. And it *sucked*.

The water was . . . I can't even describe how freezing it was, but I swear they could've rented that pool for cold-plunge sessions. And my trainer wanted to meet me every day at 6 A.M., which for me meant getting up at 5, which was a full hour and a half earlier than I'd normally be awake—just so I could meet him at 6 and jump into this freaking freezing-cold water.

It was *not* comfortable.

And, again, I hated it.

But I had no choice, not if I wanted to train for this race. The swim was nonnegotiable. That stressful state, that freezing-cold water, was part and parcel of the whole event—I couldn't do two out of three and still call it a *triathlon,* after all. Besides, I wasn't going to quit on Day 1! I had to face some big fears. I had to get uncomfortable . . . and stay that way.

So I committed to swimming three days a week. Literally just 30 minutes per session, which still felt like forever. I'd get there early to take these bordering-on-scorching showers beforehand just to get myself into the water.

But after a few weeks, my body began to acclimate to the stress. I started to get used to getting up early, so I didn't need the shower to be blazing-hot to shock myself awake. Soon after that, I could zip through a cold shower and jump right in. Soon after *that*, my muscle memory kicked in. I found myself instinctively hitting the strokes like a mermaid gliding through the water. And then one day I got up and actually looked *forward* to my early-morning work-out—the ice-cold, misery-drenched swimming workout that stood between me and the *fun* parts of triathlon prep—because I was eager to see how far I could push my limits while celebrating my tiny imperfect wins along the way. I was rising to the challenge of the stressful state, and then leveling up after that. I ended up liking those cold pool plunges (and didn't need extra cryotherapy either)!

Lo and behold, six months later, I completed my very first tri-athlon. I didn't win any awards or anything like that—I'm very much a novice—but for me, even being in that environment was a major win. My personal comfort zone had been "anywhere BUT laps in the swimming pool," and forcing myself into that new and challenging environment was a huge boost to my Bounce Factor. Why? Because of my exposure to good bouts of daily stress.

My client Cruz also found ways to challenge himself in his new environment. Over time in our coaching sessions—and in the daily journaling practice I had him start—we began to identify moments when Cruz felt judged. What did those moments have in common? What precipitated them, and how did Cruz react?

Eventually, we homed in on what made the world of moti-vational speaking so triggering to Cruz: he'd grown up with a slight stutter, and he was convinced people would pick up on it and judge him. A career where *speaking clearly* was a major part of the work was a way more stressful environment than one where he could let his fists do the talking. Cruz needed to internalize that the world of personal growth was an environment where his Bounce Factor would be a little lower at first—and work to build it up. That meant continuing to pitch himself, continuing to put in the work, gently pushing his comfort zone little by little the same way I gradually got used to the cold pre-swim showers.

It worked. Over time, Cruz got more and more accustomed to the environment, and more able to anticipate and manage the particular stressors that held his resilience at bay. But in doing this work, he also improved his craft as a speaker. Beautifully, when Cruz was able to say, "Yeah, I've had a gun pointed in my face, but what *really* scares me is rejection," he found a whole new way to connect to his audience.

BOUNCE FACTOR DEEP DIVE: THINKING ABOUT YOUR ENVIRONMENT

To make the most of the environmental influence on your Bounce Factor, you should basically be saying, "More stress, please—the good kind!" And that good kind of stress can come easily from small, new changes. So start by thinking about places or times you can simply do something new or different during your day. How can you welcome those good challenges and stressors as a way to make that environment work for you?

If you're an aspiring author, maybe this small, novel change looks like getting up earlier to write a scene every day, even though you'd be much more comfortable sleeping in. If you're working on fitness, it could be walking the mile to pick something up from the drugstore instead of driving. If you're working on being visible and present, it could be signing up for an open mic and performing for strangers.

It also doesn't have to be something major or intense (like training for a triathlon). It could simply be putting yourself in a context that challenges your assumptions, or removing yourself from one that isn't serving you.

Good stress encourages you to be better, whether at handling disappointment, embracing unmet expectations, building muscle, getting more creative, or becoming a better public speaker—all of it begins with taking courageous action.

Quick Good-Stress Boosts

Want to challenge yourself and put a bit more daily good stress into your current environment? Try one of these!

- Do five random pushups today.

- Have a difficult conversation—namely the one you've been putting off.

- Hold your breath for 30 seconds, and then take 3 sips of air, and hold for 10 seconds. Exhale while slowly counting back from 8.

- Set a timer for 10 seconds and scream. Just let go!

- Hold a plank position for 30 seconds.

- Put your favorite dance tune on and shamanically shake and move, not giving a fuck who's watching.

- Purchase something special for yourself, especially if you always hold back.

- Go live on social media and share your unscripted thoughts for five minutes.

- Sign up for that Toastmasters class.

- Pay for two of your friends' meals/coffees today.

- Set a timer for 30 minutes and write down what's on your mind—no judgments allowed.

- Record a voice note to yourself on what you love and appreciate about your body: your legs, your abdomen, your feet, your breasts, your lips, your forehead, your eyes, your age, your height.

*

Recap & Reflection Corner

1. Describe the difference between the good stressors in your life and the bad stressors. What good stressors can you add that can help shift your current environment?

2. Recall a time when you did change your environment (for example, you took the longer route to work, tried an acting class, did a personal growth training, rearranged your room, began a new and challenging workout). What came up for you during the change? How did you feel afterward? How do you think the change in your environment contributed to your Bounce Factor?

3. Now, think of a time when you felt less confident or you failed terribly. What did you learn about yourself during that time? What good stressors could you have used back then? What in your environment at that time might have affected you?

* * *

Chapter 7

Your Emotional Capacity

When Marianna came to me, she was completely burned out.

She'd been top of her class at med school, but now, a few years into being a practicing doctor, she was struggling with her next chapter. So, as an outlet from her workday, Marianna had begun writing a blog about life as a physician, chronicling the (anonymized) stories of the people who came into her office, focusing on the humaneness around those stories, and healing her patients through unconventional ways. Gradually, she realized she wanted to create a community around wellness and well-being, one that treated patients like human beings and could prescribe things like nature and meditation instead of falling back on the prescription pad no matter what.

When we first met and she shared her mission, I was inspired, and obviously super excited to work with her. Given the professional exhaustion that had led her to question her career path, I figured there would be a lot of emotions to unpack as we helped her heal from her burnout while also forging a new plan for her work life.

But it turned out Marianna wasn't too interested in talking about feelings.

"My first virtual event had only five people in the audience," she told me, right off the bat. "Out of 50 RSVPs! I just tripped over my words for a few minutes and ended it early."

I replied that 1.) that sucked and I was sorry to hear it, and 2.) it sounded like navigating the fear of failure would be a good place to start, along with any other emotions that surrounded this big life shift.

Marianna laughed and shook her head. "Oh, I don't need to talk about emotions," Marianna said. "I need to go *viral*. Can we talk social media strategy?"

Marianna was a perfectionist, or, as she would put it, she *strived for excellence*. She'd admit that much herself—she was gifted at medicine, and school and study had come easily to her, so she prided herself on getting the right answer the first time. But she also had a clear issue with her emotional capacity. Her "perfectionism" was masking an inability to healthily process any feelings of failure. So when things didn't go as planned—for example, her first event— she would stumble on her words and literally disappear for days because she could not handle the intensity of her emotions. As a result, her Bounce Factor needed a serious assessment.

We've already touched on how emotions serve a real, useful purpose in our human lives, but as we explore this component of the Bounce Factor, it's time for a bit of a deeper dive. For a refresher on the basics, look no further than Pixar's *Inside Out*. I love this movie—as far as I can tell, this was the very first film that really portrayed emotions the way they truly work. For those of you who haven't seen it yet, the CliffsNotes version of the setup is that the characters in the movie live inside the mind of a girl named Riley, where they represent the primary emotions: There's Joy, who, as you probably may have guessed, is always super happy. And then there's Anger, who is, as you may have guessed, always angry. And then there are Sadness, Disgust, and Fear—same thing for all of them. The core theme of the movie is the complexity, breadth, and scope of human emotion: Sadness is just as good to have around as Joy, because Sadness has important signals to send us, and the people who love us, about when we need to take care of ourselves. In its beautiful and hilarious story, this children's movie taught audiences more about emotional intelligence than generations of self-help gurus. It taught children that it's okay to not be happy all the time. That emotions aren't good or bad, they just *are*. It's okay to experience a wide array of emotions. It's okay to feel *anything*. And that is why I love, love, love that movie so much.

In reality, though, identifying and processing our emotions isn't as cut-and-dried as picking one out of the five simple feelings in a lineup. If we don't have a lot of practice naming our emotions, of recognizing them mindfully as they arise, it's hard to conjure up the exact feeling we're feeling out of thin air. Are we sad? Angry? Hangry? Nostalgic? Jealous? Embarrassed? Ashamed? Even bothering to ask ourselves these questions is an exercise in *emotional capacity*.

Emotional capacity is our ability to anticipate, experience, and modulate our feelings across different situations. Like the other components of the Bounce Factor, this varies from person to person, but also varies depending on context: a tough guy who never cries might still turn on the waterworks when meeting his new grandchild for the first time! Regardless, when we have a strong, well-developed emotional capacity, we are deeply in tune with what we're feeling in the moment and can see feelings cresting on the horizon. We can nip things in the bud or prepare ourselves to ride the wave. When we have a diminished emotional capacity, we're often not aware of our feelings until we're swept away by them—if we notice them at all.

Emotional capacity is a blend of nature and nurture. It's not as instantly changeable as your present environment, but it's also not as hard-coded as your upbringing—yet ultimately, it's intertwined with both.

For starters, there are some strictly biological and neurological components to your capacity to deal with hard life shit and learn to expand your emotional capacity. But the good news, loves, is that this is a skill that can be trained and cultivated (woo-hoo!). Babies and toddlers (aka the most emotionally expressive kind of human) are less capable of keeping feelings in check because the prefrontal cortex—the part of the brain that manages impulse control—isn't fully developed (and won't be until after their teenage years). So, on a certain level, our emotional capacity grows as we mature—especially after our exposure to our lived experiences: breakups, betrayal, loss, separation, failure, adversity, setbacks, family dynamics, unexpected outcomes, personal expectations, et cetera.

But, by the same token, we can learn over time, through our experiences, to forcibly narrow the emotions we're feeling, or to cast them in a particular light. Marianna's perfectionism was rooted in the experiences she'd had in her life and work so far. Her years of schooling as a medical doctor had been all or nothing, do-or-die. Exams were graded on a strict curve: when Marianna got an A, that meant someone else had to settle for a B or lower. With that goal of success so narrowly defined, she naturally winnowed down the emotions she felt to a stark set of options. Either she was successful and could feel happy, or she wasn't successful and therefore a failure, leading to a panicked fear of scarcity. But instead of addressing that fear, feeling it fully and contending with it, Marianna's emotional capacity was restricted to simply mobilizing that fear toward her goal. The lens of her emotional capacity turned everything into either a sign of triumph or a sign of defeat, with no middle ground: *If this person and this person have 20,000 followers, then I need to snatch up even MORE or there will be none left to go around!* Personally, I know my emotional capacity was shaped out of similar necessity: to survive, there were some feelings I had to process one way or the other or else I couldn't move forward. Grief was an emotion I mastered early on because of the sickness, caretaking of my parents, and the sudden loss of my brother. Joy was an emotion I celebrated at length whenever I could, to keep the peace and to get us out of the constant turmoil of stomach-dropping, panic-ridden phone call moments.

Moreover, some neurodivergent people, such as people on the autism spectrum or with processing disorders like ADHD, don't recognize and label their emotions as easily as neurotypical people, even as adults. Hormones, too, are major modulators of our feelings: surges in progesterone during the premenstrual phase or pregnancy can cause weepiness and mood swings. (I totally rode the waves of ALL of that during and after both of my pregnancies, and phew! Glad it's over!). For some, meanwhile, increased testosterone can "shorten the fuse" and make them more prone to angry outbursts. It's also been theorized that evolutionary differences in men's and women's emotional processing comes from hunter-gatherer societies, where women would naturally multi-task as they gathered food, connected with the herd community, and tended to children, and men would be more stoic, focusing single-mindedly on pursuit of prey.

At the same time, emotional capacity is deeply intertwined with our upbringing. And because our upbringing affects emotional capacity in particular—our ability to self-regulate and understand our feelings—the cultural and gender expectations that surround us early in life can calibrate our sense of how we "should" react to given events. In my Asian family (my father was from India, and my mom was from the Philippines), our emotions either had to be happy all the time, or there were huge blowouts of screaming and anger. Not only that, I don't think my parents even had the self-knowledge to identify their own emotions between the two extremes, let alone communicate their emotions to their children. This attitude is common in a lot of different Asian and South-Asian cultures, and other societies around the world as well. Emotions should be stoic. Emotions should be kept internal. Emotions aren't meant to be shared, unless there was some trauma bonding happening (which in my world came between the ages of 10 and 19, when there were lots of emotional roller-coaster events). If a similar story and set of cultural values were present in your younger years, it may have a profound effect on how you are currently able to handle your emotions.

In Marianna's case, she had a good relationship with her parents, but had grown up as an only child, so she was accustomed to being the center of everyone's focus. Her problems were everyone's problems, and there was no need to share the spotlight. As an adult, when that spotlight shifted away, she found herself in uncharted territory, and her emotional capacity had no built-in solution beyond *panic*. She'd also internalized the narrative of some of the cultural myths of entitlement that we looked at in Chapter 3. Her time in med school validated her sense that *persistence pays off,* but when the events in her life didn't follow the beats of those stories—in other words, when suck happened—she didn't have the emotional framework in place to deal with it healthily.

Our upbringing can also influence our relationship with our emotions by imposing gender, birth-order, or situational expectations. For example, in most parts of the world, men are absolutely discouraged from sharing emotions or being vulnerable, being told to "man up" instead of shedding tears—like they're all auditioning for a hard-core action movie. Women are, *of course*, seen as much more emotional, and the first to be criticized in any leadership role or business role: "She's too soft." "She won't be able to handle it." "She's too temperamental." These constructs are so destructive: not only do they limit us, but they also paint negative pictures of emotional management in general, when sometimes, in the context of a truly tough situation in life, we *do* need to hold back tears or anger in order to build our resilience. There's also the phenomenon in certain parts of the world of putting the lion's share of pressure and responsibilities on the firstborn, all but demanding they put their emotions to the side. In still other cultures, over-the-top emotions are ritualized as a way to grieve or celebrate, and being calm and collected is seen as odd!

But our upbringing isn't the only component that influences emotional capacity. Our environment can have a small but meaningful impact on how we recognize, experience, and regulate our emotions in a given moment. Environments full of physical stressors—annoying noises, bright lights, bad smells—can make even a coolheaded person a little grouchy, while calming sights and sensations (hello, weighted blanket!) can ratchet down the parasympathetic nervous system (aka fight-or-flight pathways) and get us feeling less anxious. And, again, context is crucial in how able we are to hold back a reaction or process it productively: My ability to be patient and loving when I'm watching my toddler put his shoes on the wrong feet and adamantly insist he tie them himself is pretty decent when we're just going on a lazy Sunday walk in the park. But when we're already 10 minutes late to get him to the dentist? Not so much.

In our work, I helped Marianna expand her emotional capacity so that her Bounce Factor would be primed and ready for whatever her new career threw her way. We started by simply reframing a lot of her perceptions: I pointed out that all of these overnight stars that she put on a pedestal had been working for years. For all the time she was in medical school, these guys were putting in their own long hours at their chosen careers, and that success compounded for them. With the same amount of work, there was no reason she couldn't get there too, so any panicking she was feeling was premature.

Next, instead of moving on to new tactics for her online presence, we looked under the hood of her desperate need to take action and tapped into the deeper fear of *not being enough* that was lurking beneath. From there, we worked on reframing her mindset from a place defined by lack and urgency to a place of empathy, gratitude, and savoring the moment.

"You know what I've been missing?" Marianna said. "I was so focused on the 45 people who ghosted that I didn't even take the time to feel good that five people *did* show up. Like, five is more than zero, which is how many I thought would show up!"

I asked her how she felt about it now, seeing it from this new perspective.

"I mean, I'm disappointed," she said. "I'm not going to lie. But I'm also excited." She paused. "Is that a thing? Can I be both?"

I'll tell you what I told her: absolutely. When your emotional capacity is expansive and flexible, it has room for all kinds of feelings, even contradictory ones. Living within that contrast, within that *paradox,* was a huge step for Marianna on her path to audacious resilience. In reframing her situation, she grew her emotional capacity to make room for empathy—and her mission to expand wellness to people the medical system had let down—to lead the way instead of her ego.

BOUNCE FACTOR DEEP DIVE: EXPERIENCING YOUR EMOTIONAL CAPACITY

What's your capacity to handle, or even just sit with, those B-I-G uncomfortable feelings? How do you react when things don't go your way or when your expectations are not met? How do you react when feeling betrayed or taken advantage of by others? How comfortable are you showing affection and appreciation for others? How hard is it for you to stand up to someone who is treating you crappily?

Do you shut down? Get aggressive? Feel like bursting into tears? Do you shy away from the world, fully avoid others, and try to hide yourself under a rock? Or do you go on a tear and start raging at anyone who happens across your path? Or maybe you allow the feelings and emotions to envelope you until you break down and start to dry heave. How long does it take you to return to feeling stasis within yourself?

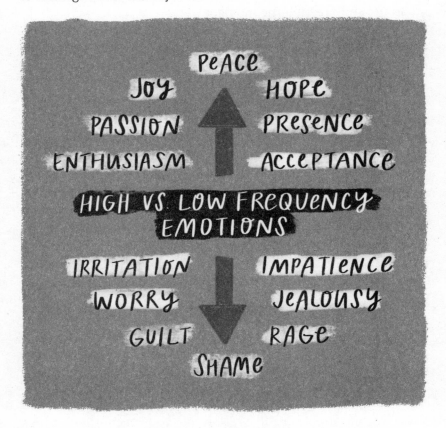

How good are your vibes? The higher the frequency of your emotions,
the better you feel.

✳

Recap & Reflection Corner

1. Freewrite on how you handle big emotions when they arise. Try completing the following sentences as quickly as you can, without self-censorship or judgment:

   - Disappointment makes me . . .

   - When my expectations aren't met, I . . .

   - I know I'm angry/sad/hurt when I start to . . .

   - When I see someone else getting upset, I tend to . . .

   - I only raise my voice / cry / do a happy dance when . . .

2. Review the high versus low frequency emotion chart on page 104. Journal for a few minutes (or record a voice memo to yourself) about a time when you fell into lower-frequency emotions when something didn't go as planned. Write (or talk) about how you navigated that experience. Create as much detail as you can—imagine you're writing a scene in a novel or telling a story live onstage. Take a break (at least an hour, or up to a day!) and revisit your writing or recording. What does this moment reveal about your emotional capacity at the time? Write (or talk) about your insights.

3. Get a rough sense of how you emotionally self-regulate (that is, calm down from a big breakthrough of feeling). Jot down a recent major emotional event—whatever comes to mind first is fine. Then jot down the next five to seven things you did immediately afterward (texted a friend, took a nap, went to a meeting, drove home in traffic, et cetera). Next to each one, write a (+) if that

action made you feel calmer or cooler, and a (-) if it made you feel more stressed or upset (or had no effect). What do the calming actions have in common? Did they each get you alone time? Did you have a chance to vent to someone else? How can you incorporate these kinds of self-regulating strategies regularly and with intention?

4. Next time you feel a major emotional storm welling up inside you, try consciously regulating your body to be *with* your emotions but not ruled *by* them. Take deep breaths, maybe putting a hand on your chest to steady and ground yourself. Close your eyes. Don't actively try to calm down or change what you're feeling, simply let it flow through you entirely.

* * *

Chapter 8

Your Self-Awareness

You've already seen this component at work—you just might not have noticed it.

Serena, the badass working mom who felt stuck in her career, grew her self-awareness not just by nurturing past wounds, but also from taking an objective look at her skills and abilities. After I encouraged her to send out a résumé to a new job, just as a test, the amazing compensation she was offered showed she was worth so much more than she'd realized. Her stronger Bounce Factor led her to finally sit down with her boss and ask for a raise.

For Cruz, self-awareness came in realizing that he was something of a paradox—a guy from the school of hard knocks who wouldn't sweat at a fistfight but got nervous at the thought of giving a speech by himself for a few minutes. His owning that reality, along with his sense of humor, made him run toward environments that challenged him instead of avoiding them. And his stronger sense of who he was helped him connect to the people he wanted to work with in an authentic, meaningful way.

Marianna's self-awareness came from reconnecting with her values. Her transition from doctor to wellness coach came from a genuine desire to heal her patients in the way that was truly best for them, whether that was through traditional Western medicine or something more holistic like time in nature and gentle exercise. Reconnecting with that side of herself—and striving to stay in tune with those values by expanding her emotional capacity—helped keep Marianna grounded and her Bounce Factor strong.

Self-awareness, our fourth and final Bounce Factor component, is a kind of meta-component. Not only *can* you apply it to the other three, you actually kind of *have* to in order to make changes! This is where you integrate the past triggers. This is where you realign with your true desires within yourself at your core. Self-awareness is what allows you to see what's at work within yourself. It lets you observe situations with ease, compassion, and no self-judgment. It's also maybe my favorite component in the Bounce Factor, because once you can tap into self-awareness, nothing is beyond your reach.

Even better, of all the components of the Bounce Factor, your self-awareness is the one you control the most. It's the one that can be directed, that can be changed, that can be shifted, in how you experience a particular situation—especially in interpersonal dynamics with family, friends, colleagues, and even the jerks who cut us off in traffic. Plenty of the micro-components of our Bounce Factor are hard-wired, or, if they are something you can change, they're not something you can change right this instant: for example, maybe you're stuck living somewhere for the next three months for a job assignment, so that part of your environment is kind of nailed down.

But you can always cultivate more self-awareness.

You're doing it right now, just by reading through these sections and reflecting on your own Bounce Factor.

And you've exercised it already if you've ever had a thought like . . .

I don't really know myself.
I've been living for everyone else BUT me!
I guess I don't know much about that subject after all.
I thought I was okay with that, but now I'm actually not.
Wow, I was choosing the same patterns in dating partners, huh?
I really have a bad spending habit.
I just don't know enough about that to comment.
I emotionally eat, and I don't know why.

Self-awareness works in tandem with your upbringing because it allows you to start the introspection and healing of any trauma or lingering resentment you might have. It can open your eyes to why certain things or people or places are triggering to you. It can give you compassion for yourself as you recognize things that you had no control over.

Self-awareness of your environment can take the form of mindfulness, of checking in with who and what surrounds you in a given moment (and help summon your emotional capacity in doing so). It can show you how and where your values and the values of those you surround yourself with align or clash. It can help you tap into where you do your best writing or thinking or painting, and where you feel confined or dampened or suppressed.

Self-awareness of your emotional capacity empowers you to step outside your emotions and see them with curiosity, compassion, and neutrality. It digs an anchor into the ground to stop you from being swept out on the tide of your feelings. It helps you express yourself when you need a moment to cool off, when you're in need of quiet time to unwind, or when you need some attention and conversation.

Yet, strangely enough, self-awareness is probably also the easiest aspect to gloss over. Most of the time, when life throws up roadblocks, we react reflexively, and fall into one of the patterns from the first three chapters. We say, "Why me?" instead of saying, "Huh, how did *I* play a role in this?" When we don't have that self-awareness, and we get into our very basic nature, when our primal brain is activated and we don't want to take personal responsibility, that's when we go into the victim mode. That's when we get into blaming, that's when we get into defensiveness, and that's when we get into entitlement.

This isn't some kind of spiritual failing on anyone's part. It's just human. There's a lot going on around us! Most of the time, we don't give ourselves permission to check in with the decisions that we make, with where we actually are and how we're actually feeling, or we simply have too much on our plate to take on a deep dive. In fact, just before I sat down to work on this chapter, I went to pick up my son with Ajit, and I found myself spontaneously saying, "Hey, you know what? These three months were really, really tough. I'm so glad we're on the other side of that."

The three months *had* been tough. We'd moved across the country, dealing with ongoing logistics because of pandemic restrictions; remodeled a house; had a new baby; and kept a thousand balls in the air for our new ventures and new projects in our businesses. There wasn't time in the moment to have that awareness because I was, in a lot of ways, on autopilot. Sometimes life is like that. Being in a holding pattern, running like a hamster on the wheel . . . we're all guilty of this because we're human. This is the human experience, right? But once the dust has settled, and we regain the ability to breathe, reflect, and ask questions of ourselves—that is so vital and so important.

Finally, I'll say that arguably, self-awareness isn't essential to a healthy Bounce Factor. Because sure, some people, if the stars align, might get themselves a nice, enriching childhood, a healthy environment, and a naturally easygoing and flexible emotional capacity, and end up pretty capable of going with the flow and weathering various storms.

But most of us are not that lucky.

Most of us are human.

And more importantly, without *self-awareness*, their Bounce Factor will never reach its full potential. They'll never fly as far forward as they could if they took some time to reflect. This is where your Bounce Factor can stretch and expand infinitely on what you're capable of. Your self-awareness is bringing to surface your likes and dislikes, what is in full alignment with you at this stage and season of life, and, most of all, how you are able to integrate the healings, and notice if and when things are totally off. That's why it's so important to cultivate all of the aspects of our Bounce Factor, not just the ones that come naturally—because if we want to break through, achieve more, and reach greater heights, we can't be content with just bouncing back.

We have to be ready to fly forward.

BOUNCE FACTOR DEEP DIVE: SITTING WITH SELF-AWARENESS

What kind of person are you?

What roles and spaces do you occupy in the world? How did you get to where you are today? How do you *feel* about where you are today?

Can you (lovingly) laugh at yourself? What's funny or amusing or endearing or cringeworthy about how you've made your way in the world this far? What's irrational or illogical or paradoxical about the bundle of traits that is *you*? Maybe you're incurably clumsy and have tripped in public more times than you'd want to admit . . . but you also know it's pretty hilarious. Maybe you still watch Saturday morning cartoons (even though you don't have kids around) or get incredibly competitive playing Monopoly (even though you don't really care about the game) or always put your eyeliner on just a tiny bit crooked (even though you've tried a billion times to keep a steady hand). What habits and details make your life exactly what it is—yours—and no one else's?

Do you still like doing those same things you used to? Or have you noticed a change in yourself while engaging in those activities? Where does it show up in your body? When you think of visiting your hometown and seeing the people you grew up with, how does that make you feel? Does your throat get choked up? Does your stomach tie in knots at the thought of saying no to the guilt trip of old friends?

What would your kid-self think of you now? What will your 90-year-old self think of you now? What have you done or changed or left behind on this planet that never would have come about otherwise?

Maybe you don't feel like you really know yourself. Maybe you feel like you've changed a lot and are still getting your bearings, or maybe you're not sure you've *ever* been tuned into who you are or want to be. Maybe you're not the you that you were five months ago or five years ago. That's okay too. Give yourself empathy and grace, and take the pressure off. There's no rush, and you have all the time you need.

✳

Recap & Reflection Corner

1. When we are building self-awareness, trusting our instincts and decisions is key. Journal about the last time you had a strong "gut feeling" about something, perhaps a relationship, friendship, move, or job. What decision did you make based on your "gut feeling" and self-awareness of the situation? What did you learn about yourself?

2. Being fully embodied in your physical self is a major part of self-awareness. For a guided grounding meditation, visit thatsuckednowwhat.com/resources

Want to see your Bounce Factor up close and personal and perhaps see how high you bounce during tough times? Take the free Bounce Factor quiz at bouncefactorquiz.com, and you'll see which aspects of your bounce factor need a little more attention.

✳ ✳ ✳

Part III

FLY
FORWARD

Life's a challenge, but that's the best part.

— VENUS WILLIAMS

Get Ready to Fly Forward

It's not enough to just survive something, right?
That's not the point of life. You've got to thrive.

— MEGHAN MARKLE

I know you're probably excited to get into this next section. (And I am too!)

But first, I have some questions—and a story—for you.

What would it feel like to not judge yourself after you screwed up a presentation?

Or to admit you'd been wrong to your partner without wanting to melt into the floor?

What would it feel like to conquer your fears and dance or sing or give a speech in public, regardless of how people react?

Or to tell your toxic friend, "Enough is enough, and I won't tolerate the way you speak to me."

Or to say *no* to the next work project that comes along, because you've been running on empty and you need to say *yes* to yourself?

Because those moments, my dear, are you having a sexy AF Bounce Factor.

That's when you are fully embodying all the components, not shaming or judging, rather embracing and welcoming all the chaotic, messy, and magical moments in between.

So, love, *what does audacious resilience feel like* when it's at its biggest and bounciest?

For me, it felt like a breeze on the beach.

I had a huge breakthrough in my own Bounce Factor a few years back, when I was traveling around the world with my husband, Ajit. We were doing the nomadic thing, but still working, conducting events, serving, and keeping up our respective coaching practices, and we had just started collaborating on our first joint coaching book. One afternoon, we sat on a beach in Thailand, discussing ideas and drafting notes for a new chapter. The waves were crashing gently in the background, the warm sunlight surrounded us, and an unfamiliar feeling took me over.

I'd been through so much. Survived so much. Fought for so much. And in retrospect, I don't think I knew what actual joy felt like until that moment on the beach.

I didn't really know what it looked like to not be in this state of constant battle. Of struggle. Of just putting one foot in front of the other and trying my best to keep things stable. I grew up with my parents in and out of hospitals all the time. I was raising my younger brother.

But that afternoon on the beach, that feeling of bliss was completely different from anything I had experienced growing up. I'd been constantly in that survival mode, always alert and activated, with no pauses for reflection, no chance to stop and take in any small victory because I had to charge right on to the next problem: the next bill to pay, the next doctor's visit, the next bombshell, the next terrifying phone call.

But the bliss didn't come purely from that contrast—from the soft sand and warm air and sunlight. It didn't come from "moving on" or from cutting ties with all that pain. It came from using the moment as reflection. It came from looking back and thinking, *Wow, that stuff sucked. But I got healed through it.*

That was what gave me that feeling of bliss.

Not that I'd loved going through the shit I went through— because I didn't.

Not that I was pretending it had never happened—because I couldn't.

But that I'd been through hell and come out in one piece. Maybe a little singed around the edges but still standing.

I'd come out on the other side of adversity.

I'd bounced back.

And I don't think I've ever experienced a sense of joy as profound as I did right then.

So the answer to that question, and the moral of this story is: resilience is joy.

I wish that joy for you. I hope you start to uncover it through the pages of this book, and I hope that you don't have to wait for decades, like I did, to experience the full, bright spectrum of joy.

Of course, my experience was very, very chaotic, messy, and crazy intense. For you, resilience can be built with simple, everyday brave moments: getting cut off in traffic, having that difficult conversation, saying no to obligation, or going live online and completely, fully bombing because you blanked on what you wanted to say. Your specifics, your Bounce Factor, and your path to flying forward will be just that—yours.

What's important is that resilience can develop in many different ways and areas of our lives, but once we have it, it applies almost anywhere.

The Fly Forward framework is like resilience in stop-motion. At every stage, I'll show you exactly what's going on when you're making resilient choices instead of default ones, how you can propel yourself onward at every turn, how you can first bounce back and restore stability, and then fly forward into new and greater things.

But each stage will also give you guidelines and boundaries for your thoughts and actions. The key to learning resilience through this framework is to *take it one stage at a time.* You don't have to floor it and figure out how to get from a weeping, angry mess to a confident, carefree badass all at once. You can just jump to the next lily pad. When you're Falling, you only need to focus on understanding that stage and breaking through to Igniting. When you're Rising, you can take a few deep breaths and ease your way into Magnifying without rushing right to Thriving. Each stage matters.

Breaking it down like this is what makes the Fly Forward framework sustainable. Too much advice about resilience-building is the personal growth equivalent of a crash diet: it might work really well at first, but there's no way you can live your whole life that way. And when the habits start to slip, you end up back where you started—or worse.

But this framework also encourages you to slow down, just a touch, and *live* each stage. To be present. To welcome the high-vibe feelings and the low-frequency feelings alike, with no judgment or shame. We've covered a lot of what it means to examine your experiences, whether it's reflecting on your upbringing or simply regulating yourself in a heated moment, and those concepts and skills are integral to every stage of this framework. Even as you're flying forward, you're living each moment one after another. Because those moments—the sucky ones and the backslides as much as the little victories and the triumphs—make up your life. When you can relish and feel gratitude for everything that falls in your lap—maybe not right away, and maybe not very much or for very long—then you're living your human life to the fullest.

Once you understand the conscious (and unconscious) forces that affect your baseline resilience—your Bounce Factor—you can start to approach those sucky moments in life with a whole new attitude. You can empower yourself not just to bounce back to your former self, but to fly forward to a new state of thriving.

I can't wait for you to feel that breeze on the beach.

Welcome to Part III, love.

Chapter 9

Falling

"I know you came into my life for a reason. I just didn't know that it was going to be in this capacity."

I got the note in the morning from a woman who was an acquaintance of mine. Luna was a friend of a friend, but not someone I knew super well, and it had been at least a year since we'd last really spoken. She'd been interested in being a client, but for whatever reason, had decided not to sign on—which was no big deal; people often decide coaching isn't right for them. But I don't usually get this kind of follow-up a year later.

"I've finally had this awakening," she said at the end of her e-mail. "And I just had to reach out."

Of course, I immediately wrote back, and she filled me in on the rest of the story. While moving into her new house, she'd fallen down the stairs and hit her head on the concrete steps. In the emergency room, doctors diagnosed internal bleeding and rushed her to neurosurgery.

"I have to take a leave of absence for three months," she wrote.

I was stunned. Luna is an absolute superwoman: two wonderful kids, type-A personality, nothing-can-stop-me-attitude, but thoroughly nice and agreeable. She'd just bought a beautiful dream house—the same house where she had the accident while moving in. And while this accident would be traumatic and painful for anyone, for Luna, the added leave of absence from work was a huge shake to the foundation. Because, as I knew, Luna did not do change.

So what had happened here?

Luna had a Fall. Literally, but also on a deeper level.

If you don't know what a "Fall" is, don't worry—I bet you've heard one of the other names. Wake-up call. Last straw. Rock bottom. Reality check. Slap in the face, punch in the gut, "oh shit" moment.

It's the big screwup at work. It's the divorce papers left by the coffeemaker. It's the car accident (and the medical bill). It's the lost pregnancy, the massive layoff, the friend breakup, the social media dogpile.

It's that something that makes you take stock of what's around you and reexamine your situation even for just a second.

In other words, the Fall is an unexpected situation that throws you off balance. Now, it was pure chance that Luna's Fall was itself an actual fall—I'd already named this stage when she reached out. But the truth is, in this stage it can feel like you're falling, even if you're physically on firm ground. Time slows down, and your heart seems to beat everywhere in your body at once. Your stomach plunges; your skin tingles. Everything about you is screaming this is it. Adrenaline is surging to keep your body on high alert. Your stomach might feel uneasy like you're literally on a roller coaster. You can't quite ever relax your muscles, because you have no idea where you're going to end up or how fast you'll get there. You feel a force, just like gravity, that signals to you: *This is totally out of my control.* And when you feel like the outside world is beyond your control, you go inward, retreat, and—many times— you start feeling like a victim. You're ashamed of yourself. You're unable to accept where you've landed. Your brain cues up a victim mindset soundtrack:

Why does it always happen to me?

They screwed me over again.

Obviously, I'm not cut out for this.

I must have failed more than anyone else on the planet.

You feel defeated; you're hurt. There's defensiveness and there is blame. But there can also be so much more. There can be change.

Think of the old saying about how anyone can change if they want to badly enough—it's true, but it's only half the story. What makes us want to change? It's not usually a calm afternoon sitting by ourselves alone with our thoughts, contemplating our future. It's the rug-pull that sends our world into chaos. It's that split second of "oh shit" where you know things won't ever be the same, in a small way or a huge one.

It's the magical moment of suck.

The difference here is that a Fall isn't just that sucky thing happening. It's that sucky thing transformed into the start of an opportunity. We need to fall because real change, lasting change, audaciously resilient change, needs a catalyst. Before this framework, before you started cultivating self-awareness around your Bounce Factor, a disastrous event would just be the start of a pity party, a pouting session, or casting blame outward. But when you're choosing to see what happens as a Fall, you're not retreating to those unproductive (though protective) default reactions.

To be clear, the bad luck or bummer moment or tragedy doesn't change. It doesn't get any less awful. It's not something you have to sugarcoat for yourself. But now, when you see it as a Fall, you know it's showing you something more. It's a door opening. And just beyond the open door of the Fall is what you want, what you need, what wounds in your heart are still tender and what dreams are still unacknowledged.

So take care of yourself in the aftermath, but realize all the same that you have been given a gift. A chance to make choices that are wiser and more constructive for you. An opportunity, not just another screwup.

Let's try that now with Luna. Luna might have had a literal fall, but what made it a Fall? Plenty of people have taken serious spills without that accident leading to long-lasting change in their lives, after all. Of course, they need to recuperate and heal from the physical injuries, but afterward they might be perfectly content to go back to life as it was before (albeit maybe with a newfound gratitude for the small things). So how did Luna step into the Falling stage instead of withdrawing into old habits and staying stuck? How did she start to change?

For starters, she employed one of the skills we discussed in Chapter 1: she shifted perspective. Recall that when I first spoke with Luna, she "didn't do change." She was pretty cool with things as they were. At the same time, however, she did know something was off in her life: namely, she was anxious AF. But any "changes" suggested to address that anxiety didn't interest her: she thought meditation was a joke (not uncommon!) and had a busy lifestyle that didn't seem to have a place in it for the commitment to change.

That had been months ago, though. Now her e-mails told a different story.

"I just had this wake-up call," she wrote. "I see it all so differently now. Like how I feel like I want to be there for my children, and I haven't been. I'm not out of the woods yet—still a lot of healing to do—but I wanted to let you know I'm already doing visualizations."

She told me she'd been spending concentrated time picturing herself out of the hospital, healthy again, going on vacation with her kids. And then she told me all her plans for when she was finally back home: the things she'd let go of, the things she'd take time for, the changes to her trajectory she was suddenly so eager to make.

Luna had shifted her perspective. Instead of seeing her anxiety as something free-floating, something she wanted to extract quickly and move on from, she realized that it was interwoven with her life. There wasn't going to be a silver bullet that would wipe out her anxious feelings and leave the rest intact: the picture was bigger than that.

Which brings me to the second skill she was employing: a healthy reflex. Instead of pushing herself to get back into her old life, back into the routines and rhythms that had ultimately left her in bad mental shape, she'd recognized she needed to rest. To heal. To pause and not feel any shame for it. This kind of constructive course of action is what helps us turn a mundane sucky moment into a Fall because it staves off the unproductive, unhealthy reactions we might be prone to.

Finally, Luna's e-mail showed me that she had started to understand her emotions—maybe even without realizing it. Leading up to a Fall, we're usually carrying a growing awareness that we're not happy. We may be questioning our job or questioning our life's purpose or just wondering, *Why am I doing what I'm doing, again?* But that essence of unhappiness can exist within us for a long time without coming to the surface. Like Luna, we might initially seek help, but decide (rightly or wrongly) that we're not ready to take the steps to change. We might make excuses, or feel ourselves in a tug of war, where a few good moments offset our discomfort, or numb ourselves with substances or other harmful behaviors to quiet that unhappy essence. But in simply recognizing that this sucky moment has caused a seismic shift in how we feel, we're leaning into the Fall. We're allowing our emotions to do their job of signaling that we need something, instead of tamping them down for being inconvenient, scary, or otherwise overwhelming.

If we can be like Luna, use those skills and draw on our self-knowledge of our Bounce Factor, we can let our shitty moment of fail be so much more. We can let it serve its purpose as a call to be more aware. We can use it like the gift that it is in our journey toward resilience. We can let our Fall propel us into the stage of Igniting.

Let's take a look at some stories of people in the throes of this stage, and how it changed their path going forward. Each of the case studies represents a story from my work and my clients, but also a general type of crappy luck that you may have encountered yourself. You may not have been head of a start-up, like Mohammad, but maybe you have seen your bank account dwindle to single digits. You might not have had to care for newborns, like Naiya, but maybe your living situation and routine was upended by something else. You might not have been bullied online like Monica, but maybe you've felt the sting of social rejection or toxic friendships.

In addition to noticing moments of personal connection between these stories and your own, reflect on how each Fall reveals the magic in the magical moment of suck—how each one bears the seeds of a new, more optimal way forward for the person in question. Take in those story moments that especially resonate with you, that ping your emotions, and pause there. Put yourself into their shoes and practice cultivating a reaction to those moments that isn't wallowing, lashing out, or sulking.

Acknowledge it: that sucked.

Then look to the future: now what?

FAILING A TEST: LARA

"My friend told me I could use some of this," Lara told me, and held up a copy of my book *Emotional Grit* with a small smile on her face. "So, I guess that's why I'm here."

From the time we first met, I could tell Lara was brilliant, accomplished, and single-minded about her goals. She'd known from the age of five that she was going to be a lawyer. After all, her father, grandfather, and eldest brother were all lawyers. At age 10, she was put in debate club, and by her teenage years she was captain of the high school debate team. She excelled in school, earned straight As—basically, she did all of the right things, because, as she put it, "Our family motto is: *We don't fail.*" Her father prided himself on being well read, and mistakes weren't really an option. So Lara grew up into more than just an overachiever; she was an over-*doer*, and a hard worker to boot.

So, when at last it was time to take the bar exam, Lara thought it would be a breeze. After all, she'd crushed it in school, and this was basically her birthright.

Except she failed.

Needless to say, the failure was humiliating. More than anything, she was embarrassed to break the news to her father, since he already was prepping an office in his prestigious firm with his daughter's name on the door.

Instead, she kept her mouth shut and buckled back down. The next exam wouldn't be for another six months, so she made some excuses and studied up once again. By the time the test came around, she'd convinced herself the first time was a fluke and went in with even more confidence than before.

But she failed again.

After a night of pity-partying and bemoaning things with her friends, Lara got a copy of my book from her friend. This friend had been going through a self-discovery journey of her own—ultimately deciding that, after law school, she wasn't going to practice law—and saw the hyper-competitive Lara getting stuck in a similar "why me" story she recognized from *Emotional Grit*.

"My father, grandfather, and brother are all waiting for me to join their practice," Lara told me. "And here I am, grinding everything to a halt. How can I be anything other than a failure at this point?"

Lara failed. For all life's gray areas and ambiguity, there are some things—tests, races, competitions—that are zero-sum, black-and-white. You pass or you fail. You win or you lose. You make the cutoff or you fall short. As Falls, these absolute "you failed" moments are so painful precisely because there's not a lot of room to reason your way out of them. Even worse, they usually come after months of intense preparation—studying, training, practicing—that wear you out mentally and physically, leaving you vulnerable to a victim mindset and ready to stack all kinds of chips on your shoulder.

BECOMING A PARENT: NAIYA

Like many professional couples, Naiya and Max waited a while to have children. But once they decided they were ready, they unexpectedly found themselves waiting some more.

In the five years since they'd decided to start a family, they'd done things the "old-fashioned way," then moved on to an attempt at IVF. When that didn't work, they went for another round. Then another. Each time, Naiya dreaded facing the window on the pregnancy test. And each round was more and more expensive. It was devastating and demoralizing.

When they gave IVF one last try, the couple was already thinking through other options: fostering, adoption, even surrogacy. They headed to Naiya's OB-GYN appointment with low expectations.

Then they got the news: they were having twins.

Obviously, they were ecstatic. Naiya in particular was over the moon. But the celebration and excitement quickly turned into intense preparation. Since she was a high-risk pregnancy, she was put on bed rest at just five months, and because she wasn't allowed to work, she had to take a leave of absence from her job.

Eventually, the babies were born—three weeks premature, but healthy—and brought every possible ounce of joy to the new parents. Through the first few weeks, there was a whole baby-care operation going on, with both sets of grandparents on hand to cook, do laundry, and change diapers and everyone's sleep schedules rearranged into shifts to provide around-the-clock care of the newborn twins.

As things settled down and the grandparents packed up to head back home, Naiya decided she would be home indefinitely caring for the babies. This was now her life, she reasoned—she'd more than signed up for it and wanted to go all-in on Mom mode. She'd wanted these babies so very badly, and now she was going to rise to the occasion.

Gradually, friends started dropping by. They'd always ask how she was doing, or commented, "Wow, you are Super Mom! How do you do it all?" Naiya smirked and brushed aside their remarks with some breezy excuse. She was working so hard at being this perfect mom: breastfeeding her twins, dressing them neatly every day, and caring for them singlehandedly when Max worked long night shifts as an ER doc.

But the truth was, she didn't have an answer. She didn't really know how to articulate how she was doing beyond that . . .well, she didn't want to articulate it. She, who had struggled for so many years, been through so much heartache trying to conceive, simply couldn't bring herself to acknowledge the hard time she was having.

But deep, deep down, she was crumbling inside.

Her hormones were out of control, so much so that she could start crying uncontrollably at the drop of a hat. She felt guilty for craving sleep or wishing someone else would carry one of the babies just so she could get a bit of rest. But her martyr/Super Mom complex left her no room to have compassion for herself.

Having children is one of life's greatest gifts and biggest joys. But, as any tired parent knows, it is hard freakin' work! As I've worked with clients with small children—and become a mom myself—I've realized that, hidden in all the chaos and upheaval and celebration and stress of welcoming a newborn, there is *definitely* a Fall happening. We new mamas in particular are contending with so much after childbirth. Our bodies have just been pushed to their physical limits, our hormones are running rampant, and our attention and energy are tightly dialed in to keeping this small new person (or people!) alive and safe. But psychologically, there's also a huge shift in identity going on, one that, if society acknowledges it at all, is always made out to be an unquestioned positive. You're a mom! That's the best job there is! You're *supposed to be happy.* Tired, sure, but not *desperate* and *scared.*

Well, take it from this mama: desperate and scared is real life. Naiya's story adds another layer of guilt, shame, and heartache by coming at the end of a long journey to motherhood. Like so many new parents, the arrival of her babies brought on a Fall—and an opportunity to move forward to the next stage.

HITTING A FINANCIAL WALL: MOHAMMAD

Mohammad was a brilliant and talented tech guy—but he'd hit a wall. A few of them, actually.

When I started working with him, he'd already cleared a big hurdle. At that time, he was leading a small but mighty team to develop an app for a new start-up. Prior to our work together, he'd gotten everything in place to get his first round of funding—slide deck ready to go, meetings all scheduled—and given his pitch over and over again. But he just couldn't get these big investors on board for that first round of funding. In the end, he made the first round happen by raising from friends and family, which is a really hard thing to do. Mo was able to make it happen because people believed in him and he believed in his team.

The next step was to keep developing the app and building the team while getting ready for another season of fundraising. Mo had built a really amazing team, and as they'd collaborated, they'd really come together for the app. By that point, Mo was paying them salaries, because he knew their hard work definitely deserved it. But it also meant he'd have to raise the second round of funding pretty quickly to keep this start-up going and thriving.

Mo got back to pitching—slide decks and meetings all over again. The first folks said no. Then the second. Pitch competitions, teams, individual investors would hear his presentation and it'd go great. They'd even go out afterward and seem to really click. But then a few days later, the rejection would roll in.

This went on for days, and then months. His team kept working, and Mo kept paying them. Finally, one day, a rejection came in literally as Mo was running payroll.

And he was short.

He closed the rejection and opened up a new tab to look at his bank account. Not the start-up's funds, but his *personal* bank account, just to make sure his team got paid.

Except he was still short. His personal account had barely more than a thousand bucks left ($1,023.00, to be exact). And he had to pay three other salaries.

"I have to make some kind of decision," he told me. "But I don't know what."

The thing that struck me about Mo was that he wanted to make his goal happen so badly—but it was *not* entitlement. He put blood, sweat, and tears into an idea that he really thought was going to just take off and help people. He had a team who believed in the app and even a host of first-round funders who believed in it too. He was qualified and prepared and putting in the time. So in one sense, he had everything going for him.

But in another, he was hitting the bottom of his Fall.

When our financial reality bottoms out, it can be a hell of a wake-up call. Whether it's having our card declined at a fancy restaurant or finding an eviction notice on our door, money troubles can confront us in pretty dramatic ways. This kind of Falling stage can start much earlier than we realize. Small purchases add up to a massive amount of debt. Or we keep scraping together funds to build just enough runway so that we don't have to think about the future . . . for a while. Money troubles are also usually tied up with so many other threads in our lives: our relationships, our business and creative goals, and our family's origin story all can have effects on our finances.

But what all money Falls have in common is that cold, hard, dollars-and-cents reality check. As Mo stared at his personal bank account page, he was staring at the facts. There was no way to excuse what he saw on the screen: the small four figures he *personally* had left weren't enough to keep him going for the next three months, let alone pay his employees.

Mo was right: it was time to make a decision. And as he came to that decision, he also (spoiler alert!) moved into the Igniting phase.

SOCIAL MEDIA SHAMING: MONICA

Monica, a junior at a prestigious high school in the Bay Area, did everything right—always.

Her father was a founder of a prominent tech company and served on a few elite boards, so the pressure for Monica to do the same thing, achieve as much as she could and then some, was high. For as long as she could remember, she'd been going at a high-octane level: running for student government, competing in young entrepreneur showcases, traveling miles and miles for debate competitions, and piling on AP classes.

I came to work with Monica through a few mutual connections—I had worked with a friend of her father's, and had spoken at another (rival) high school a few months prior—so I was pretty familiar with the pressure cooker that was her school and social world.

Still, when I actually met Monica in person, my first thought was, *Wow, this girl is incredibly smart.*

And my second thought was, *And even smart people make dumb mistakes.*

Monica, like generations of teenagers before her, had made a misjudgment. She'd broken a rule. She'd screwed up. But unlike previous generations of teenagers, her mistake could be broadcast and rebroadcast to her peers 24/7.

Basically, Monica had been canceled.

It had been an intensely long week in the thick of a busy semester, and Monica had just gotten back from a debate competition, exhausted. She could barely keep her eyes open, let alone study—except she had an AP Statistics test the next day. So when her friend messaged that she had gotten hold of the answer key, Monica wavered.

She knew many of her classmates cheated on tests. It wasn't openly talked about, exactly, just a sense that everyone does it. Still, Monica was terrified she'd get caught. She wasn't exactly practiced at cheating, after all—she was the good girl, the one who always did everything right.

Then again, she was so tired. And she promised herself it would only be one time.

Monica thought she was being incredibly careful. Yet, somehow, her worst fear came true: she was not only caught in the middle of the test, but humiliated in front of her classmates.

And that wasn't even the worst of it.

Her classmates took to social media and used post after post to blast her for what she'd done. Everyone's feed in the small student body was slammed with insults, cruel memes, and what seemed like genuine glee—as if her peers had just been waiting for the "good girl" to come crashing down. Monica had been in the running for student affairs officer—her dream—but because of the sudden backlash online, she withdrew. Her close friends stopped texting and even unfollowed her on social.

Of course, there was a punishment from the school, and Monica accepted it—she knew she'd done wrong. But the social media punishment was unending. It was as if her classmates and former friends couldn't do enough to take her down. It got to the point where Monica thought about changing schools—not because it might clean up her academic record, but because she simply couldn't bear to walk the halls anymore. She even went into a spiral of depression, which genuinely scared her. Just a year before, she had lost one of her dearest friends to suicide after struggles with bullying and mental health.

It can be easy to write off social media bullying—or any kind of bullying—as just drama. Pettiness. Snark. Not something "real" to get upset about. But if you've lived through something like Monica did—or seen it happen to someone you care about—you know that shaming, bullying, or being canceled online can be a huge, and very real, Fall.

What makes this kind of Fall so delicate and wounding is that often, there *is* a mistake at the core of it. Maybe we posted something embarrassingly personal to a work account by accident or had an angry venting text screenshotted and tweeted by someone we thought was a friend. Maybe we even said or wrote something genuinely offensive. Monica definitely made a mistake, and a pretty big one—she purposefully compromised her academic integrity. She cheated. But she also was punished by her school (as she should have been). The punishment did what it was supposed to: it reinforced the lesson that cheating is wrong. With time, Monica would heal from her guilt and make better choices going forward. She could separate herself from her mistake and not be defined by it.

Social media isn't calibrated for that kind of punishment. Social media is calibrated for speed. Social media simply moves faster than humans can meaningfully change.

Worse, social media is designed for snap judgments. Our superfast feeds make it easy to flatten our judgments. We conflate *a person* with *a person's worst mistake* so we can move on to the next post. There's no space to consider them separately.

But that space is essential. Without that space—without recognition that we are *not* our mistakes—no one would ever learn or grow. After making mistakes, human beings need grace, time, and privacy: grace from others around them, time to process what happened, and privacy to reflect inward. Social media gives us none of those. In fact, it actively engineers them away. The apps and networks might be inhabited by regular people, but they're run by corporations, and corporations have bottom lines. They know there's a direct pipeline from high emotion to engagement to advertising dollars. So they build us a framework designed for outrage, because outrage makes money. But in the end, we're the ones who pay the price—in shaming and bullying and Falls like Monica's.

Fortunately, as we'll see, these social media Falls—just like any other Fall—can still be the first step to a new beginning.

FEELINGS OF FALLING

As Luna's story showed us at the beginning of this chapter, being aware of our emotions is a key part of transforming a sucky moment into a Fall. In fact, emotional awareness is instrumental at every stage of the Fly Forward framework. We need to stay in touch with how we're feeling in order to stay honest with ourselves, to know when to rest and when to push through, to check in on whether what we're doing is really best for us.

But it's not always easy to pinpoint emotions—especially in the aftermath of a crisis. Depending on your emotional capacity, you may or may not find that identifying and processing feelings come naturally to you. And depending on how the other components of your Bounce Factor come into play through all the stages, that emotional capacity might be stronger or weaker at different steps in your journey to Thriving.

To help guide you through each stage, you'll find some typical emotions at the end of every chapter. This isn't an exhaustive list of *everything* that *every person* could possibly feel at this stage, of course, but hopefully it gets you thinking if you feel stuck or unsure. You can use these feelings and the associated descriptions to guide you in the Recap & Reflection questions that come afterward, or simply learn about them now and revisit them when you find yourself in this stage.

So, now that we've seen what Falling looks like across a variety of life experiences and challenges, let's dig into what it makes us feel.

Failure

When we don't achieve what we want or expect ourselves to, a sense of failure is a natural reaction. This reaction holds us back the most when "I failed at this one thing, this one time" turns into "I *am* a failure." Differentiating between the two is a big part of moving into Igniting. Lara was so deeply entrenched in her family tradition of being a lawyer, and her self-worth was so tied up in that identity that she was striving for, that failing the bar exam felt like a failure to be the right version of herself. And that sense of personal failure-ness is a perfect setup for a pity party (aka a victim mentality). To move forward, she had to take her ego out of the equation and make the failure *less* personal. And, as we'll see, in peeling back the layers of the story that ended with "I *am* a failure," she started to uncover the real, hidden values she'd been burying for too long.

Associated thoughts:

- *I totally bombed it.*
- *I messed that up so badly.*
- *I never get anything right.*

Ashamed

There's been a massive, wonderful growth in awareness around shame and shaming thanks to the work of Dr. Brené Brown and others, but it still can be so easy to let shame eat us up. This is especially true when we find ourselves at a certain level of success, even Thriving, only to be knocked down by a Fall. We let

THAT SUCKED. now what?

our ego become conditioned to being "high-achieving," to the point where coming up short in any way isn't just insufficient, it's *embarrassing*. Shame also comes with a social aspect, a sense that others are negatively judging us—again, a ding on our ego. For Mo, the start-up founder, there was a lot of shame swirling around his all-but-bankrupt business—all his life, he'd excelled at whatever he tried, so explaining to his employees that he wasn't able to make payroll was excruciating. For new mom Naiya, the shame of *not* being happy and overjoyed 24/7 with her babies was unbearable to the point where she was pushing past what she could realistically take on—and then she felt ashamed on top of that for not doing the impossible. And for Monica, shame was the biggest and most immediate driver of her Fall.

Associated thoughts:

- *I can't believe I let this happen.*
- *What will everyone say when they find out?*
- *I can never show my face here again.*

Defeated

Feelings of defeat in particular can come through when the Fall is some kind of competition or zero-sum game—in other words, when we are literally defeated. Lara, after bombing the bar exam, could retake it, but that particular instance was *not* a pass, and it was hard to see any kind of silver lining. The key to moving past feelings of defeat is to understand that no defeat is total and all-encompassing in every aspect of our life. That self-awareness will be key to Igniting in the next stage.

Associated thoughts:

- *Fine, you beat me. Happy now?*
- *Guess even my best isn't good enough.*
- *I had one chance and I blew it.*

Helpless

Mo felt helpless when staring at that bank statement. He couldn't conjure up more money out of thin air. He couldn't draw on backup funding that didn't exist. When a Fall leaves us feeling helpless, it's a good time to take a step back and look at what we're trying to do. If we can't come up with the right answer, maybe the question is the problem. As we'll see, once Mo stepped out of wondering, "How can I keep this company going?" he was able to move to the Igniting stage and see a path forward.

Associated thoughts:

- *I'm trapped.*
- *I have no choices left.*
- *Nothing I do would make a difference.*

Depressed

Depression can come over us at any point in the Falling process. Losing interest in things, feeling empty, and just plain sadness can all present themselves—sometimes, as in Monica's situation, coupled with powerful shame. There's also a physical component in depression as both a contributing factor and a symptom: for Naiya, her already exhausted body wasn't able to give her mind and spirit a physical anchor of rest and calm. However, it's important to note that serious depression (especially with any thoughts of self-harm) should be addressed with a mental health professional. When in doubt, reaching out to a qualified therapist or psychiatrist is never a bad option.

Associated thoughts:

- *I don't want to get up. What's the point?*
- *I hate having to fake a smile.*
- *Nothing feels worth it anymore.*

An Embodiment Practice for Embracing the Suck

After my daughter, Aiyla Rae, was born, I was quite keen on embracing the 40-day "sitting in" period, as it's called in several cultures around the world. In India, postpartum moms aren't even allowed to leave the *bed* for the first 40 days, so as to allow for proper healing, replenishment, and nourishment from the elder women in the family. As a new mama, it allows you and kiddo to form a nurturing bond while the matriarchs step in and do the caretaking for *you* now that your body's gone through *quite* the drastic transformation. (Side note: I was absolutely against the sitting-in period when I had my firstborn, so this time, I was more than ready to surrender to the extra help.)

For those first six weeks I was in and out of the newborn daze, feeding Aiyla every 90 minutes while trying to make cuddle time for my then two-and-a-half-year-old son—and while my husband and I were trying to find a groove together in the midst of all the diaper changes, bottle cleanings, and feedings.

During one of those late nights, I told Ajit, "Hey, when we hit the three-month mark, let's celebrate with a little date night together." Sitting in was all well and good, but I was already dreaming about being a grown-up again—even if just for a night. Ajit was all for it, and so I eagerly googled "date night experience Austin" and came upon an experience called Dinner in the Dark. Immediately, I could picture it: the first time in who knows *how* long that we would get all dressed up, that I'd actually brush and blow-dry my hair, put a cute dress on, and strap on my sparkly heels.

I instantly booked the last two tickets available. Excited, even with weeks to go, I began organizing all of the details for our "first date"—which included trying to find childcare. My Austin mommy groups on Facebook recommended some caretakers who could handle a two-and-a-half-year-old *and* a three-month-old for a few hours, and after a few conversations with candidates, we decided we'd hire a woman named Aimee. We were ready to go—locked and loaded!

As our date night neared, I was so excited I texted Aimee constantly: to make sure she had the address to our home, to send her the schedule for the kids, to let her know what they liked to have as snacks, and, of course, to share the bedtime routine. When the big day finally came, I put on my makeup, curled my hair, and strapped on my first postpartum little black dress. Ajit was stoked that we could finally take a break for an evening and see each other for what felt like an eternity. Before I knew it, it was almost 5 P.M., and Aimee would be there any minute.

But 5 P.M. rolled around, and Aimee didn't show. I texted and called her at 5:15, then at 5:30. *Did she get lost? Is everything okay?* No answer. An hour—and many panicky text messages later—she finally answered: "I'm sorry, something came up. I'm not going to make it."

Those words went straight to my heart like a dagger. I had been waiting, wanting, planning, dreaming about *finally* getting alone time with my husband—for months. I was dying to celebrate the newborn bubble we'd just emerged from. And now it was all ripped away.

Tears started rolling down my face . . . and the victim mentality started to seep in. Instantly, I turned into my toddler self, shouting out loud, "I can't believe she did this!" and "We planned this for months!" and "I confirmed everything!" and "Why would she cancel last-minute?!" My voice got louder. "I'm feeling SO angry right now!" I was now full-on pouting, stomping my feet, and just feeling awful.

Then I heard a little voice with a question. "Mama, why are you stomping and shouting like a dinosaur?"

My son, Arie, had noticed my victim spiral (it was kind of hard to miss). He could clearly tell how upset I was. And now I realized it fully too. So I took a big breath . . . and I told him the truth. "Well, Mama and Dada were supposed to go on a date, and I was really excited," I explained. "But now we're not going to go out after all. So Mama has really big feelings right now. Big feelings that needed a little stomping about."

I paused for a moment. "Do you want to shout and stomp like a dinosaur too?" I asked Arie.

He looked at me with the biggest grin and started laughing. "Yeaaahh, Mama!"

I asked Alexa to play the "Dinosaur Dance" by Boots and Cats, and together, we danced and stomped and roared over and over again, embracing the suck, feeling the suck, moving the suck, transforming the suck, and releasing the suck.

It was that day that birthed this embodiment practice. It acts as a reminder that every day will bring moments that suck, things that don't go as planned, or even bombshells that bring on a falling stage—but we get to choose whether we sit in the suck or move in it and around it. We can feel those feelings everywhere in our body and maybe even find some dinosaur-tastic magic in them. We can laugh and be silly even when we're disappointed. C'est la vie.

As Arie and I stomped and roared, I looked over at Ajit. "Babe, can you go out and grab some vegan chocolate chip ice cream for us?"

We didn't end up on our big date, but we *did* end up having the best ice-cream party with our family of four, jamming to "Dinosaur Dance" on repeat.

Want to try your own embodiment practice? Here's what to do during moments of suck.

1. **Anchor the suck.** Simply say it out loud: That sucked, now what? Embrace the sensations you're experiencing. Where do you feel it in your body? Back, head, stomach?

2. **Feel the suck.** Say it out loud and acknowledge the suckiness of the moment. Say, "I am feeling . . ." and name the emotion out loud. Use sounds, words, or even scream and shout it out if you need to.

3. **Tap into the suck.** Play music—the more ridiculous, the better—and shake, shimmy, or stomp like a dinosaur.

4. **Move the suck.** Now really start to move around. This is where you can dance, jump, and move the energy through your body.

5. **Transform the suck.** Giggle, belly laugh, repeat "that sucked, now what!" three times while laughing. (Laughter helps activate the calming vagus nerve in your body!)

6. **Breathe and integrate the suck.** Breathe in three times, exhaling each time on a buzzing sound with your lips. Then do three rounds of deep belly breaths, exhaling with an open mouth. Then go back for one more set of breathing in and exhaling with that buzz sound three times. *Phew.*

You can move that suck all around—seriously!

For a list of videos and resources to take you visually through the That Sucked, Now What? embodiment practice, as well as a list of ridiculous songs to move the suck, visit www.thatsuckednowwhat.com/resources.

*

Recap & Reflection Corner

1. Recall a crisis point or sucky moment from your past.
   What made that moment especially powerful for you?
   What weak spots in your Bounce Factor did it hit hard?

2. If that moment led you to retreating into a victim
   mindset, entitlement, or blaming others, how could
   you have made it into a Fall? What emotions were you
   feeling? Did you make time to pause and rest your body,
   or did you push through? How could that moment have
   been part of a bigger, or different, picture or perspective?

3. If that moment was the catalyst to a big change in your
   life—a Fall—how did that come about for you? What
   feelings or sensations clued you into the potential for this
   moment to lead to newer and better paths forward?

* * *

Chapter 10

Igniting

When I was 12 years old, I went to the mall with my dad. As we passed by Limited Too, I saw this pair of jeans that I *had* to have. They were baby blue, kinda baggy, and had a little rip across the knee in true '90s fashion. And they were *glittery*. Basically, they were the kind of jeans that would make me the coolest girl in the sixth grade.

So, of course, I asked my dad if we could buy them.

And, of course, Pa said no. "You have so many clothes already, Neeta!"

I was heartbroken. I *needed* those jeans. I begged him—*please, please, they are SO in style right now*—but it was no use. His only response was that when I made my own money, I could buy my own clothes.

Seriously? I thought. *Make my own money?* Frustrated and upset, I stomped off.

Still, I wanted those jeans *so* bad. I couldn't just forget about them. I had to get resourceful and creative. So, as I stewed in my room, I took out my diary and made a list of all the ways I could make money as a 12-year-old: *babysitting the neighbor's cat, selling home-baked cookies door to door in my building* . . .

As I wrote, my gaze drifted to my closet. The closet where I had "so many clothes already." And then, almost without thinking, I wrote down another idea: *selling my own clothes.*

Immediately, I circled it on my diary page. I jumped up, screamed, "I can sell my own clothes!" and started going through my closet and drawers. I pulled out everything I wouldn't mind parting with: a red top with ruffles on it, a blue crop top that some

141

of my girlfriends liked but I didn't care for anymore. I grabbed a few shirts, skirts, and sweaters, stuffed them in my big bookbag, and brought them to school.

In class, I passed notes to my girlfriends, letting them know I was having a "garage sale" and I'd brought some things I thought they may like. The teacher caught wind of my disruption, but I didn't care. During lunch, I told a few friends to try on some items from my collection. One friend asked if her crush in school would notice her wearing it (of course he would!); another friend asked if she could swap it with another sweater she liked in my closet (sure, we could make that happen). Without realizing it, I'd basically invented personal shopping on my own—and I felt good making my first few sales.

At the end of the day, I rushed home to share the news: "Pa, guess what?! I sold my clothes at school today and got 10 dollars for two of my shirts!"

My father gave me a curious look. "You sold your shirts to your friends and they gave you money for them?"

"Exactly," I said.

The curious look on his face turned to a big grin. "Well done, *beta*. I'm proud of you for thinking outside the box. In fact, here's another 10 dollars to match your earnings."

I'll never forget the first time I put on those baby-blue glitter jeans—jeans I bought with *my own money*. It made me feel on top of the world (and was the start of a lifelong entrepreneurial journey). But it was also the first time in my life I remember having that realization. That flash of clarity. That lightning-quick insight that, "Oh, I can *do* something about this." When I hit on the idea to sell my own clothes, I'd Ignited.

Igniting is when we state clearly and definitively what we want. Who we are. What we will or won't stand for. If Falling shows us that an exit door exists, Igniting kicks it open. It's when you go from saying, "Maybe things could be different . . . somehow" to "*This* is what I want to change." That could be a single, short statement of what you want—or don't want. It could be a judgment that you've been holding back or suppressing for too long. It could be a brilliant solution you've finally hit upon (like selling your old sweaters to buy glittery jeans). It's your own personal the-Emperor-has-no-clothes moment, when you call out what's not going right, speak truth to power (or to yourself), and do so in no uncertain terms. Thoughts and questions may arise in your mind like:

Do I really want to keep living the life I'm living?

I can't do this to myself anymore.

What will my life look like without . . . ?

Is this the time—finally?

Something has to give.

You know what? I don't have to do that.

Is this all there is to life, to work, to marriage?

I can't keep waiting.

I don't need (him/her) anymore.

I'm stronger than this.

Why am I putting up with this?

I'm in bad shape.

I want change.

It's a subtle shift, but it's one that gives you so much more agency. Your wants, your desires, your innermost thoughts are now part of the equation. And usually, those thoughts and internal questions will become action.

The moment I went from *How can I make money?* to *I can sell my clothes!* got me from insight to action almost instantly, and I had my endgame in sight: glittery jeans. But Igniting hasn't always had that clear endgame for me. Leaving my first marriage was abrupt and happened all in one night: on December 31, I packed as much as I could and got out. I couldn't foresee the next few days, let alone weeks, but I *could* see one thing very, very clearly: *I need to change my situation, NOW.*

Putting my dental practice up for sale came with a similar revelation. *What will my life look like without this?* I asked myself. On a practical level, I wasn't *really* ready, but what I knew and felt viscerally in my bones was this: I didn't want to be chained to one location, to one city. So I came to terms with leaving everything that I had built from the ground up. I came to terms with disappointing my family. I came to terms with what was crystal clear in my mind: I was meant for more. That clarity was all I needed to fully dive in and take action.

When we Ignite, we see that, one way or another, we have been playing small, and we can no longer deny it. We can't deny that we have been ignoring parts of ourselves that need attention, or neglecting our relationships, avoiding having that conversation.

Because for so much of our lives, we hold our tongues.

We hold back.

We deny, repress, squash down.

We don't tell bullies we're sick of their shitty treatment of us. We don't confess to our boss how much our job sucks. We don't declare we have a choice and we're finally going to take it. We don't admit to our weaknesses, to having too much to get done or too little time to ourselves.

Instead, we just stay quiet. We swallow our hurts. We reinforce the wall between our experience and our assessment of it.

Igniting burns that wall down.

In the first stage, you took a sucky moment and reframed it as an opportunity for change. Now you're going to crystallize exactly what that change needs to be.

But you don't have to act on that change—not yet. Igniting is taking the spark we felt in our Fall and giving it our time and attention and energy so it can grow—just a little more—into an intense firecracker of positive change. In this stage, it is enough to simply feel and own our eager desire to change. It is enough to step out of the comfort zone of ignoring and pushing aside and into the relative *dis*comfort of staring the truth down. It is enough to speak our realization and let it echo in our heart. It's enough to embrace all the big human emotions, to feel them, break down, let them fully enrapture us, and know intuitively that change to your entire core is coming.

As with Falling, the moment of Igniting goes by a few names: a lightning bolt or thunderclap, a flash of insight, a moment of clarity, an epiphany, an awakening. What's fascinating is that there's something actually happening in our brains and bodies when we feel that jolt of clarity. Researchers have conducted whole studies on what makes for an aha moment! In MRI and EEG studies, they've hypothesized that insight-based problem-solving is most likely to occur when we turn our attention internally and away from external information. When we rely less on the visual parts of our brain, and more on the parts of our brain primed to process abstract ideas like word meanings and relationships, we hit on those aha moments—the solutions that are lurking in our subconscious but still only weakly activated and below our conscious attention threshold. Science further shows that when we experience those flashes of insight, we also tend to feel a greater sense of processing fluency and positive affect—aka good feelings—as well as a greater sense of agency (yay!).

But enough about brains—let's take a look at how other people have experienced Igniting in their own lives. As you read these stories, look for the moment that the overall feeling snaps into a realization. Lock in on that #nofilter statement. See which statements—of needs, of wants, of pure frustration—resonate with you. More than anything, remember that Igniting is about achieving clarity. That's all this stage needs to do. Clarity fosters your sense of agency, yes, but you don't need to *take* any major, sweeping actions—not just yet. In each story, look for how articulating that want, need, or can't-take-it-anymore attitude is a powerful act in itself.

"I NEED HELP."

As we saw in the last chapter, Naiya, the new mom of twins, was starting to feel her struggle. After a long fertility journey, she finally had everything she'd ever wanted, and was determined to be Super Mom. Everything in her life was swirling into a perfect storm of exhaustion, hormones, guilt, and emotional upheaval.

Naiya was barely hanging on. But in feeling her grip start to slip, she was finally about to Ignite.

One day, her husband, Max—the busy ER doctor—left for work in a hurry while Naiya was busy with the twins. As had become routine, they barely had time to say good-bye, both distracted and with their hands full.

A few minutes into his commute, Max realized he'd left his lunch on the counter. Since he wasn't too far from home, he swung around back to grab it. When he came through the door, he stuck his head into the living room to say one last good-bye to Naiya and the babies.

But Naiya didn't see him—she'd fallen asleep with one of the babies and left the other on the floor, crying alone.

Gently, Max woke Naiya up, and when she realized what had happened, she burst into tears. All the frustration and shame of the past few weeks came cascading out, and for the first time, she fully broke down, confessing she wasn't even sure she was fit to be a mother.

"I just can't do it," she admitted. "I don't know what to do or who to talk to and . . . I need help."

Are there any words more humbling to speak than *I need help*? It is one of the purest expressions of our desire to change, the core of almost every lightning bolt we feel before we Ignite. For Naiya, she literally woke up and saw her reality clearly: the house strewn with baby things, the three-day-old sweatpants she didn't have the energy to change, the messes and spills she'd really meant to clean up. But she also saw her *emotional* reality clearly: the concern on Max's face, the fear in her own heart, and the two precious babies she'd do anything for.

There was simply no way for her to do it all. She needed help.

Admitting we need help can be empowering, as counterintuitive as it seems. It lets us recognize the limits of our own abilities and use those newfound boundaries to draw a clearer, more defined picture of what we *can* do. When we're striving for something outside those boundaries, denying or ignoring that we need help only makes things worse. Not only do our goals and needs not get met, but we also feel a compounding sense of shame for failing to do what we think we *should* be able to do.

In Naiya's case, even as she was being outwardly self-sacrificing by devoting all her time and energy to her children (even before they were conceived!), she was also letting her ego call some of the shots. She wouldn't (or couldn't) ask for help because she needed to be Super Mom. She needed to validate all the anguish and trauma of the long, drawn-out IVF process by being the most kickass, capable, *worthy* mom to ever raise kids. Her victim complex (from her and Max's fertility struggles) had launched her directly into a sense of entitlement (that motherhood should be easy) that was impossible to fulfill (because motherhood is *never* easy!). The chip on her shoulder she carried from the wounding years of being unable to conceive, from feeling like the universe was telling her, "You can't be a mother," left her determined to prove the opposite true.

Deep down, I think *all* our lightning bolt moments can be boiled down to "I need help" one way or another. It's an admission that we're not perfect. That we can't do it on our own. That we're not Superman (or Super Mom) and we're okay admitting it—even if it's just for a hot second. When we say "I need help," we Ignite by simply opening our minds to a possibility and a truth we've probably been shutting out for a long, long time. And by opening our minds, we create space for that help to come in as we move forward to Rising.

"I HATE MY JOB."

Remember Marianna, the doctor from Part II who was starting a new side hustle as a holistic wellness coach? Her moment of Igniting was as simple as it is relatable. Being a doctor was exhausting, and it wasn't living up to what she really yearned to do: take time with patients, see them as people, help them however she could, whether that was with Western medicine or not. Looking through her patient notes one day, frustrated that she had to speed through each one, she casually muttered to herself, "Ugh, I hate my job—why do I even do this?"

It stopped her dead in her tracks. Because it was so true.

She hated the conveyor-belt approach to treating patients.

She hated the demanding hours.

She hated the red tape of insurance policies keeping her from getting patients what they needed.

Probably all of us have the thought *I hate my job* at one point or another. (Hey, work is hard!) But, like many of these flash-points, the thought only becomes a revelation—a lightning bolt that Ignites us—when it comes at the right moment, in the right context: when we really just can't take it anymore.

Marianna knew being a physician was stressful. But it took that moment of clarity to realize she didn't have to let that job stress—or even that job—rule her life. For others—like working mom Serena who had serious self-doubt about her worthiness—the trigger moment might be yet another performance review without a raise, a shakeup in leadership that changes the culture for the worse, or even a promotion, if it's to a position we realize too late we are *totally* not suited for. The COVID pandemic inspired many knowledge workers to quit their jobs in the "great resignation," because once they got a taste of a flexible work schedule (or could finally save a few bucks thanks to their stimulus check), they realized life was too short to stay stuck in a particular job.

"I DON'T WANT TO DO THIS ANYMORE."

Lara, the aspiring lawyer, felt like a massive failure. (It was hard not to, after flunking the bar exam twice!) But she knew she didn't *want* to feel like a failure, and that's what led her to come work with me.

As she told me her life story, how she got to this point in her journey, I noticed something in how she *told* that story—quick, to the point, direct. She didn't ponder her answer or stop mid-sentence and start from a different angle; she just plowed straight ahead. I could totally see why she was the star of the debate team.

I was listening to *what* she was saying, too, of course. But coupled with *how* she said it, I realized something about Lara: she *never* paused. Not in her speaking, not in her thinking, not in her life. She'd dove into one activity—debate team—and stuck with it for years, all the way to the top of the roster. After high school, she'd gone straight to college, and after college, she'd gone straight to law school. The next step in that chain of events was to join the family law practice, where her father, grandfather, and brother were waiting for her, ready with her own nameplate.

So I did something Lara was *not* used to: I interrupted her.

"Can you make a list for me?" I asked. "What are the things that you're *curious* about? You know, the things that make you feel alive outside of work and school."

Lara, ever the dutiful student, quickly came up with a few things: singing, running, cultivating a yoga practice.

With those potential pursuits in hand, I suggested Lara lean into this pause in her life. She'd stepped off the conveyor belt for a while—because the next bar exam wasn't for a few months—and she could take advantage of this unusual (for her) period of waiting to explore those things that made her curious. And perhaps that time off would give her space to reset and take the bar again when the time came.

Lara was game for it in a big way. She decided she would go all-out and take on a yoga teacher training course in Costa Rica. A few months later, she came back to take the bar exam.

And third time's the charm, right?

Nope! She ended up failing again. Yet this time, she had clarity. Instead of staring at her results and thinking, "I'm such a failure—again!" Lara had a new thought: "I don't want to do this anymore."

She'd glimpsed what *else* she could do with her life once she'd stepped off that conveyor belt. She'd gotten a taste of charting her own path. She'd glimpsed what success could be on her own terms—because she'd finally learned what *her own terms* were.

Naturally, I was beyond psyched for Lara, because I could see that she had Ignited. I had a sneaking suspicion that she wanted to seriously reevaluate her pursuit of a career in law, but I also knew there was no way she'd be able to do that if she didn't *pause*. Something as simple as, basically, a vacation to try something she'd always been curious about had been enough to trigger that lightning bolt moment for her.

When we are locked into a particular goal, objective, or test, it's so easy to keep those blinders on and never look at the whole picture. Our ego gets so swept up in the need to Do the Thing that our deeper, spiritual needs get buried or rushed past. Like Lara, we step onto a conveyor belt aimed at a destination and structure our mental landscape around it: you're either at the end goal, or you're on your way there, with no alternatives.

The power of "I don't want to do this anymore" isn't in discovering our life's purpose for once and for all. That's just stepping from one conveyor belt to another. The power is in rejecting what we *don't* want, what we know *isn't* right for us. It's in honoring our spiritual needs and values—even when they're murky and uncertain—over the locked-down commitment to something dependable but wrong for us. It's letting our happiness (not our *ego*, and definitely not anyone *else's* definition of success) take over as a guiding force.

It's also important to remember that "I don't want to do this anymore" is perfectly sufficient for the Igniting stage. Remember, this stage isn't about instantly bursting into your new, better, actualized self all at once—it's Igniting, not Spontaneous Combustion! All you have to do is get to that moment of realization: in this case, that whatever it is you want to do with your time on earth, it *isn't* this thing.

"THIS ISN'T GOING TO WORK OUT."

Mo, the start-up founder, needed to make a decision.

Except both of his options, as far as he could tell, sucked.

He could shut his business down because he hadn't paid salaries for a month, and basically throw out everyone's hard work. Or he could pay everyone, but out of his own pocket, still not covering payroll *and* essentially throwing himself into bankruptcy.

This was a crossroads of epic proportions. The financial straits were dire, and either way, he lost.

At first, Mo did what a lot of us do: he gravitated toward what seemed like the easier way out (since neither way was straight-up *easy*) and tried to rationalize that potential choice. *Not* closing the start-up seemed simpler in a lot of ways. He wouldn't have to have the uncomfortable all-hands meeting to make the announcement. He wouldn't get branded with the stigma of a "failed start-up." He wouldn't have to let down so many of his friends and family who had gotten literally invested when he couldn't get first round of funding from investors.

In other words, he wouldn't have to do a lot of uncomfortable stuff. More than uncomfortable—folding his company was pretty much his nightmare.

But at the same time, pretending everything was fine didn't feel right. It felt against his values—the very values that had convinced so many small-dollar, first-round investors to chip in for the company. His integrity. His honesty. His commitment to the cause.

"How much worse does it have to get?" he asked himself, frustrated. "We're broke, I'm exhausted, and I'm compromising on core values. Like, if this isn't when I quit, then when?"

He'd asked the question. And he was about to spit out the answer—to hit that lightning bolt of truth moment.

"Maybe this *is* it," he said. "Maybe this . . . no. *Probably, very* likely, this company just isn't going to work out."

Saying it out loud was a huge relief. Mo didn't have to equivocate or justify or walk any fine lines. He didn't have to work until he was literally starving. He could let his ego go, read the writing on the wall (or on his balance sheet), and move on.

Moving into the Igniting stage doesn't mean we have all the answers. It just means that we finally have the courage to tell ourselves the truth (out loud or otherwise). And the thing about courage is that it's not always balls-to-the-wall dedication at any cost. Sometimes it's tolerating that brief *discomfort* so we can stop things from getting worse. Then we'll be ready to act, knowing we can get up, dust ourselves off, and stoke those embers of positive change.

"That moment," he remembered later, "was such a powerful, pivotal decision for me. I mean, I felt just devastated. Crushed. I was like, 'Fuck, was I ever even meant for this? Am I the guy who just burns out?' But in the end, it was so illuminating."

"WHAT DO I WANT OUT OF LIFE?"

There's one more client I'd like to introduce whose story so perfectly illustrates Igniting. Sheena was a bright and beautiful newlywed, yet behind the scenes, her marriage to her husband, Arjun, was crumbling. Small cracks had turned into deep fissures, and they were fighting almost daily.

But Sheena felt paralyzed, held in place by a single question: *What will people think?*

Or, more accurately: *Log Kya Kahenge?*

This Hindi phrase, popularized by comedian Hasan Minhaj in his Netflix special, resonated with the entire South Asian diaspora for a reason. Sheena, like so many of us, has felt the struggle of "me vs. family obligations—and the opinions that seem to come with them."

Those obligations felt impossible to ignore, even as Sheena realized she was on the verge of living out all the mistakes she saw in her parents' relationship. To quote her mother: "After the wedding, you get settled, there is no more fun, and it's time to get pregnant."

Sheena didn't want that. And she certainly didn't want it with a partner she couldn't get along with. But what other option was there? How could she dare to say no to this marriage? How could her picture-perfect dream of proposal, wedding, and pharmacist career not make her happy? How could she *give up* like that?

Log Kya Kahenge?

The rhetorical question was enough to keep her stuck. The only part of Sheena's life that *wasn't* wrapped up in her tightly-knit community and marriage was the growing ecommerce website she'd just started. She desperately wanted a compromise between her new business and her crumbling marriage, but the more she grasped for it, the more *both* sides suffered. She hated the idea of saying *no* to her marriage, but when she said *yes* to her marriage, to her husband, to her family, she was effectively saying *no* to herself and her dreams.

Basically, she realized, it was either-or.

And for the first time, instead of "what will people think?" a new question popped into Sheena's head.

What do I want out of life?

Learning that we can choose ourselves over others in our lives is *huge*. Whether it's our parents, our partner, or our peers, other people can seep into our lives and color our whole worldview, to the point where their dreams and desires become enmeshed with ours. Like a fairy tale princess in a tower, we assume the little space around us is all we can ever have, even if our souls long to open up, escape, and breathe some fresh air. Sheena's worries over "What will people think?" were keeping her frozen in place. She was letting their viewpoint dictate *her* story.

At the same time, though, she wasn't incorrect. Because the thing is . . . if she asked for a divorce? Yep. People *would* think she was saying no: to her husband, her family, her duty, her destiny. They *would* judge her. I struggled with the exact same reality when considering my own divorce. If the question is paralyzing, it's only because the answer feels so painful.

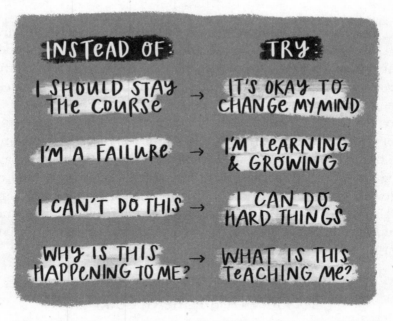

When you Ignite, you start to see potential where you used to see defeat.

The thing is, Sheena didn't need to find the right answer to *Log Kya Kahenge*. She needed to let herself ask the *real* question.

As Sheena started to Ignite, she allowed herself to start rewriting the story based on "What will *I* think?" In Igniting, she turned her story into a tale of bravery and overcoming, a tale of *yes* to herself instead of *no* to anyone else.

FEELINGS OF IGNITING

As we can see in the stories of these folks evolving from Falling to Igniting, it's a special time—the quintessential lightbulb moment, the initiation that sets the hero's journey into full swing and gets them that much closer to healing. Let's pause and dive into some of the feelings that can crop up for all of us in this stage.

Courage

Real talk: you have to be brave AF to get to Igniting. (Trust me—I navigate this a bunch on *The Brave Table*, my top-rated podcast where I help you have more brave conversations.) This is the stage where you come to the truth, have the big scary thought, feel the *realest* feelings. You aren't deceiving yourself anymore—and you're the hardest person to be straight with. But because Igniting comes from that moment of facing your fears, you're also going to feel so damn courageous. Sheena got a surge of courage in saying yes to herself, because she knew pretty clearly what kind of blowback she would get and *still* wasn't shaken from her decision. Naiya admitting that she was vulnerable and in over her head was hugely courageous, because she'd spent so much of her life building up an image of self-confidence and capability.

Discomfort—But the Good Kind

If there's one feeling that sums up the overall vibe of the Igniting stage, it's this one. You might be acutely, super-consciously aware of how *un*comfortable this stage makes you—but in a totally good way. This isn't a place you've been before. But, as we've seen, discomfort isn't something you've got to avoid at all costs. Positive stressful states are what help our Bounce Factor adapt and handle new environments. More than that, sometimes avoiding discomfort just makes things worse—like if Mo had decided to keep his failing start-up going just so he wouldn't have to make the deeply awkward "we're closing the company" speech. You'll feel like you're *juuuust* over that boundary of what you're familiar with, and maybe even excited by the mystery of what's out there.

Snapping to Life

I called this stage Igniting because it's just that: the moment of spark. You don't have to know how big a bonfire you're going to light in your life to know that you're going to light *something*. Lara felt ready to do something different in her life, even if she didn't know yet what that positive change would be. She still leaned into the excitement and possibility. This feeling can even come through as an actual sensation of warmth, like your body is priming itself to get up and go do the thing.

Strength

We talk so much about "building" strength, like it's a tower of blocks we're stacking one on top of another. I like to think of *cultivating* strength instead, of gently tending to the growing feeling of power inside us, giving it what it needs but also getting out of its way. Yes, this stage will test you. It won't be easy, as there may be obstacles and uncertainties along the way. But thing is, queen, when you're Igniting, you might sense the presence of that strength in yourself, growing bit by bit, day by day. Sheena knew the answer to "What would people think?" but she also felt grounded in saying yes to *herself*. Now isn't the time to demand that your strength perform for you just yet—in this stage, you're just the steward of that growing strength, welcoming it to take root inside you. It's stretching you in ways you never even imagined: maybe bringing on the tears as you feel yourself expanding, as well as a whole new appreciation of your capacity to transform.

Awakening of Your Soul

Sometimes, we feel ourselves Igniting on a spiritual, even profound, level. The call to change feels at once deeply personal and bigger than ourselves, and while we may not understand where that call is leading us *just* yet, we embrace the sense of opening. Marianna was already curious about new pathways for healing people when she hit a boiling point with her physician job, and that new, refreshed calling to serve others made it that much more seamless for her to look beyond her job as a doctor and take the next step into wellness coaching.

*

Recap & Reflection Corner

1. Can you recall a time when you were Igniting in your personal or professional life? Describe how you navigated that powerful awakening.

2. What did it open doors to? How did your mindset shift? What other changes did you notice?

3. What was the phrase or question that came up when you had your moment of Ignition? (You can use the ones from this chapter as a guide.)

4. How did it contribute to your relationships, or career, or health now? What were you able to change in your life?

* * *

Chapter 11

Rising

At some point in those hazy days right after my toxic first marriage fell apart, when I was just trying to sort out what to do next, I was out in Chicago on a coffee date with my friend, commiserating in classic pity-party fashion.

"How did this all even *happen*?" I asked him, practically holding my face in my hands.

Now, he could have patted my shoulder or launched into a diatribe about how terrible my ex was.

But instead, he answered my question *with* a question.

"Neeta, didn't you ever think of how *you* played a role in this?"

Um, sorry—did I ever *what* now?

Deep down, I want to think that I knew he was being encouraging. That I knew he was trying to get me thinking outside of the little bubble that I was so safely encased in.

So I thanked him for his question, and took it as an opportunity to pause and reflect on the habits and patterns that had brought me to that point in my life.

Just kidding. I didn't know any of that, and I got *super* defensive. Probably even rolled my eyes.

We all have that friend. The truth-teller and straight-talker. The one who doesn't bullshit. They aren't trained as a coach or a therapist, but they low-key seem to have the same skills. They're the friend who asks good questions—who asks *the* question, the one that makes you instantly stiffen up and think, *Oh, I do NOT want to answer that. Because you might be right.*

And then, maybe because you're so close to them, you just get mad.

Now, in the immediate aftermath of my divorce, I went through a *rough* couple of months. Eventually, I took baby steps out of wallowing and recognized that I had a chance to change things. I'd had my Fall. I felt the clarity and urgency of what I wanted next. I'd Ignited my dreams for my next steps in life (professionally, at least). But I still wasn't fully Rising—not yet.

Rising is the stage of action. Falling opens our eyes to possibility. Igniting defines our dreams into something specific. And Rising sees us start to make them happen. It's the stage where what we want to do (from Igniting) and why we need to do it (from Falling) combine into *doing something*.

But that *something* isn't a grand, sweep-the-table-clean gesture. Rising is a process, and a process means small, everyday action. It means forming habits and taking personal responsibility. And to get there, we have to clear out the last of our excuses. We have to start where we are, and that means owning where we are for once and for all. We have to cultivate radical self-acceptance, a "warts and all" brand of self-love. Instead of softball questions, the kind that we ask so our friends will console us, we have to ask ourselves those tough, new questions—or have a friend put those questions to us directly.

Back with my friend in Chicago, I managed to keep a lid on my bubbling feelings and respond. "What do you mean?"

"Just to take a look at all your relationships over the years," he said. "I think maybe you should ask yourself a different question."

At that point, I was still clinging to a lot of unhealthy mindsets. I had to pack up and leave. I had to present my case in front of a judge. I had to get a restraining order. What else could I possibly *have* to do now?

But my friend's interjection gave me the perspective I needed. Prior to our coffee chat, I was in my Igniting stage—I had strong feelings of what I wanted but hadn't taken action. I didn't want to go back to where I was before my Fall. But in order to Rise, I had to face those questions. Questions like:

What could I be doing differently?
Is there something bigger going on here?
Does this stir something up in me that I'm acting out on?

You may not be ready when these questions start to unfold for you either. Taking action is scary. The self-knowledge it takes requires *vulnerability*. You have to look at your past and *your* role in shaping it instead of ignoring it or suppressing it. But when you can look at your experiences and choices with the conviction of Igniting, of "I'm never going back there again," you can tap into a powerful motivator for action.

Recognize that the oh-so-sucky human experiences you've suffered through are the *opposite* of what you want for your life, and harness the clarity of that mission to keep you going on day to day. Every successful star can tell their own version of this story—Tony Robbins talks about never wanting to be poor again. My husband, Ajit, talks about growing up in less than ideal conditions and vowing that he'd do whatever it took to make sure he could always provide for his parents.

But when we ask those questions, when we own the whole picture of our past, we can sink into the heart of the Rising stage: discovery. We are ready to learn something new and take steps to pursue it. To say Y-E-S to new (and scary) opportunities—to being able to do the hard things with awe and wonder. And when we tackle those things, our fears are minimized or even curbed. Suddenly, the excitement of exploring new frontiers within ourselves is much more compelling than the fears that could hold us back.

Six months after that coffee date, when I'd gotten more soul-searching under my belt, I found I was acting with compassion more and more in my daily life. And in the midst of all that growth and activity, my memory jolted me back to that chat with my dear, kind, *incredibly perceptive* friend.

Oh, yeah, I thought, seeing him in my mind's eye. *You know what? You're right, actually.*

I saw the pattern that I'd followed in my life and relationships.

I saw how my Bounce Factor had been compromised for so much of my life.

I saw that my dear friend, who'd known me since high school, was a mirror to who I was and what I'd been doing.

And I saw that the clarity he pushed me toward was what spurred me to say *yes* to myself, exactly as I am.

For me, saying *yes* opened up a world of possibilities. I finally took the chance to let someone run my healthcare business on the day to day, which freed up more of my time. I became curious about different types of remote businesses, and began studying and joining networking groups just to learn about the intersection of online businesses and wellness start-ups, and get a peek outside of the halls of medicine. Those small, gradual changes in my everyday life were all ultimately giving birth to my next chapter—of travel, of new kinds of work, of real action toward what *I* wanted.

Saying yes may look like signing up for that weekend breathwork workshop you've always *said* you wanted to try: *now* you make an effort, reserve your spot, and get it on the calendar. Or maybe it looks like stepping out of your comfort zone and attending a Toastmasters class to improve your public speaking (which still kinda freaks you out, but you say yes because you are committed to the action and discovering you). It could look like embracing all kinds of healing: getting a full blood panel drawn to learn about your overall health or exploring alternative therapies to quit that caffeine or alcohol habit. It could look like booking that trip across Europe, perhaps backpacking solo. Or taking a course on attracting the right partner. Or working with healers, therapists, and somatic body workers to dive into trauma work.

Whatever that *yes* of discovery is for you personally, Rising is the stage where it happens. This is embracing this new reality of truly getting out of the funk. It's about reconnecting to your authentic values and letting those be the drivers of your day-to-day.

In this chapter, we'll look at what it takes to form those new habits through the lens of self-discovery, and see how radical changes don't have to be hard, and how to loosen those final constraints of judgment to be truly open to what's next.

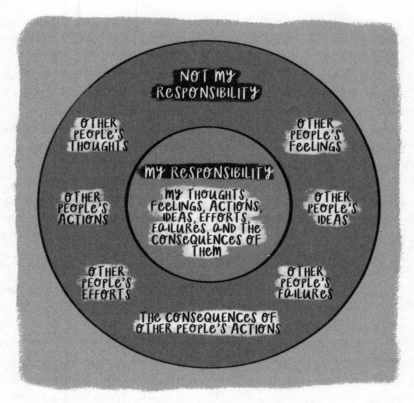

Knowing what's truly your responsibility and what's beyond your control is a key part of Rising.

FLOSS THE ONES YOU WANT TO KEEP

Let's talk flossing.

When I was a practicing dentist, I'd tell my patients, "Remember, only floss the ones you want to keep!" and send them on their way with a sample-size box of floss. When they returned six months later, some of them had started flossing regularly (and had the healthy gums to prove it), but most of them hadn't. So we'd go through another cleaning, another mini box of floss, and another promise to pick it up—rinse and repeat until, eventually, I'd break the news that they needed a filling, an extraction, or even treatment for gum disease.

Two things tended to happen at that point: the patient was totally surprised, and they took flossing a *lot* more seriously after that.

Fast forward to years later, when I was well into my coaching career and teaching my son how to brush his teeth on his own. He'd mastered holding the brush and squeezing the toothpaste (with a little help from Mom), but, like most toddlers, he wanted to know *why*. Why did he have to brush his teeth? Why was it so important? Just . . . why?!

Now, I could have given him a whole peer-reviewed Power-Point presentation on the long-term effects of brushing. But the other thing about three-year-olds is that they have short attention spans. They like immediate rewards. So I kept it kid-friendly: "Well, if we don't get the sugar bugs out, they'll start eating away at your teeth and make your breath all stinky!"

That logic worked for him. There's that instant reward—no yucky breath, and no icky sugar bugs. Two minutes of brushing and the results speak for themselves.

I started thinking back to my non-flosser patients. I'd given them a *why*, and they'd understood it intellectually. But that still wasn't enough to get them to adopt flossing as a *habit*. In other words, the action with a short-term reward—brushing—was easier to make a habit than the action with the long-term reward—flossing. It wasn't until a wake-up call—like a root canal—brought the long-term consequences front and center that they saw the light, felt that jolt of clarity, and *actually* changed their ways. They'd floss the ones they wanted to keep.

When we Rise, part of what we're doing is shifting to that long-term mindset. We're growing beyond our immediate-reward, toddler-level mindset and thinking about our best interest now *and* in the future. Thanks to our Fall, we've seen how pursuing our short-term fixes screws us over as time goes on, and in Igniting, we claim our need to change course.

The Rising stage gets us to that long-term mindset in two parts. First, we key into a clear sense of cause and effect. We put together some personal pattern recognition: "When I do (or don't

do) X, then Y is going to happen (or not happen)." We understand what we've been doing and take personal responsibility for
the outcomes of our actions. This sense comes with observing our
lived experience, as well as developing our intellectual maturity
(so toddlers aren't too good at figuring it out).

Second, we *feel* those consequences. Our Fall has given us a
taste of the long-term results of our actions. The bad things aren't
just theoretical anymore. The emotional urgency, *personal* urgency,
is there. Again, this comes from lived experience, an acute sense
of what precisely you will feel if A leads to B. This visceral anticipation of sensation (whether positive or negative) is a potent motivator. Without it, the consequences can seem vague or unlikely or
not too major to worry about. Hear your dentist tell you to "only
floss the ones you want to keep!" and you won't cringe thinking
about what might happen. Hear them say, "Open up for the drill,
please—this might pinch a little," and you're going to get a clear
gut reaction—one that you won't soon forget.

It's the combination of that personal responsibility and that
powerful emotional charge that gets us to Rising. Knowing what
to do, and feeling deeply *why* you should do it, together make for
more positive habits going forward—even flossing.

But this isn't just coach-talk, or even dentist-talk. There are
neuroscience and psychology findings behind this.

Researchers have described successful behavior change as com-
prising two domains: the cognitive and the motivational. The cognitive is the *way* to change your behavior (that is, the exact actions
you need to take) and the motivational is the *will* to change your
behavior—the drive to actually follow through on the actions you
know are part of the goal.

For most habits, the *way* is generally pretty obvious: cut out
foods that don't nourish you to lose weight, or take up a daily
meditation practice to feel calmer. Yet it's the *will* that gets harder
to summon. This is because the *way*—the actions to take—comes
from the logical, problem-solving, time-managing parts of our
brain. But the will comes from a more ancient portion of our
brain: the reward system.

The reward system is inherently short-term-focused. It's there to help us survive *right now,* because if we don't make it through the next 10 minutes, then something two years away won't really matter. This is why, in books and media, we tend to hear about the reward system in a *negative* context: how the cascade of new content on TikTok and Instagram reels triggers feel-good dopamine in our brains, and so our thumb scrolls again, and again, and again until it's 2 A.M. Yikes!

But the reward system *can* be put to use in achieving longer-term results, and the strong emotions that get stirred up in Rising can help it happen. To engage the reward system, you have to tap into something that matters to *you,* when you're by yourself and there's no one to be accountable to but you. This could be avoiding a kind of unpleasant outcome you've already experienced, or it could be building toward a happy outcome you're eager to experience. The more you associate the action with the emotions that come with visualizing those outcomes, the more you spark the reward system into gear.

To get back to our flossing example, flossing because your dentist tells you to isn't a strong motivation because the reward system isn't engaged. I knew my patients would *tell* me they'd start flossing, because they wanted my approval in the moment—that's a reward of sorts. But once I was out of the picture and they were back at the bathroom sink, that urgency was gone. There was no Dr. Neeta to give them the reward of a thumbs-up. But if you're flossing because you know you *really* don't want to get oral surgery, then each time you do it, you'll get more satisfaction out of it.

So that's the basics of how Rising helps us take new, more positive actions based on our past experiences. But the science doesn't stop there. To level up your habit formation, and make it truly lifelong, you can tap into your *personal values.*

Your values are the high-level beliefs that define what matters to you on a large scale. Articulating those values and applying them to individual situations can rev up your motivation from something generic to something personal—*and* bring in the reward system. It really can be that simple. Our brain has a built-in system that *wants* us to live by our values, and all we have to do is ask it to kick in. Here's a few more science-backed insights that can help you maintain positive action as you Rise.

- **What you focus on expands—big time.** Studies have shown that our willingness to take action—and our willingness to sacrifice or pay something to do it— grows as we direct more attention and focus toward it. Keeping a new behavior top of mind with a few simple visual reminders (like a vision board made on Pinterest, or photos posted on your fridge or on the lock screen on your phone) are a huge help to cementing those new habits in your life. After having my son, I made a big, audacious goal: getting back to my pre-baby weight, but this time even *stronger*. I thought signing up for a 3-mile Tough Mudder (literally running over obstacles through mud and around barbed wire) would do the trick. I had to keep my eyes on the prize for *six months*. But I worked that focus. I created my vision board with female athletes post-baby. I blocked out the time four days a week for 45 mins of intense training, the kind where failure to complete an obstacle earns you 30 burpees—it was nuts! But that vision got me through. (I definitely have a new appreciation for those dirty races, and yes, six months later I'd built an extra 5 percent of lean muscle mass and finished the race!)

- **Your intentions rewire how your brain works.** Our minds have this sweet little setup called the reticular activating system (RAS), a network of nerves between the brain and the spinal cord that essentially wakes up the brain and gets it ready for action when it notices any sensory stimuli. It kickstarts the process of focus, and you've probably already seen it in action before— like when you're considering a new white two-door sports car, and suddenly all you *ever* see on the road is white two-door sports cars! Priming your RAS with your intentions allows your mind to subconsciously be on the lookout for moments and opportunities that lock in that intention, and tug your focus toward them (and away from other, less essential things).

- **Your lived human experience counts and helps you choose well.** The perspective and views you hold after going through heartache, pain, loss, and the spectrum of wild human emotions we process when shit hits the fan—that all matters! For years, after losing my parents and brother, I took up a major interest in all things wellness and geeked out on biohacking, directly motivated by what I'd been through. Research has shown that your lived experience prompts your prefrontal cortex, which helps in decision-making. Fun fact: Meditation actually helps thicken the parietal lobe (in the pre-frontal cortex) to increase your awareness in this area. Look at your life through a lens that's optimized for whatever healthy choice you want to make and your decisions to act expansively become no-brainers.

- **Declare it loud and proud.** Choose your words wisely, friends, because when it comes to motivation, nouns are more powerful than verbs. Behavioral studies have found that thinking of your actions in terms of "being vegan" or "being paleo" or "being a yogi"—as opposed to "not eating meat" or "not eating sugar or grains"—make you more likely to follow through. (And the opposite is true as well—people who identified with negatives like "I'm not good at math," "being a night owl," "addicted to my phone," or "everything is *so* hard for me!" stuck to *that* reality too.) It's the same as manifestation and the laws of attraction. As we begin to start verbalizing and identifying with the behavior we want—"I'm an early riser," "I'm a powerful public speaker," "I'm a fighter"—as declarative statements, we begin to rewire parts of our brain, the crucial initial steps in true and long-lasting behavior change.

For a full list of 50 declarative statements that may help you make shifts and spark new pathways in your brain, visit thatsuckednowwhat.com/resources for a free guide on making sure those habits stick along with journal prompts to keep you accountable.

- **If you're stuck, just "do the opposite."** In dialectical behavior therapy (DBT), a method designed to help with emotional regulation, there's a technique called "opposite action," which is basically what it sounds like. If you find yourself paralyzed by choice, overwhelmed by emotion, or otherwise flooded and unable to think straight, simply choose to do the opposite of what that burning emotion is begging you to do. For example, if you're having one of those mental health days, feeling the feels, and just want to stay cooped up with the covers over your head, *do the exact opposite*: spring yourself out of that bed, take a shower, and go for a walk—or at least elevate your mood by playing some tunes and pull open the curtains and let that good natural light in.

- **Remember: you're human and life happens.** When clients tell me, "Okay, I'm ready for my next chapter. I'm finally going to focus on me! I'm going to start that side project! I'm going to launch my painting collection! I'm going to begin my morning routine at 5:30 A.M.!" I am all for those are big, audacious goals, and I know the dopamine and excitement around the newness of the project will jumpstart it. Just remember that if you rely *solely* on a huge surge of excitement and enthusiasm to tackle a new habit, it will be hard to *sustain* that habit over the long term. Why? Because you're human! Life happens! The key is to adjust as

you go and not let any one "miss" make or break your
new behavior.

Knowing *why* something matters to you, and then doing it,
will give you that feel-good rush—positive emotions. The value
behind that action makes all the difference. In other words, your
core values aren't something to cultivate and understand *independent* of new habits or healthier behaviors. They're intertwined.
And Rising is the perfect time to put those values into words.

By thinking long term and being wholly invested in the
behaviors that will optimize our life, change your habits for good,
and help you work toward being a better human, you can live
your Rising stage to the fullest and make those everyday actions
with lifelong benefits (like, you know, flossing) integral, easy
parts of your day-to-day. To jumpstart your journey during the
Rising stage, join the free five-day habit reset challenge here:
thatsuckednowwhat.com/resources

FROM JUDGEY BITCH TO BRAVELY OPEN: SMALL SHIFT, BIG CHANGE

"How about you, Sierra?" I asked. "What are you going to try
this week?"

We were in a group coaching session, and I was setting up the
students to tackle a "conquer challenge." I'd told them that this
week, they had to go do something that scared them, step out of
their comfort zone somehow, and then come back and share. For
accountability, they not only had to report on how it went after
the challenge, but also share an idea for what they could try as the
official kickoff.

Sierra was a lovely, bright woman in her mid-30s, and in retrospect, I'm not sure what I was anticipating as her answer—but she
definitely surprised me.

"Moms' groups," Sierra said without hesitating. "I dread those
kinds of things."

When Sierra joined the coaching group, she'd just had a Fall of epic proportions. She'd built her whole life around her husband and her family, focused the past five years on her children, and with the kids now in school, she had been working on rekindling her romance with her husband when the bombshell came: her husband was cheating on her.

Obviously, her world was rocked.

"I realized I've been in my own little isolated bubble," she'd explained earlier. "I only do things for the kids or the family. And it's like . . . it's like I don't even have an identity of my own."

From that perspective, it was easier to see why Sierra was equal parts terrified and disdainful of those coffee-chat, meet-in-the-park, mothers' social groups. Still, I asked her to share more about why these groups were outside her comfort zone.

"They're just . . . not me," she said. "I look at the women who hang out in the middle of the day, and it just seems so selfish. But," she added, "I might be being a little judgey."

That all made plenty of sense. Before her Fall, Sierra was used to playing it safe, flying under the radar. Her social life was about serving, whether it was volunteering at the kids' school or entertaining her then-husband's work colleagues at their house. She didn't have *time* for those kinds of grown-ups-only meetings—not if it wasn't in service to her husband or kids.

In Igniting, though, she'd been starting to focus on herself for the first time.

And now she was ready to Rise.

"Go for it," I told her. "Hit up that moms' group. Conquer it. And let us know how it goes."

When I say that openness is part of Rising, I don't mean you have to suddenly dump everything you ever were and make a radical pivot to a new value system. Sierra is a perfect example of how seemingly small the openness can be—she wasn't opening up to a major lifestyle change like, I don't know, extreme minimalism or moving across the globe or going 100 percent vegan. She was literally just opening herself to a slightly different social group. She was becoming a teeny-tiny bit less judgey. For her, Rising was just taking these baby steps of intentionally seeking out new people and committing to that effort.

When we reconvened, I was eager to hear from Sierra. "So? How was it? How were the moms?"

"You wouldn't believe it, Neeta," she said. "I met three other women who *also* just broke up with their boyfriend or husband. All of us are navigating the single mom life now."

Sierra was practically glowing as she spoke, like the courage she'd found with these other women was lighting her up from the inside. And what was most beautiful is how, in being open to something she'd written off for so long, she was able to grapple with the fears of putting herself out there and the fears of being vulnerable.

"I never really needed to do that before," she explained, "to reach out, or test the waters with new people. Or I thought I didn't. I had those excuses, my husband, my kids . . . I wasn't really asking myself if those were real excuses. I just assumed that my thinking was right. That my judgment was sound."

The moms' group was just the beginning. After that, Sierra went on to sign up for spiritual retreats and meditation. She had never done anything like that before: "Honestly, I made fun of self-help!" she said, and laughed.

Slowly but surely, this was the reckoning that she needed to come back to herself. Her Rise was just that series of small openings, small invitations to connection: having coffee with somebody, then wine night with a couple of new friends, then having people over to her house, and then a full-on crying session as she empathized with these incredible new women in her life.

In her openness, Sierra was also asking new questions as well. Before, she would ask questions designed to keep her squarely where she already was: "How am I supposed to make time for myself and my friends if I have to pick the kids up after soccer and have dinner on the table at six and throw in another load of laundry?" But as she began to Rise, her questions reframed her situation and invited her to that sense of open possibility: "What if I put my activities first and then filled in everyone else's needs around that? What if those women hanging out are onto something? And why am I so afraid of what they have?"

What was perhaps most interesting about Sierra's Rise is that even though her life was busier, she also found it easier to prioritize herself. In fact, this whole season of uncertainty and divorce, of shuttling the kids to their father's house and having those nights totally to herself, clarified for her that she didn't want to be alone—and didn't deserve to be alone either. That sense of worthiness even let her have compassion for herself.

"I probably should feel pretty stupid," Sierra said. "Five years of my husband being gone once a month for business trips and I never realized that it wasn't actually business?" She shrugged. "But I wouldn't judge my girlfriends for that—I don't judge them for that. And I don't judge myself either. Not anymore."

Rising is the stage where we can make huge leaps forward by taking tiny steps, and ultimately, as Sierra's story shows, it's that openness to new experiences, to new questions, that multiplies our efforts. Something as simple as a cup of coffee with strangers can literally change your life. And we can all probably stand to be a little less judgey.

YOU (STILL) CAN'T SKIP THOSE SETBACKS

There's one thing I want to be super clear about: in Rising, you will still stumble.

Maybe they'll be small stumbles, or maybe it'll be a full-on Fall that lands you back where you started.

That is totally, completely normal.

Carmen was a client of mine who had struggled with health problems. A former college athlete, she had just been through months of seeing doctors and, although she'd gotten a diagnosis of Lyme disease and was undergoing standard treatments, still wasn't *feeling* better. This was endlessly frustrating, because she identified strongly as someone *healthy* and *active*. She valued working hard to find solutions. So, after Igniting, Carmen decided to take matters into her own hands.

Carmen began to research everything she could about Lyme. She reached out to experts and interviewed people. She sought out far-flung clinics and alternative therapies, healers, and bodyworkers so that she could begin her true healing journey and find answers, treatments, and therapy that actually worked. She tapped into her identity as someone energetic, competitive, and always up for a challenge and channeled it toward new healing approaches. There was no way this diagnosis was going to keep her down. She'd do whatever it took, put in whatever time for the treatment she needed.

But it *still* wasn't easy.

Of the new therapies that she tried, eight of them were not for her. Each time, the new treatment gave her hope and optimism, and each time, she felt a slow creep of disappointment when it didn't end up helping. There was definitely a sense of hopelessness in the air. But the difference was that Carmen now immediately knew to step out of it. She could shake out of her funk and say, "Okay, I'm going to just try something else."

She kept up the research, kept exploring, finding new pathways, and asking different questions. "What haven't I considered yet?" "What else might be going on here?" These questions led her to information on physiological manifestations of trauma, and how the body can hold on to negative experiences and emotions long after they'd passed. And from that came a new question for her: "What am *I* still holding back?"

She went in for Reiki sessions, talk therapy, and Tapping (formally known as Emotional Freedom Techniques, or EFT). She talked to people in support groups and joined online forums to connect with others on the same journey. She even tried a bee-sting therapy—literally putting bees on her skin to sting her!

Not everything worked. And of the things that did work, some worked better than others. But Carmen was willing to try anything, because she told herself, "I am going to be this open vessel and welcome all possibilities for healing." She was willing to *experiment*, to go through trial and error.

That's the way to handle setbacks when Rising.

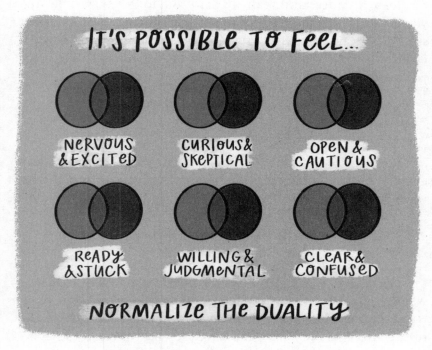

So much of this stage is a paradox. Embrace it!

We already know that setbacks are a part of life. But when we get to this exciting stage of Rising, and we start to see ourselves making those small changes, taking those little bits of personal responsibility day by day, we can get so hyped up about our progress that we forget that setbacks can happen at any time, for any reason and *to* anyone—including us.

Even though we're Rising.

Even though we're already seeing change.

This is why Rising is only halfway through the upward cycle. It's exhilarating to be here, but it's also not the ultimate expression—not yet. And it's okay if you hit a setback.

It's okay if life rips the rug out from under you—again.

It's okay if *you* screw things up.

Ultimately, all that matters is how you recover. All that matters is whether you're ready for this new ride, and this new adventure.

Yeah, it's uncertain. Yeah, it's scary. But in this stage of Rising, you are still going to fumble through some changes. You can even still Fall, because the Rising stage is so new. But the good news is, when you Fall, it's not going to be as bad as that first Fall that got you started. Because you *are* on this upward trajectory.

FEELINGS OF RISING

Now that we've seen what happens to you as you Rise, let's explore the feelings going on internally as you're progressing through this stage.

Acceptance

The biggest aspect of this stage is that you're finally accepting where you are. Instead of giving up and refusing to see your situation for what it is, you're able to say to yourself, "Nope, this is the reality, this is where I'm at, and I need to take that on for myself." When I had that conversation with my friend about my relationships, at first—before I really started to Rise—I *couldn't* accept the fact that I held some responsibility for what had happened to me. But once I could accept that truth, it was liberating.

Confidence

You have a little bit more confidence when you Rise. Saying no to things that don't serve you and saying yes to things that do is no longer such a daunting prospect. As you try out new actions and habits that feel right to you, and as your view shifts to a long-term one, you reap the rewards of incremental gains, and bolster your sense of agency and ability to make your own changes happen. And that feels *good.* It's a confidence booster like no other!

A Sense of Ease

When we Rise, sometimes things actually start feeling easier for us! As those habits and actions kick in, and we let ourselves be guided by our values and our true identities, we don't have to struggle so much to pursue what we want. Clarity reduces friction and helps us glide. You might find that sometimes the path forward that involves "less work" might actually be the one you need to Rise—because it's the one that speaks to your confident sense of who you are and what matters to you.

Openness and Curiosity

Rising brings us new experiences, and as we explore and undergo this newness, we kindle our sense of curiosity. Sierra's decision to do something challenging and join up with a mom group was a beautiful example of openness in action—she let go of her preconceived judgments and just let herself be there to receive the experience. Carmen, in trying new healing therapies and seeking answers for herself, was also open to new options even when prior "new" options hadn't worked out for her. Both women were able to stay buoyant and keep Rising because they held onto that curiosity—and *dropped* the judging.

Readiness

Rising isn't the final stage—there's lots more good stuff to come. That's why readiness is such a key feeling to experience, usually as you're about to leap into Magnifying. You might not know exactly what's coming around the bend (because, really, when do we *ever* know that for sure?); but you feel ready for whatever life will bring you next. You're staring it down head-on instead of peering anxiously around the corner.

✳

Recap & Reflection Corner

1. Ask yourself some new questions. Look at your present situation and wonder: What was your role in getting to where you are now? What personal responsibility will you need to take moving forward? What might you need to reevaluate, or see in a new light, like Sierra did? What might you be pursuing that you don't *really* need to see through?

2. When you are in the Rising stage, creating new habits that serve you is exciting! Reflect on your current inventory of habits right now. List one or two habits you wish to create or let go of that may cause some shifts where you are right now.

3. Your personal values and your sense of identity is key in forging habits that feel like part of you. What are *your* values? How do you see your best self? What identities are present in that version of you? For example, if you're seeking to improve your physical health, you can claim your identity as a runner, a swimmer, a Pilates obsessive, a gym rat—whatever speaks to you! If you're breaking through in your career, try on a new title for size: writer, designer, entrepreneur, CEO, mentor. What actions and habits does that identity connect to? How has channeling those values—or failing to channel them—gotten you closer to your goals in the past? How could reconnecting with them find you fresh motivation? For example:

   • The woman who tried every diet fad to feel more "worthy" in a thin body vs. the intuitive eater who improved her diet to have more energy with her kids

- The young lady who vowed to wake up at 5:30 A.M. every morning because she wants to feel virtuous and hardworking like her peers vs. the morning riser who realized that her anxiety is calmed with a slow morning routine

- The executive who was burned out and always on her phone because her imposter syndrome wouldn't let her unplug vs. the high performer who kicked ass by day and disconnected at night because she prized the *other* activities in her life

4. Having setbacks in this stage is part of the process and is totally normal. It's okay to feel curious yet skeptical. Open yet cautious. Excited yet reserved. This is the spectrum of the human experience! You will have optimal days, and you will have your sucky days. What self-care rituals are going to be nourishing and helpful for you in this stage? List two to three. For example: Going to bed 30 mins earlier. Winding down with my self-care lounge playlist.

* * *

Chapter 12

Magnifying

When I met my client Anand, he was 25 and feeling *incredibly* conflicted about what to do with his life.

Anand had a bunch of cousins living across the globe and kept in touch with them on social media. As they'd all gotten older, he'd started to notice through their Instagram posts and Twitter updates that, unlike him, many of his cousins were dating casually, pursuing passion projects and short-term work instead of dutiful careers, and essentially doing what they wanted to do and living in the moment.

It *looked* amazing.

But for him, it *felt* impossible.

Anand was a child of immigrants. His parents had struggled to come to the U.S., leaving their homeland and what was comfortable to head into uncertain and uncomfortable circumstances—all to provide a better life for their family. Yet this "better life" didn't come without its own stressors. As for many of us whose families left their countries in pursuit of better, the American Dream came with a duty to family and an obligation to lean into more stable careers like medicine, law, or engineering because those sectors are "safe." For the generation before, education was the "safe" way to get out of struggle and find a way to thrive. So can you blame them for wanting the same path to thriving for their children? I mean, they had to leave—often many times—everything they knew. They left their families, homes, culture, language, friends, society, and sometimes faced violence, terror, and oppression—all to travel uncharted waters. To battle against a fast-moving current, and then start over from the bottom. They had audacious resilience all their own—they didn't know how to fail, because failure wasn't an option. All their choices were about survival.

So, Anand's parents valued education and had a family-first mentality when it came to his career and, basically, his whole life. Anand was kind and considerate, and he took into account everything that his parents sacrificed for him growing up. His mom worked nights at the gas station his uncle owned for years, just so Anand could fit in with his friends and take swimming and tennis lessons. So it was only appropriate that he wanted to please his parents and get the external validation of being a "good" and "smart" son; he went to school to be an engineer.

But shortly after he graduated and started working, Anand realized that he didn't *want* to be an engineer. He was talented enough at the work, but for him it wasn't—for a lack of a better word—*fun*. It wasn't letting him use what *he* felt he was best at: his sense of humor and personality. (No one cares if an engineer can crack a joke; they just want the project to end up structurally sound.) Fortunately, the pressure about studying to be an engineer had let up—he'd checked that box. Unfortunately, the pressure to get *married* took its place.

That was what got Anand spiraling. It was one thing to bite the bullet and go with their wishes for his professional life, but marriage wasn't *just* about him—there'd have to be a bride involved. And he couldn't in good conscience commit to another person if his heart wasn't truly in it. It just didn't feel right. He didn't know how to tell his parents that he truly wanted a life more like his Western cousins, a "love marriage" instead of an arranged path they expected.

So, for a while, he *didn't* tell them. But he did start working his way up to Magnifying. Through our coaching together, Anand took a look at his Bounce Factor, and was able to identify how he had gotten in the habit of saying yes to his parents over and over again, and how his attempt to please everyone was undermining his own potential and desires. He experienced a ton of shame and guilt at the thought of letting down his parents—after all, they did everything for him. He literally owed them his life! After experiencing the Fall of the not-so-subtle hints about getting married, he worked up to the Igniting stage when he started toying with the idea that he could make decisions separate from his family, and then started Rising when he took up his own pursuits and hobbies. On almost a whim, he created a new Twitter account where he started posting witty jokes and one-liners about the world around him, and to his surprise, people seemed to like it. After that, he got the courage to take a stand-up comedy class.

But he was still working as an engineer. And, as far as his parents knew, he was still signed on to get married soon, to a woman his parents would select for him back in India.

In our work together, Anand had to acknowledge and accept that he had to upset people, at least temporarily and maybe permanently, to have the kind of life and career he truly wanted.

He had to Magnify.

Magnifying is the stage where you put your power on full display. Like an Avenger or Wonder Woman ready to face down whatever's next, you are standing on your own two feet, your cape blowing in the wind and your emblem shining on your uniform. You've cultivated change on your own through Falling, Igniting, and Rising, and now you're ready to show that change to the world. You're unafraid to be who you are, do what you're doing, and say what you think in a greater, public context.

In other words, Magnifying is when you just *own* it. You own what you're doing. You own your past. You own exactly where you are and where you're going. And you change your relationship to expectations—your own and others'—for good.

For Anand, that part was painful.

It was revealing.

It was confronting.

Yet, until he could get to a wild reckoning of standing up for what his values, dreams, and actual gifts meant, then none of those would ever really reach their full potential. *Anand* would never reach his full potential.

This was where his Bounce Factor came into play in a big way. He knew very clearly what the values of his upbringing had taught him, and also how a shift in environment was a game-changer: online, a few mean tweets sent his way from randos were easy to brush off, but in person, a disparaging or disappointed word from his parents could emotionally wipe him out. He had to build up a tremendous amount of courage—and fortify his emotional capacity—simply to utter the word *no* to a single request from his mom and dad.

But he'd gotten as far as Rising, and with another look at his Bounce Factor, he knew what he was up against inside himself. Guilt for even thinking he would be tearing his parents apart. Shame for lying to his parents about his rawest, deepest desires. Ultimately, what brought Anand to the Magnifying stage was a conversation with his mother. He bravely asked her to stop setting him up on dates and pursuing an arranged marriage on his behalf.

Culturally, this was a huge ask—almost unthinkably so. It was a courageous conversation. It required thought and planning, which we did together: since Anand knew disappointment was on the table, he wanted to speak with tact, assertion, and respect. After several drafts, and role playing, he got the courage to lay out his boundaries and have the difficult conversation with his parents. Surprisingly, his mother ended up being wildly supportive. As it turned out, Anand's father was the parent who needed more time to accept that his son didn't want the life and "help" he was supposed to have from his parents to find his life partner.

Still, the support from his mother was incredible—something he never would have received if he hadn't said yes to the Magnifying stage. He discovered his desires and values and was able to choose his own happiness for his career and life over potentially being unhappy for the rest of his life just to please his parents. This was hard work! No one wants to disappoint, or even disrespect, their parents. So many clients of mine from immigrant backgrounds don't use their voice or share their truth for fear of disrespecting, shaming, or just rocking the boat with their caretakers. Yet there is magic to the art of giving yourself permission, to unshackling yourself from fears of disappointment, and exploring what it means for *you* to be happy.

In the end, Anand's mother giving him support was exactly what he needed to stand in his power. When he no longer felt like he had to walk on eggshells around her, he could take ownership and responsibility for his desires—and their relationship grew closer as a result. Soon thereafter, he started saying no to other career expectations that didn't match what fundamentally mattered to *him*—like being an engineer. Anand was Magnifying, beautifully—and I couldn't have been more excited for his evolution. Each decision he made, each no he shared, defused his tendency toward people-pleasing and gave him more unapologetic confidence and audacious resilience. Bit by bit, those decisions propelled Anand into a career that he would have never ever expected—as a stand-up comedian.

As the name suggests, Magnifying is defined by *expansion*. You may feel like your heart is expanding— that you have so much more compassion, so much more forgiveness for yourself.

But Magnifying isn't simply "more growth." When you look through a magnifying glass, things *appear* to be growing larger; when in fact, you're just gaining a closer view, a greater sense of detail and context. This deep recognition means you're able to unlearn what you *thought* you knew, to pull apart even deeper patterns buried in your Bounce Factor. You feel a desire to recognize what you've been through without lapsing into a victim mentality or feeling resentment.

By the same token, the Magnifying stage is where you come to a sense of forgiveness. Forgiving the other person, forgiving the situation, forgiving the environment around you. Because you have such compassion for yourself and what you've been through, and you've cultivated your own power, you see what you are capable of. You can forgive whatever has happened. For example, when you've just been fired, you can easily cling to anger and misgivings about your former boss.

They were so cruel, and I'm a good person who didn't deserve it.
They were just being greedy, and I was working out of passion.

They made mistakes all the time, and I was the one to pay the price.

But if you can work your way past that Fall and let yourself Ignite, and then Rise, you'll come to a point where your focus shifts to yourself and your gifts.

I'm going to get those books, because I'm worthy of improving myself.

I'm going to hire that coach, because I care about investing in myself and my career.

I'm going to study for this certification, because I know I have the foundational skills already.

I'm going to get my feet wet and start freelancing, because I'm a badass, and can hustle like nobody else.

And then I am going to start that business, because I care about following through on my dreams.

You're living for yourself, unapologetically you, and not hiding from anyone.

Finally, Magnifying creates a kind of ripple effect. Because even though Magnifying is the stage at which you stop living for other people, it isn't about tuning the world out entirely. In fact, it's the opposite. It's letting your light shine so brightly that you draw others closer, share the gifts you've cultivated, show by example how wonderful and enriching a life on the way to Thriving can be. Just like that superhero standing bravely atop a city building, their signal in the sky, you're a shining example to everyone who sees you. You're confident, brave, and excited to do what you're doing.

Yet at the same time, you're not fueled by your ego. You're fueled by purpose, by your values. You ask, *How can I share this with others? How can I Magnify other people?* You become the leader. You become the one people ask, "Hey, are you doing something different? Your energy has changed . . . something new with you?" You begin attracting a new, more expansive vibe, because you are magnetic and Magnifying your big bright light, and people become curious and want to tap in to this new frequency.

You see that it's not about *me*, but about *we*.

And from there, you're well on your way to Thriving.

"NO" IS A COMPLETE SENTENCE

Magnifying is the stage where we make it clear that we're living on our terms and not anyone else's. But, as we saw with Anand, that doesn't just mean getting clarity on what we want and don't want for ourselves. It means expressing that to others—and holding the line.

Very recently, I was working with a well-known CEO in coaching his top executives. In order to hit a deadline for one of this CEO's projects, we needed to sit down for a collaboration session to get his input. My team was going through a really busy season, so scheduling was already tight, and the CEO kept blowing off calls, blowing off e-mails, not responding to pretty much anything.

Most of the folks on my team were afraid to push back on his flakiness. This was a really big-deal person, after all. As one assistant told me, "I know I *could* say something, but what if he stopped working with us?"

Now, I completely understood where she was coming from, because ideally, no, we wouldn't want to lose our working relationship with this client! But at the same time, the whole thing wasn't sitting right with me. I mean, how could I look at my employee and say I valued her time and efforts while at the same time I was wasting that time and effort by not laying down the law for this guy? And how could I expect her—or any of us—to operate at our best if we were going in circles?

Well, I couldn't.

In order to Magnify, I was going to have to say no.

No, this behavior isn't acceptable to my team.

No, you can't keep giving us the slip.

No, I don't let my team get the runaround from someone like this.

Magnifying means owning ourselves, standing in our truth, and taking action—and sometimes that action is saying *no*. I don't love confrontation (who does?). This wasn't some kind of ego trip for me. In fact, I fully recognized that this client might react badly if I gave him an ultimatum. But ultimately, I care more about standing up for my values, and Magnifying to others around me, than I did about one client's opinion of me. I felt firm in my truth: that for us to do what he'd hired us for, we needed more accountability from him.

Getting comfortable saying no is not easy for a lot of people. It feels mean, harsh, negative, and can push on a lot of weak spots in our Bounce Factor (especially when it comes to things like cultural or gender expectations). But saying no doesn't mean we don't have empathy or compassion. It means we're channeling that empathy to stand up for the people we care about—or for ourselves. Saying no to what *doesn't* serve us, to what we won't stand for, allows us to make time and space for interactions with people who respect our time, and it honors our needs in the moment, as well as the journey that we're on.

Saying *no* to what's wrong lets us say *yes* to what's right. It's stating your boundary of what you deem is acceptable and tolerable.

SAYING NO TO WHAT'S WRONG LETS US SAY yes TO WHAT'S RIGHT

Never forget that your "no" to others can be a big fat "yes" to yourself.

So I gave the CEO client an "ultimatum" (which was just a firm but polite e-mail stating that we needed better accountability or we'd have to reconsider the project). And everything completely changed. The CEO wrote back and actually said, "You know what? No one has ever put me in my place like that, but you're completely right. I dropped the ball. I appreciate your being forthright and will strive to do better. I have great respect for you and your team holding me to my word."

In the end, my assistant's fears were unfounded—by saying *no* to what wasn't good for us, we actually made our client *more* eager to work with us. Win-win! But even if things had gone the other way, I would still have held strong. If that client had either continued to ghost us or he responded poorly, then that would just confirm that we needed to say no even more—maybe even ending the relationship. And if I had caved and accommodated his ghosting my team, I would have said *yes* to the client, but *no* to my team. I'd have sent the message that I cared more about pleasing the "important" people than I did about my own team's well-being—and my own! That would be disrespectful to myself and my entire team. And *that* is wildly inconsistent with my values. Like I said, it wouldn't have been fun to cut ties with a client, but I knew I could do it if I had to, because I knew what I valued, and I was willing to hold tight to that.

Saying no is incredibly simple, but that doesn't make it easy! So here's a quick cheat sheet for the next time you need to draw a line in the sand.

1. Describe the behavior that is not acceptable. *You have not answered the last five e-mails my team has sent you, and you have been unavailable by phone.*

2. Express what you need in simple, direct terms. *Please respond to the outstanding questions by the end of this week and to any future e-mails within two working days.*

3. Don't defend, don't justify, and do not overexplain. Be simple. *We need your input in order to proceed with the project. These communication lapses are holding us back.*

4. When you are faced with resistance, just restate, reiterate, and repeat what you just said. *We appreciate that your schedule is tight, but if this behavior continues, we are in danger of missing the deadline entirely.*

5. Know what your course of action will be if your no is rejected. *At this point, it seems like our goals are not compatible here, and it'd be best to part ways.*

LEAVE IT ALL BEHIND TO FIND YOURSELF

We can make huge strides in Magnifying by simply changing the context around us—transporting ourselves somewhere where we are a stranger, alone, and independent. Where the sights, smells, tastes, and rhythm of life *aren't* what we're used to. Where no one knows (or cares) what we do or don't do with our time.

I remember vividly my study abroad trip to Italy as a time when I could connect to a whole new sense of myself, no longer weighed down by heavy emotions, dark times of uncertainty, and obligation after obligation. But even as I repeat that story, I realize how maybe the whole "woman seeking growth and insight on a trip abroad" sounds like a bit of a cliché. But you know what? I'm fine with that. I *wanted* my few months of "eat, pray, love."

Now, I think for anyone who's Magnifying, traveling on their own terms is an irreplaceable experience, but I also think that's especially true for women.

One of the reasons I came up with the Bounce Factor and its four aspects was as a way to address and unpack many different parts of our human identities and how those can both empower and limit us depending on our individual experience, makeup, and surroundings. In the Magnifying stage, we come back to a lot of those initial boxes that we've been put in by our upbringing and our current environment, and start to re-evaluate and even reject them. We've seen this in many of my clients' stories throughout this book: Serena, the working mom who felt torn between family and her HR position. Naiya and her impossible goal of being both a perfect, available, hardworking mom, and recovering from a physically and emotionally taxing pregnancy.

But no one exemplifies the Magnifying power of travel quite like Sheena, who was in an unhappy marriage and struggled with "What will people think?" before realizing she needed to ask "What do *I* want?" instead. Sheena had discovered, in Igniting, that she needed something that wasn't the fairy-tale marriage she'd been raised to desire. She had a business she wanted to pursue, and she had herself to consider. There was too much she wanted to invite into her life to stay confined in a box. In her Rise, her beliefs about her own worth had shifted: she was eager to start living for herself, independent of those boxed-in definitions of "good daughter," "dutiful wife," and "happy" (aka married).

But as Sheena started to Magnify, the upper bounds of her shifted beliefs emerged. It was one thing to tell herself she wasn't going to fall for all the trappings of what her family and thought life was about: get married, have a child, rinse, repeat. It was another thing entirely to show them that truth.

Sheena had great admiration and love for her parents. She was always so reverent of her parents' journey—first-generation immigrants, coming here for a better life, laying down the path—and this wasn't something she wanted to forget or disregard. The reason she'd wanted the "happily ever after" in the first place—she now realized—was ultimately to do her parents a favor. To prove to them that they'd succeeded. To give them a good daughter whose life they could proudly share with their friends.

But Sheena's new beliefs helped her see how uneven this bargain was. Living her life on her parents' terms might have given them something, but at the expense of her whole sense of self. She was letting herself be caged up.

And Sheena wanted to fly.

So she said, "You know what? I've never been to Paris before."

And just like that, Sheena planned an entire trip for herself. She found a girlfriend who wanted to tag along. She packed her bags. She grabbed her passport. And she left—for three months.

Mind you, this was the first time that Sheena had ever left her family—not just moving out and establishing independence, but going across the world for months at a time.

That was the right choice for Sheena. But, of course, a drop-everything-now trip abroad is a huge privilege. If you can, especially if a trip is something you've longed for and dreamed of but were held back from taking because of *other people's needs* or *other peoples' expectations,* then this is your sign. Go. Now.

But there are still a lot of ways you can capture the spirit of "Fuck it, let's buy a villa in Spain" without up and leaving right this instant.

- **Shop at a different grocery store.** One client shared that she'd taken to driving an extra 10 minutes to a less popular store where she never ran into neighbors or colleagues. No nosy, judgey peeks at her cart. She could relax, and shop for herself and herself alone.

- **Order your Starbucks coffee under a different name.** It's the little things, okay? If you're usually Beyoncé, be Sasha Fierce at the cafe.

- **Go see a movie, play, or concert by yourself.** How many times have you missed out on an event you're dying to attend because you can't get anyone else interested? Next time, just go by yourself. It's much less weird to do stuff solo than you think.

- **Take a day-cation.** Go completely incommunicado for a full 24 hours. Put your phone on Do Not Disturb, get away from Wi-Fi, and do whatever *you* want to do. Everyone else will manage.

- **Take a break from the Internet.** A digital detox is a remarkably effective (and totally free) way to rededicate yourself *to* you. If you can't go cold turkey (e.g., for work), try small steps like removing the social apps from your phone, or installing a browser extension that replaces your newsfeed with cute kitten pictures (yes, it exists).

- **Learn some creative skills.** Whether it's improv comedy, oil painting, or salsa dancing, learning to make, perform, and share art can be hugely liberating. Not just because you'll build new skills (and maybe discover a new passion) but because you'll become even more at home feeling like a beginner—an anti-perfectionist, someone who's clumsy and just getting started and *still* doesn't care. A class setting is a beautiful place to meet other people who share your values and show your new, Magnified sense of self to the world.

- **Mentor someone.** What better way to share your insights and values than by guiding someone else? Living your truth and Magnifying your impact can happen even if it's just one-to-one—in fact, sometimes that's the most powerful way to shine your light. Take on a protégé at your work, become a "big sibling," volunteer at a career clinic, or even lead a workshop if you're feeling bold.

- **Take a course or earn a certification.** On the flip side, becoming a student yourself can reap huge benefits in this stage. If you've been considering leveling up your professional skills or developing personal growth with accountability and expertise right at hand, look for some courses (online or in person) that speak to you, and dive in. Visit thatsuckednowwhat.com/nextchapter for a list of certifications that may just help with your next chapter.

EXTREME MAKEOVER: MINDSET EDITION

If you've ever watched HGTV, then you've probably seen this episode.

(Doesn't matter what show. I guarantee this happens on Joanna Gaines's *Fixer Upper* as often as on *Flip or Flop*.)

A nice couple decides it's time to redo their kitchen, maybe add a back patio or three-season room, and gets a quote. The house seems to be in pretty good shape, so the project should be relatively quick and fairly affordable. If nothing goes wrong, they should be done on time and on budget.

Spoiler alert: something always goes wrong.

Turns out that the house that looked to be in "pretty good shape" has a lot going on once the demolition starts. Peel up the linoleum—the subfloor is rotten. Scrape off the wallpaper—is that lead paint under there? Chisel off the popcorn ceiling—um, that's definitely asbestos.

Suddenly the costs shoot up. The dream house becomes a nightmare. Nothing was as solid as it seemed.

But it *looked* solid. At least until they got to peeling back the layers.

Magnifying is the stage where we do that peeling back.

This stage is when you put yourself, your values, and your boundaries under the magnifying glass.

Magnifying

Sometimes our motivational statements, our mantras, our self-pep-talks are doing us a disservice. Magnifying is when we have to scrape away the layers of "resilience" we've accumulated and see what they're really made of. We pare back to what we've really been telling ourselves, those patterns we've been carrying along, and see how our old version of self-assurance, no matter how good it looked to everyone, or even to us, was only papering over a bigger crack in our confidence and our beliefs.

Naiya, the mother of twins who'd realized she was far too overwhelmed, came to a point of Magnifying by peeling back just like this.

Naiya had always been tough. She knew that being a working mom was going to bring on judgment from all sides—that colleagues might see her as less committed to her work, and fellow parents might see her as less committed to her babies. She'd made the choice to delay having kids in order to focus on work. When she and her husband experienced fertility issues, it felt like just another way of being judged for her choices.

As a result, her mantra for motherhood was *I can do it all*. But it was almost a mantra she was repeating for other people to hear. If there was an extended edition of her mantra, it would have been *I can do it all even though you* think *I can't—just watch me*.

For a lot of her life, that *I've got this* attitude had worked pretty well. She *had* been able to do it all: build up her career, form a loving marriage, be a total trouper through IVF. Even the first few weeks with her new babies were fairly manageable, thanks to the help she had from family.

But when she hit that Fall and had her moment of Ignition, of realizing she did need help, it peeled back a layer of her mantra. Now it was something more like *I can do it all—wait, shit, I got caught. And maybe I actually can't.*

When she got to Rising, and asking a different question, she went from "If I can do it all, then why can't I fit this all in one day?" to "If I really can do it all, then why is everyone around me suffering?" She peeled back another layer of that mantra.

And when she got to Magnifying, she peeled it right down to the foundation.

She realized that her core value wasn't about proving to the world that she was this supermom.

Her core value was caring for her family.

That was why she'd built a loving, respectful partnership with her husband, Max. That was why she'd been through those exhausting, expensive fertility treatments.

That was why she was seeking help to take care of her children—and herself.

For long stretches of her life, Naiya had been in environments where weakness was unacceptable. Her Bounce Factor was shaped by that kind of competitive culture. She'd imported that fear of weakness to her current environment—only to be worn down physically and spiritually by the exhaustion of parenting newborn twins and recovering from a taxing childbirth.

Peeling back revealed to her that "weakness" wasn't what she thought it was. She had to look at her own values as she uncovered them, and then redefine what weakness meant to her on her own terms.

Her ego had told her that being weak meant failing to prove herself to other people. But in Magnifying, she realized that her ego had it wrong.

In fact, *real* weakness would be selfishness, putting her ego and its need to prove itself and justify the chip on her shoulder above her own and her children's well-being. Weakness would be *not* asking for help.

Indulging her ego about being an amazing, mom-who-has-it-all was like putting up beautiful wallpaper over a rickety, splintering wall. It might look okay to people passing by, but it wasn't safe to live beneath it permanently.

Naiya did get that help: a therapist, professional childcare, and more active parenting from her husband, who reduced his work hours to be home more. And that help wasn't selfish, not even remotely.

Because the beautiful thing about Magnifying is how it draws in other people, ones who see us in our expansiveness and are overjoyed to see that transformation.

In Naiya's case, the added help at home and the active treatment for her postpartum depression brought her and Max even closer as a couple—it rejuvenated their marriage. As her babies got older, and started to babble and smile and act more and more like tiny humans, Naiya saw how their lives, too, were getting better.

"I want my babies to have a mama who smiles more than she cries," she said. "I want to give them that gift."

In Magnifying, Naiya's old mantra got a down-to-the-studs renovation. No longer was her controlling thought a desperate *I can do it all*, but an expansive, generous, genuine *We can do it all—together.*

WHEN FLYING FORWARD MEANS GOING IN CIRCLES

"I was always the one getting in trouble," Katie told me. "Total black sheep. I always knew that out of all of my siblings, I would probably be the one to leave."

Katie was one of our new students at Dharma Coaching Institute, and she came from a small town and an even smaller religious community—so small and restrictive it had basically brainwashed her.

Even within her conservative upbringing, Katie found ways to express her inner fire. She studied dance, and that environment was the one place where she felt free to move and take up space and just exist without so much judgment raining down on her. Like lots of little girls, she decided that being a dancer was her dream career. Costumes, music, using her body to create art—it sounded perfect.

As a teenager, Katie stayed stubborn and headstrong, but her family still saw her dancing as an acceptable pursuit, so she kept it up. Finally, as everyone around her was starting to talk about jobs and college and next steps, she felt brave enough to share her dream with her father.

It was a hard no.

He said there was absolutely no way his daughter would be a professional dancer. Katie was meant to go to a tiny, two-year religious college that for generations had been the only acceptable place for women in her community to get an education. Then she'd get married—or better yet, get married before graduation and drop out to save her family the tuition money—and have children of her own.

The people closest to you can sometimes be the ones closest to the edges of your boundaries.

Katie's hopes were dashed. This moment was her Fall. But despite her upbringing having such a tight grip on her Bounce

Factor overall, her natural expressiveness and curiosity gave her the emotional capacity to question norms even when no one else did. She almost immediately Ignited and knew one thing for sure: "I can't stay here."

So she ran away from home.

And ran *to* Los Angeles.

The big city was the perfect backdrop for her Rise. Katie was constantly entertaining audiences as a kid, to the point where it was practically a job. But when it came to getting an actual grown-up job, she didn't have a ton of professional skills, and her first wave of rejections were humiliating. For all her feistiness, she still had serious doubts about her worthiness—a result of how her upbringing had stunted her Bounce Factor.

So when she saw an ad for DANCERS WANTED, it was like a dream come true—a big pro sports team was holding open auditions for its female dance troupe. Katie jumped at the chance (and probably did a midair split).

Of course, she landed the job. This small-town girl with the sheltered, strict upbringing was now sporting a spandex uniform and shaking glittery pom-poms on national television. Katie was officially a professional dancer.

At first, it really was a dream come true. And life in LA was so much more than she'd ever imagined. The glitz, the glamour, everyone wanting to be in Hollywood or working on a screenplay or starting a fashion line—everything was a lot faster paced than Katie was used to. She was fully in the swing of her Rise, meeting new people from different backgrounds and experiences and asking different questions left and right, from "Why am I always the black sheep?" to "What if the people judging me were the ones who were wrong? What made them so right?"

But for Katie, the next stop wasn't Magnifying. At least not right away.

Sometimes, Flying Forward isn't a linear path. And that's totally okay. Not only okay, that's *normal*.

We saw how Carmen's determination to address her Lyme disease meant exploring new options. When Carmen was Rising, she was trying different courses of action, figuring out which treatments her body would respond to and which didn't do much for her. She understood that setbacks, however frustrating, were part of the game when it came to figuring out what exact actions would get her where she wanted to go, to a place of health and strength.

Katie, on the other hand, locked on to the course of action for her Rise pretty quickly. What could be more validating to her vivacious, can't-keep-me-down energy than dancing on TV in a sparkly costume? It's a picture-perfect happy ending for the small-town girl who was desperate to express herself.

But it also wasn't sustainable. For one thing, the stress and demanding pace of the dance career started to take its toll, and life in LA was exhausting and expensive. So much of it was new, so much to learn on the fly. For another, her heart just wasn't in it anymore. Dance had been her outlet, her rock, and suddenly it felt like work. Her passion was gone. She was just plain burned out.

Instead of finding the Magnifying stage, Katie had been triggered back into a Fall.

Katie's story isn't unusual (well, not many people end up as professional sports team dancers, but you know what I mean). Sometimes the choices we make in Rising help us break through to a better version of ourselves, yet aren't exactly right to carry over into Magnifying. It could be that we're simply overdoing it and wearing ourselves out (as with Katie's demanding schedule). It could be that our Rise was such a hard pivot from the ways we used to act that we cleared out some actions or values that we actually wanted to keep in our life. Or it could just be another sucky moment happening and sending us tumbling back.

Fortunately, the second time around, Katie's Bounce Factor was a lot stronger. She looked at her current environment and realized that although LA was exciting, its materialism rang hollow to her. As much as she disliked about her upbringing, she realized she missed the sense of peace she used to get from regular church services and her faith. And she'd cultivated enough self-awareness to quickly Ignite and hit on the truth: she wanted something spiritually meaningful in her life again.

And, just as fortunately, LA also had plenty of options for spiritual seekers. Soon, Katie found herself trying out a breathwork class and she was hooked almost instantly. The practice was so peaceful and grounding, the people so humble and genuine. She knew she wanted more of this, whatever it was.

The workshop had been held at a yoga studio, so she went back for a yoga class a few days later. By the time the class ended, she was in happy tears. Something about yoga felt so *right* to Katie. For her whole life, she'd seen her body and her spirit as divided. Polar opposites. You could either be sexy and shake your pom-poms on the field, or you could commit yourself to spirituality, but you couldn't do both, and definitely not at the same time.

But now, once again, Katie asked a different question: "What if I *could* use my body to nourish and grow my spirituality?"

She was back to Rising, and this time, it felt really, really right. After a few weeks of regular yoga practice, Katie enrolled in teacher training, and from there, started leading classes.

By the time Katie joined us at Dharma Coaching Institute, it was clear that she was fully Magnifying—even on the brink of Thriving. Dancing on TV had been an incredible, revitalizing experience for her, but ultimately, she'd realized that she still had a chip on her shoulder—she'd still been trying to prove everyone in her hometown wrong by swinging to the total opposite of their conservative social group. It was as if she were staring right through the camera lens and back to her family, saying, *I'll show you!*

It took burnout and a second Fall for her to get to a place where she could truly live on her own terms, and display her worthiness for everyone to see. Teaching yoga was clearly nourishing every good thing that made her *Katie.* Her empathy, open-mindedness, and the gorgeous energy she projected as she practiced asana drew students to her, coming not just for a good workout and some stretching, but to share their own stories of spiritual growth and understanding. She was there to share her gifts with others, to work alongside people who wanted to learn what she'd mastered and say, with gentleness and generosity, *Here, I'll show you.*

Katie's amazing story of growth shows that sometimes Flying Forward can happen in waves and cycles instead of step by step. If you feel you're struggling to Magnify, that isn't a failure. That's part of the process. It can be frustrating, especially after pouring so much effort into what you've carried out in Rising, but it's worth it to pause and reflect. Tune into that self-awareness and look at all the components of your Bounce Factor. Are you inadvertently lapsing into less productive states, like a victim mentality, entitlement, or resentment? Where could you rewind and try a new way forward?

HOLISTIC MAGNIFYING: EXPANDING YOUR REACH

One of the beautiful things about the Magnifying stage is how we can come to expand our gifts beyond the realm that Ignited us to change in the first place. Like Anand, whose single conversation with his mother empowered him to shed expectations and roles that weren't working for him in other parts of his life, tapping into our gifts and standing firm in our values isn't limited to the initial "problem" we faced in our Fall.

Another client, Chelsea, had a similar experience of Magnifying. Her story had a lot in common with Serena's: a working mom frustrated by the lack of progress in her career, Chelsea was tired of double standards that rewarded her male colleagues for being "aggressive" while faulting her for being "pushy" or "bossy." After a Fall in the form of major storm damage to her house, Chelsea Ignited: with massive repair bills and no time off granted to clean up the mess, she knew her job wasn't cutting it, financially or flexibility-wise. She seized agency and had a fantastic Rise, redoing her résumé, taking new headshots, and hitting LinkedIn hard, eventually scoring a much better job.

But it wasn't until a few months later that Chelsea jumped to Magnifying. Chatting over the fence with her neighbor—another young mom around her age—she found out that her neighbor was also looking for a job but hadn't worked full-time since having her son, and didn't even know what she could put on a résumé.

"But I bet you've never had that problem," her neighbor told Chelsea, seeming embarrassed. "You're so impressive! Honestly, I wish I knew as much about work as you do."

Now, Chelsea didn't know her neighbor *super* well. In the past, she would have worried about coming off as too bossy or too pushy—two qualities that she'd felt had held her back profession-ally at her old job. "But," she said, "then I was like, eff that, I don't work for them anymore!"

Chelsea told her neighbor to go inside and grab her iPad. Over the next two hours, Chelsea helped her neighbor redo her résumé, filling it in with the volunteer roles and board positions her neigh-bor held at the local school and their church, and even walked her through creating a LinkedIn profile. By the end of the week, her neighbor had landed her very first interview—and then asked if Chelsea could also help out her sister.

Eventually, Chelsea found a volunteer role for herself, leading career workshops at a local women's shelter. She found it exhila-rating to help people—mostly fellow moms, many of whom had also lost work after the storm and were still struggling—redis-cover their own values and talents after years of being told they had no worth.

Your own experience of Magnifying might look like living your truth in plain sight, like Anand declaring what he truly wanted out of life. Or it might look like directly helping or serv-ing others, like Chelsea offering to mentor someone. The beauty of this holistic Magnifying is that the opportunities to shine your values brightly arises naturally from the new path you've put yourself on. Your subconscious mind is even more tuned to places and people who fit with what you're doing, yes, but your confi-dence will also be magnetic. Stay open to possibilities, to inquiries from others, to conversations you might not have had, and your Magnifying will expand further than you ever knew possible.

FEELINGS OF MAGNIFYING

So now that your Magnifying is in full swing—your boundaries defined and maintained, your self-expression expanding, your influence shining forth—how are you *feeling*?

Excitement

Above all, Magnifying is *exciting*. No matter what form it takes for you and your journey, you'll likely feel a new burst of positive, anticipatory, can't-wait-for-what's-next energy as you start to take bigger, grander, and more expansive actions to shine your values into every space you occupy. Chelsea, as she started to expand beyond her own career advancement and reach out to others, found that the "extra" work was in fact something she looked forward to—and almost not work at all. Sheena found it intensely freeing when her plane touched down in Europe—and she couldn't wait to explore what was next.

Shining bright, like a diamond

When you are Magnifying, your light is shining brighter than before. You've got a pep in your step, and everywhere you go, people tend to see it. Co-workers comment, friends take notice, and strangers on the street can even spot your energy. You, my dear, are fully radiating that light of yours. Your growth has now gone beyond even the benchmarks you set for your own goals. Your influence and drive has surged past the boundaries that you (or others) laid down to contain you. Anand, when he was able to take his personality and passion and turn it into an actual career, was showing that expansiveness in action: he'd always known he valued his sense of humor and felt his best when he could exercise it, but now he was able to let it expand into more and more areas of his life.

Blossoming

By the same token, you might feel that you're simply and naturally unfurling to a true, bright, and glorious presentation of yourself. Naiya found that after she had bounced back from her postpartum struggles, she was able to extend herself gracefully into the role of motherhood. As her husband saw her Magnify, and made small positive changes himself, she also grew that much closer to him, blossoming into a fuller expression of herself as a wife and life partner. She'd wanted to be this person for so long, and the potential was always inside her—but now that she was Magnifying, it was able to finally see the light of day.

In Flow

Magnifying is when the habits we began to establish in our Rise become truly second nature. We can slip into the moments and movements of our new, more expansive self without having to do a whole "pre-flight checklist" to get ourselves rolling. Chelsea found that she was so able to lock into a confident mode of speaking—about herself or about anything she was passionate about—that she sometimes didn't even notice until halfway through her conversation how strong and clear she was coming through to the person on the other end. It made her new pursuit as a career mentor, even though the context was pretty unfamiliar, feel easy to slip into.

Momentum

Even as you're expanding and shining brighter, you're accelerating the pace. You're looking for new places to bring your energy and efforts, new contexts to explore, and new and bigger challenges. You can sense that you're on the way to Thriving (and you are!) and you're only too eager to stay the course and discover what's next.

Alignment

Above all, Magnifying brings a sense of *rightness* to your day-to-day—not that you're "always right" (because you'll certainly still have those little hiccups!) but that the way you carry yourself, the way you reflect on events and conversations, the choices as big as the projects you decide to pursue and as small as what time to set your alarm for tomorrow morning, all feel like they're working together toward a common overarching goal—the goal of being you. Instead of feeling pulled in a thousand different directions, you can see how everything in your life is interconnected, and intuitively tap into the power to act according to your values.

*

Recap & Reflection Corner

1. When and where in your life have you experienced the Magnifying stage? What emotions came up for you? What did you notice about yourself?

2. What might you have to say no to in order to Magnify? What feelings does saying no stir up for you? Use the five steps listed on pages 187 and 188 to plan out how you might say no to this in the future.

3. In what ways can you see yourself in the Magnifying stage? How are you showing up? What activities (such as Sheena's trip to Europe) do you see yourself trying and exploring as you gain more confidence?

4. What might you be able to peel back, like Naiya did with her mantra? What core values might still be buried for you? What values might be missing, like Katie's need for spirituality?

* * *

Chapter 13

Thriving

Mo was back in the game.

It had been three years since he'd made the tough call to shut down his start-up. Three years since he'd looked at his bank account and realized that it was, basically, game over.

But over those three years, he'd been running a business again. Several, in fact.

It had taken a while for him to decide what the next step was. Was working in start-ups even going to be right for him long term? It wasn't like he had the greatest track record.

Still, a year or so after he'd closed that start-up, he'd connected with some new folks, with a new idea, and soon enough Mo was working in the thick of another start-up.

This time, though, he'd learned a *lot* about what to do—and what not to do. In fact, his bumpy history with his previous company made him an insightful, wise part of the team, able to spot potential problems on the horizon thanks to his firsthand experience. He felt *way* more confident, knowing that he'd stuck to his principles and told his co-founders and employees the truth when the money was gone, and his integrity became something of a calling card.

After one year at this next company, another opportunity came down the pike, and this time Mo was eager and ready to take on a new challenge. By year three, he was on his third start-up—not because they were failing, but because he'd found his strengths to make them succeed. He was now the one who begins these projects, gets them to a minimum viable product, and then hands them over to an experienced team to execute. Not so bad, right? The specialized employees run with the concept, and Mo is never stretched so thin that he can't employ his best strengths. He's ready to move on to the next idea.

Mo had more than just bounced back from his start-up failure. He discovered his zone of genius and flew forward into new ventures he couldn't even have imagined back when he was staring at that almost-empty bank account. And like any good tech executive, he was never content to rest on his laurels. It was always about what could come next. It was about building on success to create the next great thing, without losing sight of all the progress that had been made.

In the tech world, they call this process *iteration,* even *innovation.* But I call it Thriving.

THRIVING IS PERPETUAL MOTION

Remember when the first iPods came out?

I do. I wanted an iPod *so* badly.

No more chunky buttons to press: the iPod had a *click wheel.*

No more swapping out cassette tapes or CDs: the iPod could hold up to a *thousand* songs.

No more buying batteries: the iPod had this little white cord to plug in and charged *itself.*

It felt like the future had arrived. We'd reached peak technology. This cute, chic, sleek little music player was light years ahead of my ginormous, clunky Walkman, and I knew that once I had my very own iPod, I'd be set for life.

At the time, I was in dental school, working my butt off in class and at two part-time jobs, and saving like crazy. Every day, I'd walk through campus and the student center, where there were these weekly drawings for students to win various prizes—and of course I entered. Because every so often, the prize would be a brand new iPod.

I was still years away from my biggest breakthroughs in personal growth, but still, I felt *something* back then, a sense that if I made myself open to possibility, to abundance, good things *would* come my way. Or, at the very least, if I didn't *enter* the giveaway raffle, I'd never win it, right?

Well, I *did* win it. In fact, I won *three* times. (Yeah, I know, crazy. I guess I was good at manifesting iPods!)

Three beautiful, glorious new iPods were mine. I had my click wheel, my teeny white earbuds, my just-about-a-thousand-songs in my pocket. And honestly? It was everything I'd hoped it would be. I *loved* that iPod. Taking my music everywhere with me, and knowing that I'd been open to the possibility *and then it happened,* felt incredible. And yes, I know it was just an iPod, but for me, the young dental student Neeta, it was basically the pinnacle of existence.

In life, however, there's no such thing as "the pinnacle of existence." Making breakthroughs, achieving goals, getting the wins we've worked hard for, all of those things are incredible and rewarding. They should be savored and celebrated. But they should also be seen for what they are: a new threshold. A beginning as much as a conclusion.

Was Dental School Neeta absolutely thrilled to have an iPod (or three) of her very own? Absolutely—life could *not* have gotten any better!

But I didn't *stay* Dental School Neeta. I continued to grow and change just like the world around me. Give that same iPod to Today Neeta and, well, I honestly don't know what I'd do with it. I'm not exactly jumping at the opportunity to go back to carrying a separate mp3 player *and* a "dumb" phone *and* put a GPS device in my car (because bye-bye Google Maps). I like having my e-mail available everywhere I go and knowing I can call an Uber even in an unfamiliar city. And I kind of love Bluetooth headphones.

Again, this isn't about me being addicted to technology. It's about growth being the only constant, and about how our needs will change as we continue to grow.

It's about what it means to Thrive.

As we arrive at Thriving, there is so much to celebrate. You've come so far from your initial Fall, put in hard work and been through tough things as you Ignite, Rise, and Magnify. You should feel good about that! (I know I do—go you!) But it's just as important to remember that Thriving is not a static state. It's not a kick-back-and-rest-on-your-laurels moment. In fact, it's a constant search, to strive for more depth, more connection, more self-awareness, and more thoughtfulness around the triggers that will inevitably pop back up. What fulfills you now might not be the same thing that fulfills you in six months, five years, or at *any* point in the future. That doesn't mean you're *not* Thriving. After all, would you still be satisfied listening to your music on an old-school Walkman in, say, 2035? (Maybe they'll be retro-cool then, I guess—but you know what I mean.)

My point is that even when you've reached the stage of Thriving, you still need to take care of and support yourself—maybe more so than in any prior stage. You *have* made it here, you *did* win that iPod, but if you let go of your self-awareness now and just coast, you'll arrive in the future without the things you need to *Thrive* in the future.

The world will change, things will evolve, and your life will have its twists and turns. Sustaining your Thriving stage requires strategy and a deeper sense of self-awareness in every dimension.

So pop in your earbuds and let's do this.

THRIVING THROUGH OUR TRIGGERS

My client Chantel took my advice; she was *finally* taking a vacation.

She had been crushing it as a small business owner and decided to join a retreat/relaxation group trip to spend some time in the sun (and away from her family). This group was all self-actualized women: matriarchs, leaders in their fields, entrepreneurs, survivors, basically a rocket ship full of badass ladies. These were women who'd worked with their internal shit and unpacked their emotional baggage and put time and energy into their spiritual and emotional wellness. Some of them were in different phases of their journeys, or different seasons of life, but it was safe to say all of them were Thriving.

The first night, Chantel skipped out on the group dinner, telling herself she was tired from traveling. The second night, she hesitated again—she was a total introvert and needed some time to recharge.

By the third day, she hit on what the real issue was: this was the first time that she'd ever said yes to any kind of girls trip, let alone a fancy one. Growing up, money was always tight, but Chantel was smart and always did well in school. Unfortunately, she'd been bullied pretty badly for her thrift-store clothes and her "stuck-up" attitude (aka getting good grades). Later in life, as she started her business journey, her social groups skewed male, and she never really made any close girlfriends. When she got married, her only bridesmaid was her sister.

But Chantel had done a lot of work on herself. She'd reflected and journaled, thought through her own Bounce Factor in our online community, and knew that, because of her modest, even lean, upbringing, her business and her money had *always* been at the front of her mind. She was so focused on her career, and then owning her own business, that she hadn't ever really taken time to connect with women like herself in a *non*-business context. At a networking event, with business cards to hand out? No sweat. But chatting over cocktails? Chantel felt almost panicky at the thought.

The funny thing about the Thriving stage is that often, your inner critic will get *louder*. Your insecurities will come on *faster*. Your mind can feel out of control and unsafe because you are now living fully outside what used to be your comfort zone. Your imposter syndrome kicks in precisely because you're growing so fast.

Like Chantel, many of my coaching clients are entrepreneurs who didn't grow up with a lot of money, or had a negative relationship with money. Many have actually been chasing success their whole lives. Even after they've reached financial abundance, or even independence, their approach to money is still influenced by their fear of poverty or being broke, or proving their worth. It affects the way they look at their finances, how they hire people, and the way they choose to save and spend the cash they earn. Sometimes, an external trigger—like a client canceling or, of course, an international pandemic that affects the entire global economy—can shift their behavior. (In hindsight, it wasn't surprising that I saw a lot of my clients making haphazard and even irrational decisions when pandemic lockdowns started. That was a gut reaction after being triggered into a fear of losing money or business or both.)

We've already seen that Flying Forward can be cyclical or have setbacks, and that's true even in this final stage. Basically, even if you are Thriving, and have the self-awareness you cultivated to get here, you'll still have triggers—and plenty of them. There are still those moments that will come up to spark negative feelings in you, to poke holes in your growth and happiness. But you can still continue this healing journey that we're all on as humans.

Chantel ended up feeling good that she'd identified the reason she felt so iffy on going to the group dinner. So that night, she did some quick journaling in her room, then headed out to mix and mingle with the other women properly—and ended up having a fabulous time. By the end of the meal (and a bottle of expensive champagne) they were getting along like girlfriends she'd had her entire life. Feeling emboldened, Chantel had the waiter snap a picture of their table, which she posted to Instagram before heading to bed.

But the real trigger was yet to come.

When Chantel woke up, she saw a flood of comments on her picture. Most were pretty routine for a vacation picture, but a few stung.

Jealous . . . stuck back here taking boring road trips for vacation, LOL.
Girl . . . is that seriously Dom Perignon in that ice bucket?
Right?? Must be nice!!!

She'd even gotten an angry private message from a cousin whom Chantel had declined to loan a few thousand dollars to the month before, chewing her out for putting luxury over family.

Chantel was instantly triggered. Physically, she felt nauseated, and her heart started racing. She deleted the post, but the damage to her mindset had been done. She didn't leave her hotel room for the rest of the day, missing out on the sunshine and salsa classes and everything the retreat was supposed to be about. She was spiraling, hard.

Chantel had arrived at the retreat already in a vulnerable place. She realized that when she uncovered her reasons for avoiding the group dinners—her history of bullying, and how her dedication to her business had crowded out her social life in her 20s and early 30s. Being in this new environment—an all-women retreat of financially successful leaders and businesswomen—put a serious strain on her Bounce Factor. But she trusted in her emotional capacity to handle whatever would happen and went to the dinner anyway.

So when her reward for taking that calculated risk pushed a very particular button, she crumbled.

The IG comments and DMs were just enough to send her over the edge. They activated her feelings of not belonging, of everyone thinking she was "stuck-up," and the memories of the bullying she'd survived as a kid. At the same time, they activated her imposter syndrome (who did she think she was for taking this fancy vacation?) and feelings of unworthiness (no one she grew up with got to have expensive Champagne, so why should Chantel be any different?)

Everyone has been through traumatic experiences and everyone has triggers. Even when we are nearly through the weeds of a transformative experience like the four stages leading up to Thriving, we can be triggered into behavior that we thought we'd outgrown.

Often these triggers feel visceral.

I'm not good enough.

I have to work harder.

Who the heck do I think I am?

I'm an imposter.

I don't deserve this.

The thoughts that come when you're triggered can very easily put you right back where you began, at a Fall. Chantel was poised on the precipice of tumbling backward and going home from the retreat feeling worse about herself, her business, and her growth than she did going in. But when you key into what your triggers are and learn how to manage them effectively, you can stay in the Thriving stage for weeks, months, even years, and continue to grow even more from there.

To manage triggering moments like this, we have to understand what might trigger us, recognize the triggers as they arise, take a moment to pause and exercise awareness, and then—and only then—react. Here, however, Chantel didn't pause; she was on fast-forward. Wound up by the emotional and physical feelings that came with reading the IG comments, she reacted immediately out of a desperate need to make those feelings stop. She deleted the post and hung back to keep to herself.

Fortunately, Chantel decided to pull herself together in time for the next dinner, and as the conversation went on, she found herself sharing what had happened that day with the other women. It ended up being a powerful bonding moment for all of them, talking about everything from the mean girls they'd encountered in middle school to the financial anxieties they still had from growing up poor. In the end, Chantel avoided a full-on Fall, and kept up her Thriving trajectory—plus made some actual girlfriends as a bonus.

Our triggers, like our Bounce Factors, are highly personal. Some people, for example, can brush off social media bullying or passive-aggressiveness like it's no big deal, but are devastated by, say, public speaking. Accordingly, your strategy for managing your triggers will be specific to you. But there are some basic tools that can work well for almost everyone.

Even when you're zoomed in and Magnifying,
don't forget you're on a long-haul journey.

TOOLS OF THE THRIVING TRADE

It's an odd facet of human behavior: when things are going well for us, we ignore a lot of the practices that got us there. We don't keep up with our gratitude journal, we skip our daily self-care practices, we stop nourishing our bodies with high-quality nutrients and let more sugar cravings take over. I've seen this thousands of times with my clients and in my own life.

I distinctly remember one of these mindset slip-ups from early in my coaching career. I'd gotten an opportunity to work in-house at a prestigious firm and give a workshop. This was the very first time that I'd actually be going into a legit boardroom and speaking to top-level executives. I was so attached to sticking the landing (because, I'll be honest, I wasn't really pitching to other companies) that I got kind of in my head about it and was totally nervous. My presentation was . . . well, I bombed. Totally failed. Embarrassed myself. Even the PowerPoint slides weren't working right. I felt like *such* an amateur in front of those execs.

On one hand, I'd reached a place of Thriving. I'd been through so much growth and change—getting into my new career of coaching and landing this epic opportunity—and I felt like I had tapped into what I was really meant to do.

On the other hand, I felt super stupid, not to mention ashamed. The thoughts running through my head were along the lines of *I'm just not cut out to give big presentations. I'm just not meant to be an internal coach for an organization. I'm just not meant for greater things in general. I'm just not good at this after all.*

Whoa—slow down, Past Neeta!

This presentation didn't have to be a full-on Fall—and fortunately, it wasn't. I managed to use the tools of Thriving to keep myself from spiraling. Still, getting carried away by these triggering or sucky moments will happen, even when we're Thriving. Maybe especially when we're Thriving! After all, once we've achieved a goal and things are going well, it's so easy to get caught up in the day to day, the fast-paced chaos of life, and all the things on our plate that we ignore reflection altogether. We're too busy living our best life to check in with ourselves—until we hit a snag, like one of those triggers. But here's the thing: we have the capability to catch ourselves and bounce back, right in the moment, and we have the tools to make it happen. Know that, let any self-judgment go, and then roll up your sleeves and get to work.

Reframe the stories. We all make up stories in our minds. And those stories also influence our values, our beliefs, our patterns, and our attitudes. So if we are able to reframe a particular story, we can actually change the meaning behind it and stop it from triggering us into that Fall.

For example, I had a client who thought that she wasn't capable of giving talks on stage because she had *also* screwed up in a presentation: She tripped on stage as she walked on to give her keynote speech. She brushed it off and made a joke about it in the moment, but afterward, she didn't return to the stage for literally two years.

The story she told herself was: "That speech was a failure, so I can't give speeches anymore." But in reality, the feedback she got from her audience was in direct conflict with that story! Online and even in person, they said things like, "That was incredible—if that happened to me, I would run off the stage in tears" or "I loved that you seemed so *real* in your talk." She was able to compose herself with such grace that people in the audience were tweeting and sending her messages. They didn't even care—or remember—that she'd even stumbled.

Think about how you might take a fresh look at some of those most embarrassing, challenging, crazy moments in your life. What are some of the ways that you can reframe them? My client, for example, could've taken exactly the opposite story from her trip-and-bear-it keynote: "I'm such a compelling speaker, I can screw up my entrance and *still* captivate the audience." You can do this exercise as a journaling prompt. You can tackle past moments, of course, but it's also really good to get into the flow of doing this routinely as challenging moments arise. That way, when you're in the moment and tempted to tell a negative story, you'll have strengthened the muscles to flip it on its head immediately.

Reframe the emotion. Related to reframing the story is reframing the emotion you're experiencing. Chantel, feeling that trigger of social ostracism by trolls on IG, could reframe her panicked feelings of "Why doesn't everyone like me?!" to calmer feelings of "It'd be great to be loved by everyone, but that just doesn't happen to anyone. I'm happy that I get to be here on a trip with people who *do* understand and accept me." A simple reframing of the emotions will allow you to process the situation and not be so hard on yourself, turning the moment from the end of the world into a bump in the road.

Anchor yourself with rock-solid rituals and practices. Maybe you already have restorative practices and rituals (like putting on comfy PJs, or blasting your favorite song, or playing with your dog) for dealing with stressful situations. These anchoring practices, especially ones that engage the five senses, activate a neural pathway to the good feelings, good vibes, and good emotional cues that you associate with that particular playlist, scent, taste, and so on. That neural activation shifts your emotional state so that you can get out of that funk and not get triggered into a spiral.

Other ideas for anchors include incense, candles, or essential oils; an object that reminds you of a favorite calm place, like a seashell from your family trips as a kid (bonus points if it's calming to touch or handle); a poem, song, or mantra you can recite; or a short physical activity, like yoga or tai chi, with an emphasis on breathwork.

Be your own friend. What would you say if your best friend came to you in the middle of some dire circumstance—they got laid off, their partner broke up with them with no warning, they lost someone close to them. You would be empathetic, right? You would lean in with compassion and love and support. And you *wouldn't* chew them out for not being able to "just deal with it."

If self-judgment starts to spring up, think of yourself in the third person and actually give advice as you would to a friend. You can even give yourself a nickname and write yourself a letter (seriously).

Take baby steps. Thriving isn't a static state. There's still plenty of forward (and occasional backward) movement in your growth. Just like it's important to notice small triggers that might set you back a bit, it's equally important to see the incremental opportunities you have for growth in those moments. Taking a look at your little shortcomings without succumbing to a scorched-earth "I effing suck" attitude is really the hallmark of Thriving!

For example, looking back at my disastrous corporate Power-Point presentation, could I have practiced more with the slides? Yes. Could I have gotten there early to double-check the A/V setup? Yes. Could I have skipped using PowerPoint entirely, and focused on my strengths, like conversation and storytelling, instead? Yes and yes.

Taking the perspective that we can always incrementally get better, especially when things don't go the way we planned, is a powerful way to thwart self-judgment. Breaking an incident down into small wins and small possible improvements gives you simple proof that you're not a total failure (because there were those wins) or a total success (because there are things to step up your game on).

Take an actual assessment. Not a judgment, mind you! An assessment is about curiously seeking the truth (if there is any!) about your thoughts. Are you *actually* a lousy partner? Are you *actually* not worthy of your new job title? Okay, prove it. What are the facts?

More often than not, you'll discover that you're not an unworthy failure to your core. You just stumbled one time—like maybe you were crabby with your partner after a bad night's sleep. Or your emotional reaction to a trigger—like your boss frowning in a meeting—is blotting out the truth (that you have six years of related experience and stellar performance reviews).

Try journaling out an assessment, but *just* the facts. (Hint: If you have to assume, guess, mind-read, or jump to a conclusion, it's probably not a fact.)

Try a Personal Observation Check. A Personal Observation Check (or POC) is one of my favorite and most powerful tools for keeping yourself Thriving. A POC can be done on a weekly or daily basis (personally, I do a POC at the end of the day) when you have a chance to reflect.

In practice, a POC is pretty simple. You ask yourself five key questions.

- What went well today?
- How am I feeling?
- What could I have done differently?
- How could I have shown up differently?
- What am I grateful for in that situation?

Not only do these questions set you up for success the very next day by showing you how to improve, but they also allow you to find the smallest things to be grateful for. Even in my toughest times after I left my abusive husband, I could be grateful for a warm bed. I was grateful that I wasn't in a shelter, that I was safe, and that I had the funds to lease an apartment and put a bed in it. That was enough. I could see how things could be worse, and how I had the strength to provide myself with what I needed, and feel grateful for that.

YOU (SOMETIMES) CAN'T GO HOME AGAIN

Remember my client Lara, whose whole family expected her to be a lawyer, only for her to flunk the LSATs?

Good news: Lara had made it to Thriving. She was pursuing her passion and working as a yoga teacher, and had made huge leaps forward in her personal growth. She'd even started dating someone, and it was getting pretty serious—to the point where she was bringing him home over the holiday break to meet her parents and siblings.

At first, it was going great. The trip out was uneventful, Lara was full of energy, and she felt excited to introduce Marcus to her family. Everyone seemed to get along pretty well.

But by dinnertime, something was starting to feel off, and as Lara was setting the table, her brother made a comment about the new partner at their law firm—maybe in innocence, or maybe trying to goad her. Lara snapped first at him, then at Marcus when he tried to deescalate. Then her parents got involved, voices were raised, dinner was forgotten, and the evening culminated with Lara and Marcus arguing in the driveway.

"I don't know what got into me," she said later. "It was like I was 14 years old all of a sudden, and all I wanted to do was run to my room and slam the door."

There's one last aspect of Thriving I want to share, specifically because it's so common. As I'm writing now, it's late November, and between Thanksgiving and the rush of winter holidays, a lot of my clients and friends are spending time with their families— their parents, grandparents, aunts and uncles, and other "grown-ups" who've known them their whole lives.

Basically, families can be triggering.

It doesn't mean you're not Thriving.

It doesn't mean you've lost all your progress.

It just means families are triggering.

There are so many layers to family dynamics, and many of them are what hard-wired our initial Bounce Factor. For starters, the upbringing component of the Bounce Factor is obviously hugely influenced by our family in a general sense. But when we're *around* family in the present, our current environment shifts as well. Whether we're physically in our childhood home or simply around the familiar energy of the people who raised us, the current environment is now working in tandem with our upbringing and amplifying the same messages we grew up with. When we're somewhere that reinforces all the "lessons" of that upbringing with *two* components of our Bounce Factor, the expectation to be loyal to our upbringing gets stronger, and we're less able to push back on it.

Whether we obey this expectation or rebel against it, most of us can't simply ignore it when we're back in that context. Someone like Sheena, whose cultural upbringing had a specific, restrictive vision for her life as a married woman, might feel the renewed judgment of choosing herself over family. Someone like Katie, whose small-town religious family strongly disapproved of her dance career in Los Angeles, might get passive-aggressive attempts to "save" them from their worldly life or bring them "back into the fold." And someone like Lara, who didn't join the family business, might find that their career decision is a sticking point over and over and over, for years to come. But even people whose Falling and Igniting stages didn't directly involve their families can find themselves sliding back into old patterns of behavior when surrounded by parents, siblings, and other relatives.

In that sense, spending time with family can often be the ultimate test of our Thriving, where all our buttons are pushed and all our triggers are activated. This is because so much of our innate Bounce Factor is tightly interwoven with our family: our upbringing, certainly, but also our current environment—the wave of nostalgia that hits you when you step into your parents' living room or taste your aunt's home cooking can also catapult you back to your formative years (kind of like the anchors we touched on earlier).

THRIVING STAGE Self-CHECK

- ☐ HiRE COACHES, THERAPIST, OR HEALERS
- ☐ READ BOOKS OR WRITE IN YOUR JOURNAL
- ☐ NOTICE WHO LIFTS OR DRAINS YOUR ENERGY
- ☐ REVIEW YOUR BOUNDARIES
- ☐ REVIEW YOUR HABITS & COPING STRATEGIES
- ☐ FEEL YOUR FEELINGS
- ☐ TRY SOMETHING NEW & BE OKAY SUCKING
- ☐ LOOK AT YOUR TRIGGERS & REACTIONS

Thriving is the perfect stage to pause and take stock of all that you've done—and all you're now ready to try.

Once Lara put two and two together, and realized that the overwhelming family environment (plus the general nervousness about introducing her boyfriend) had turned down her Bounce Factor and made it that much harder to play off her brother's jabs, she was able to forgive herself for "messing up," and she apologized to

Marcus. In the end, it turned out to be a strong moment of bonding for them as a couple, prompting a whole discussion of what family dynamics meant to each of them, and making Lara feel even better about Marcus as a long-term partner and potential co-parent.

She also revisited some of the boundaries she'd developed as she was Magnifying and journaled on how they came into play in this particular hometown context. She apologized to her parents, too, for her part in disrupting the evening, but was careful not to overexplain why and how she'd gotten so triggered—keeping that private was an important boundary for her, and she wanted to be sure that boundary stuck in place as she continued to Thrive.

"I'm strangely glad it happened," she said. "Now I have a much clearer sense of how far I've come, and what I've learned about myself. I can put it into action."

FEELINGS OF THRIVING

When you're Thriving, you *really* feel it. It's powerful and exciting, but also a constant presence of reassurance and self-reliance. Let's take a look at what emotions might be coming up for you in this stage.

Joy

It feels good to be Thriving! Plain and simple, this is a wonderful stage to be in. You feel a deeper sense of joy at the things you've always loved and treasured, while also expanding your joyfulness to the truths uncovered in genuine self-acceptance. You are able to tap into that joy even in moments of difficulty or even pain, because you know that no matter what befalls you, you will always have the capacity to accept who and where you are in that exact moment.

Contentment

There's no longer a need to *rush*. You aren't as easily swayed by FOMO (fear of missing out) or false urgency anymore—you're happy to be where you are, but are also happy to grow too. You are unapologetic in saying no when you need to, without feeling shame or guilt. You have a wider perspective that has relaxed your need for everything to happen at an accelerated pace. You appreciate those little things, the small wins and baby steps, and cherish them for the progress that they are.

Limitlessness

Thriving has a sense of *what's next?* You feel as though almost anything is possible—it might not be easy, or fast, but you can make it happen.

Contribution

Thriving means it's no longer about you. Now that you've owned your dharma, you've rediscovered yourself, and it's no longer about you. The questions now become: *How can I help someone else? How can I pay it forward so that someone doesn't have to Fall and have a big old initiation like I did?* You move from micro-level focus to a community level of *How can I help change by contributing to people around me?*

Authenticity

When you're Thriving, you're bursting with radical self-acceptance and self-love—not because you've achieved perfection (ha!) but because you're totally and unapologetically who you are. You are totally okay with being *you,* even if you're not a "perfect version" of yourself—because you've realized authenticity *is* perfection.

Fulfillment

Thriving doesn't mean stopping. Often, it means going for new and more exciting goals! But you'll still get a sense of fulfillment. You're fulfilled not so much by your achievements and accolades, but by your gratitude, your appreciation for all the lessons you've learned. The external successes are rewarding, too, but as you're Thriving, you appreciate that it's the personal, internal accomplishments of deep understanding that resonate the most.

✳

Recap & Reflection Corner

1. What are some of the tools mentioned in this chapter that you can incorporate to help navigate your best self during the Thriving stage?

2. How will you incorporate your POC—as a daily activity or a weekly check-in? What other questions will you add to your POC?

3. We discussed the more "positive" or higher frequency of emotions that you may experience during Thriving, but what are some of the lower-frequency emotions or fear-based emotions that may come up here? List as many as possible and create a "Thriving Emergency Plan" for how you'll respond when those emotions do arrive. Keep your Thriving Emergency Plan somewhere safe so that you can refer back to it and welcome those emotions as they arrive.

✳ ✳ ✳

Chapter 14

Spreading Your Wings

I had a *great* plan for this chapter. But that's not the chapter you're going to read.

I can explain.

See, I'd sketched out my vision for what I was going to write—a version of the "maintenance" section of a fitness program, except for your own resilience! Perfect! I drafted a bunch of the sections. I had my schedule blocked out, my Asana boards organized. I was feeling really on top of my game, patting myself on the back for being so thorough, for crushing my word count even while wrangling two small kiddos and going through a huge launch for my business. All I needed was for everything to keep humming along and I'd basically coast to the end of the writing process.

Then one of my employees quit.

Not just quit, actually. Ghosted.

With like zero notice.

And you know why?

Because she'd read a draft of my book—this book—and realized she'd Ignited. She needed a major change.

She realized she was burned out and hadn't prioritized her self-care in a very long time.

So good news was, I knew the book was resonating.

Bad news was, my plan for this chapter—and for everything else I was in the middle of—went out the window. (Plus, my employee didn't get to finish the rest of the book so she could learn how to fly forward when things happen!)

The moral of this story is that life just keeps on happening. Sucky, unexpected things will continue. Just when you think you've reached a place of perfection and balance, *bam*: life throws a new surprise in the mix and you have to scramble to redo your oh-so-perfect plans.

Because in case I haven't made the point enough yet, difficult and challenging things are going to happen and keep happening.

And at this very moment, I'm scrambling along with you.

You've got to laugh sometimes, right? That's life, in all its glory. It's not always a tragedy or loss that throws you for a loop, either: I was chatting with a student in our online communities the other day who had gone in for her annual gyno appointment at age 42 only to have her doctor tell her, "Liz, you know you're eight weeks pregnant, right?"

"Of course I didn't!" she shared in the group. "I would have hit the ground in a dead faint if I weren't already in the stirrups. But now I can't ever imagine my life without my baby. I wouldn't have it any other way."

It's not even necessarily a single *thing* that makes things feel messy and chaotic. Sometimes it's being in an all-around stressful season of your life. A few months before I started writing this book, my family and I moved from Los Angeles, California, to Austin, Texas. We ended up buying and living in the biggest home I've ever had. As I've mentioned, in addition to being a boss and a coach, I'm also the mom of a toddler. And when we moved, I was pregnant with our second child. And the house needed renovations, which, of course, I wanted done before the baby arrived.

I created plans, spreadsheets, and schedules, but after a few weeks it was clear that nothing was going right. Contractors would show up, spend days or weeks hammering away in the house, and report the work as "finished" but leave a shoddy job behind. Because there was rework needed, there were more meetings, often face-to-face. Timelines were constantly being adjusted. Electricians and plumbers needed to be moved up or moved out. I had to take time off work to handle the reorganization of schedules and make sure our budget wasn't being blown out by extra time and labor. The date nights I worked hard to carve out with my husband were canceled by babysitters who didn't show up. Then I had to cancel even *more* work to find a new school for my son, who wasn't adjusting well to our move. Not to mention that I had all the usual pregnancy hormone ups and downs, complete with forgetfulness, massive fatigue, brain fog, and morning sickness (sometimes 10 times a day!).

I'll admit it: I went into full-blasted victim mode about my situation. I felt annoyed and even resentful that I was assumed to have a more flexible work schedule than my husband even though we tend to have similar workloads. I felt aggravated by the fact that contractors hadn't fulfilled their promises. I felt helpless that our families didn't live closer during the pandemic. And I worried about the long-term implications for my 2-year-old son.

But, exactly like I advise my clients to do, I realized there was beauty in simple surrender.

I gave up my spreadsheets. I pushed out deadlines, both for the home renovation work and for work-work. I said no to projects and shut down parts of my business to focus my energies better. By being conscious about where I was at and where my family was at, I was able to see that this is just one season of our life together. I realized I can balance being the CEO, being pregnant, being the project manager of a home renovation, and being the caring mom of a two-year-old all at the same time while supporting my husband and his work. I can find my way to Ignite here, Rise here, Magnify here, and yes, ultimately Thrive here too.

This is the chapter you can turn to when more suck happens in your life. When you inevitably face another obstacle or find yourself in the midst of a life-changing up-leveling. This is the chapter you will bookmark and reread as many times as you need to. This is where you can come for a tune-up, a refresher, or some real talk, depending on the situation. (And in case you want a study buddy for your remedial course in resilience, I'm relearning right now too. Solidarity.)

Being able to remind yourself that this is just a season or a moment in your life, that you have the tools to deal with it, and that you don't have to fall back into the trap of victimhood, entitlement, or resentment is huge.

You have everything you need to Fly Forward—now and for the rest of your life.

FLY FORWARD FRAMEWORK (THE SKINNY RECAP)

Stage 1. Falling

- hitting rock bottom
- something unexpected or a crisis happens
- you fail or feel like a failure
- a grave sentence

Stage 2. Igniting

- a sense of urgency—something requires your immediate attention
- undesirable pain
- a strong desire for change

Stage 3. Rising

- owning personal responsibility
- discovering new frontiers
- self-growth
- saying yes to new opportunities
- staying open to learning new things
- embracing and accepting your new reality

Stage 4. Magnifying

- unlearning and healing old thoughts and patterns
- exponential growth
- self-forgiveness and letting go
- self-compassion
- owning your power and confidence

Stage 5: Thriving

- flourishing
- a feeling of joy
- a sense of fulfillment
- renewed self-awareness of your Bounce Factor

YOU CAN ALWAYS LEVEL UP

When I was growing up—and still to this day—I liked playing Mario Kart. Why? Because it was always a challenge. Beat the 50cc race? Great—time for the 150cc round! Won a bunch of races in a row? Time to upgrade your character, your car, your wheels and parachute. No matter how fast your finish time is, you can always challenge yourself to smash your personal record just *one last time*. You never really *beat* Mario Kart—you just keep improving your technique.

Your journey to Flying Forward is like that game of Mario Kart. There will always be a harder level waiting for you. There will always be a chance to up your skills, to see how much better you can get, to challenge yourself a little bit more each time. And there's no ultimate destination where you arrive, hit the brakes, and stop.

Because there's no limit to how far you can fly forward.

The tools you've cultivated while reading this book will always be here for you. They aren't one-time fixes for a one-time problem. They're there for you as you level up, seek the next challenge, or revisit an old one to see if you can finally beat your personal record. They're there for you so that you can react with audacious resilience instead of victimhood, blame games, or entitlement.

Even if you stay shell-shocked by a Fall for a while and need to simply *be* with the truth of what's just happened.

Even if you need extra time to simmer in your Igniting phase before you have your aha moment.

Even if your Rising takes weeks, or months, or years to take shape.

Even if it's hard to see where or how you can Magnify once you've found stability and stasis.

You've learned so much about yourself, your natural resilience, and how you react to challenges. You've tuned into what matters to you and tuned out the influences and demands of others that go against your values.

In other words, you've grown your Bounce Factor. If nothing else, you've expanded that self-awareness by leaps and bounds. And that's what you can rely on here.

But even if you don't actively seek leveling up in every season of your life, those challenges and changes will arrive. As you go deeper in your self-discovery, spiritual practice, and growth journey, you'll encounter new people and places, discover new practices and hobbies and even careers that kindle something exciting inside you. You'll be faced with new challenges, at all new levels, at the varying different stages of your life. That's one of the most glorious things about going through life on this earth as a human—the common experiences, the sorrows and joys, the

THAT SUCKED. now what?

things you were told that "you'll understand when you're older" and now you at last see what they're all about.

So, even though you're getting close to the end of the book (wah!), you aren't at all close to *done.*

Remember: sucky things happen, and you're human. You'll be met with newer and bigger challenges as you level up through life. And you may be tempted to wallow or cast blame.

But now you know that you don't have to react mindlessly or unconsciously. New challenges and setbacks—harder levels in life—might be inevitable, but you can feel confident in knowing that you have the tools to handle them. This might be a trickier track to drive on, but the rules of the race are the same.

Life will always have challenges. You will always be called upon to level up. The journey to audacious resilience has no finish line. But when we learn to fly forward, everyone can win.

SHARING AUDACIOUS RESILIENCE WITH OTHERS

Are you excited? I'm excited for you.

Because there's an awesome aspect to the Fly Forward framework that I haven't mentioned yet.

Once you're able to master the tools I've given you and have experienced the stages for yourself, it's your turn to share and teach these techniques.

Give this book to someone you know who is going through a tough time, who is on the brink of an evolution or a major life change, or who may be stuck emotionally. Or teach these techniques to your own clients, students, friends, and family. Hold *That Sucked. Now What?* support circles, or host a book club party and discuss these inevitable sucky life moments. (If you want to know how to host a support circle of your own, visit thatsuckednowwhat.com/resources.) There's so much that comes from learning as a collective, and growing as a family and friends group, or even one-on-one with your favorite person. I believe firmly in being wildly generous with everything I teach because I believe that the secret to a better world is building stronger communities. Creating ripple effects. Starting with a spark. Especially with those who may not have access to the tiniest gift such as self-discovery and exploration. I'm highly committed and beyond excited to see transformation in the lives of others.

I know my words will go to rooms I've never stepped foot in. Or perhaps to places in the world where there may be only one way of resolving tough life situations. And so I'm asking you to take my words and wisdom with you on your own journey. Be the wayshower of your town or community, the torchbearer of the charge, the matriarch of a new way of thinking. Be the educator, guide, and mentor that your community needs, because this is a conversation for all of us as we're reframing and appreciating the wild spectrum of this human experience. As you grow and start to embody who you are meant to become, that will change the lives of people around you. Whether you realize it or not, you are a role model. People are watching you.

Our peers see and read our posts on social media.

Our close friends see our smiles getting wider.

Our loved ones recognize the positive energy that's emanating from our spiritual core.

And our children . . . well, as a mom, I can tell you that our children benefit the most from seeing aligned adults operating in a soul-centered way. Can you imagine if you'd known about the Bounce Factor and the Fly Forward framework as a kid? An adolescent? A teenager? A college student? I know I would have suffered less if I had been able to use and move through this framework back in the day. Can it spark different conversations with your parents and grandparents who came from a generation that perhaps only knew how to survive or who came from different parts of the world that only knew about oppression? This knowledge is a gift and a privilege to give others permission to begin healing old wounds—to allow for different perspectives and deeper and more fulfilling relationships.

My hope for you is that you stretch into the smallest crevices of what you are capable of, and that you share all that you've learned on these pages to everyone around you. In your actions, in your behavior, in your thoughts, in paying it forward for someone else (even if they may not agree with you). My hope is that you take the lessons and insights here and help build and grow mentally strong, emotionally supportive, and resilient communities of humans who can all thrive no matter what life throws their way. Because life *will* throw things our way—we know that now more than ever, and there may be those whom you love who will not fully vibe with your new reality. In fact, they may be quite skeptical, even resistant, toward your new journey. Just stay aligned with your newfound principles. It's not always easy, but I also know from experience that there is incredible power in the collective and its varying beliefs. It's my mission to make sure these frameworks reach everyone who is yet to use it as their greatest medicine, an awakening to their next chapter. Remember that those closest to you may begin their journey at different phases and steps, so there's definitely no need to bulldoze them into it. Patience and compassion helps your resiliency, and that Bounce Factor!

Sharing with Your Partner

No relationship is perfect, even when both of you are deeply invested in personal growth. Even when both of you are *coaches*. Take it from me: the other day, my husband and I were driving along, and Ajit said something like, "You're gonna make a left here, aren't you?"

I. Flipped. Out. "What?! Of *course* I'm going to make a left. We *live* on this road. You don't think I know where we *live*? I can't even—why would you ever . . ."

Not my best moment. *Far* from perfect. But in reality, a resilient partnership is not about achieving perfection. To Ajit's credit, he just said, "Whoa, okay." And I admitted I was touchy because I'd only slept like four hours. We both realized what was going on and brought the temperature down a bit. I apologized, we made up, and I eventually got some sleep.

Sharing the concepts and tools from this book with your partner or spouse gives you a common language to discuss the challenges you face, both as a couple and individually. And that is what will see you through every left turn (ha!) that life puts in front of you.

Sharing with Friends and Family

No one wants to be the friend who makes a huge breakthrough, or discovers a new hobby, or otherwise "sees the light" and tries to make something happen, so to speak, with their friend group, insisting that everyone try it.

But at the same time, once you've gone through the five stages here, you will start to notice that the problems your friends bring to you or even mention in passing fall into the framework. Honor that feeling! Of course, the best personal growth comes from people who are motivated to change on their own, but that doesn't mean that you can't, with your newfound insight, give a gentle nudge when needed, and perhaps strike a conversation with open-ended questions, or even organize a round-table retreat where you can lead a journey of discovery into uncharted waters.

Sharing with Your Children

As we've seen in investigating our own Bounce Factors, the first years of our lives are hugely formative for how we face challenges and develop resilience.

On one hand, kids are naturally resilient. Babyhood and toddlerhood are tough times: the world is big, they're very small, and they're growing like weeds and learning faster than a supercomputer. But at the same time, they can be delicate. Just ask any parent who's ever had to kiss a booboo or battle a monster under the bed.

So, you know, no pressure, right?

Take it from me, a far from perfect parent: anyone can teach their children the foundational tools. Just by seeking your own resilience, you're a living example of what a healthy Bounce Factor and a life of Thriving can be. As for the nuts and bolts, all the concepts like loving yourself, being unapologetic about who you are, and what perspective shifts need to happen in order to bounce back quickly after a setback are surprisingly easy for kids to grasp. Not to mention that this is the best way to *reparent* yourself in the situations you encounter with your kiddos. You can reflect on your own childhood—how Little You would've wanted to do a particular thing, and what you can now do differently with your children in the process. So much magic!

Sharing with Your Colleagues

This is not a book about work or work relationships in particular. But when it comes to challenges and stress—and people that stress us out—career and financial goals rank high up there. It's why so many of my clients' stories in this book revolve around their careers, their co-workers, or their bosses. We spend a good chunk of time with the people we work with, for, and above, and in an ideal world, we're all aligned in how we seek and cultivate resilience in whatever it is we do for a living.

In reality, we rarely are.

Most adults who've been in the workforce for a while can tell stories that make *The Office* look like an actual documentary. And Gen Zers entering the workforce are often stymied by the huge emotional and cultural gaps between them and their older supervisors.

A lot of cultivating resilience in the workplace is still very personal, and boundaries are hugely important in a professional context. But there's still a lot you can do to share a sense of resilience with your colleagues. Be the one who reframes sucky workplace moments as opportunities. Offer a listening ear to a colleague who needs advice. Lead by example—and point people to discovering how they can fly forward too.

Sharing with Your Community

Over the past two years, one of the most beautiful things to come out of all the struggle, pain, and hardship we've seen in our country and across the world is a deeper sense of connection and community in our own backyards. And wow, are we starving for it. Never have we entered a better time than now to cultivate community and support. We aren't meant to live on mountaintops alone! We're wired for connection and community gathering. We've started to see that our fates and well-being are intimately intertwined with those of the people who live on our block, whose kids go to school with our kids, who share much more in common with us than might be obvious at first blush. You get to choose your soul family. You get to choose the people with whom you'll go deeper, and the people whom you'll let go as you've outgrown them.

Join Us and Share

If you have entered an awakening, feel inspired to develop more of your gifts, or are ready to contribute to the lives of others, there are lots of ways to get started. Visit thatsuckednowwhat.com/resources to see a list of opportunities and trainings for your next chapter..

Turn your mess into someone else's medicine! There are many ways you can share this book in your community or give this book as medicine to your friends and family members by hosting a book club or a reading party.

Some of the ways clients have built upon the Fly Forward framework:

- Starting a charity to support others with a similar medical diagnosis

- Becoming an advocate for a social issue that they are passionate about

- Starting a YouTube channel or podcast around a major failure/life lesson

- Launching that side hustle/project as a way to heal their heart through crafts

- Taking voice/singing lessons and performing at open mics

- Doing standup comedy sets to share the gift of laughter with the world

- Becoming a Spiritual Life Coach or Soul-Purpose Coach and help others find their purpose at dharmacoachinginstitute.com

✻

Recap & Reflection Corner

1. Can you recall a time when you were Falling in one area of your life, yet you were Rising in another area, and perhaps Igniting in another area? What decisions did you have to make peace with, or let go of?

2. Imagine yourself six months to a year from now. It's a beautiful, perfect day. You've mastered the Fly Forward framework and increased your Bounce Factor by 10x. Yet another relationship fell to pieces. Or you got fired. Or you and your best friend got into a terrible fight. Knowing that you now have all the tools, journal out how you would respond. What practices would you recall? What insights would you now give to yourself?

✻   ✻   ✻

Afterword

Embrace and Surrender

Here's one last story for you as you get ready to fly.

When I was pregnant with my son, we had plans.

We'd planned for the full natural birth—100 percent organic, no drugs, at home, the works. We were still living in LA at the time, and the expectation there was basically, "Pregnant? Well, of course, you're going to do a home birth, preferably a water birth, and get a doula *and* a midwife."

I was fully on board. Not necessarily because I was a hardcore earth mama either. Because I really, *really* didn't want to be in a hospital.

I spent my childhood in hospitals. I saw both my parents perish in those stark white beds. I saw my brother Djay for the last time in that stark white bed. I spent a lot of time in my teen years watching both of my parents breathe on ventilators. I still remember what Thorek Memorial Hospital smelled like. The floors were dirty. The whole place had filled me with dread.

So I knew, energetically and consciously, that I didn't want to go to the hospital to bring my son into the world.

It took like six months of convincing my husband that we were going to be okay. He was downright confused at first: "Wait," he said. "Really? In India, everyone loves going to the hospital. You go to the hospital for everything! We hit up the doctor every chance we get!"

But eventually, after watching many natural birth videos and documentaries, we settled on our all-natural plan. We got the doula, the midwife, the crystals, the candles, all the pre-birth class prep, the books—the whole nine yards.

And finally, it was time. Labor started. "All right, this is it. This is it!"

That was Monday night. By Tuesday morning, the labor had paused. Then it started again Tuesday night. Then it stopped again Wednesday morning. Then it started again Wednesday night, and at this point, I was getting cranky. "Oh my God," I muttered. "Three days of anticipation, and excitement, and no sleep, for this?!"

Meanwhile, Ajit's parents had come from India to the U.S. for the very, *very* first time. So I have all of this guilt, because, of course, my "good Indian daughter" trigger pops up to the surface, and obviously I must take care of them while they're here, especially after such a long trip to a totally new place.

And then my Bhua (my dad's sister) and Uncle Glenn came that same day, because . . . why not, at that point! By now I'm having hardcore contractions, but nothing is progressing. (For the moms in the room: I was dilated to one centimeter. I had a long ways to go.)

At this point, I'm basically the boy who cried wolf with my doulas. Right—doulas, plural. I had two of them. Mind you, these are the ones in LA who deal with the celebrities and the fancy people of the world. These are doulas with *podcasts*. This is no joke. I got the cream of the crop for my baby, because *I was not going to the hospital.* I was not letting the first thing he saw in his life be one of those terrible places.

The doulas tell me to call back when I'm further along. So I call the chiropractor, who was also a doctor-to-the-stars kind of person, a big-deal Beverly Hills guy. And bless him, this guy came out to do an adjustment at two in the morning, because he had four kids, and I guess knew that pregnant ladies don't like to wait. So he helped position me so that the birth canal was aligned and basically gave me a massage.

And it was intense. It's two in the morning, he's doing body-work on me for two hours in the middle of the night, and finally I say, "All right. I'm done. I'm ready. I've surrendered. I've met my spiritual edge."

Silence. I realize I'm going to have to say it out loud.

"Take me to the hospital," I said. "I need to go."

I told my husband, and I told my chiropractor, and I told my doulas and my midwife. The three of them sprang into action. "Neeta, remember, you said if you felt like giving up, we should encourage you to hang in there." And they were *really* encouraging me: "You can do it. You can do it!"

When you sign up with a doula, they ask you in the begin-ning, "Well, how do you want us to coach you when you're at your edge?" At the time, I didn't know better, so I was super gung-ho. "Yes, keep telling me to go and to stick it out! I need that tough love!"

Except it was now Thursday, and I'd started labor on Monday. It turned out I did *not* need that tough love. What I needed was—

"An epidural," I told the doulas. "Please. I can't. I'm done. I need to have this baby. I need to sleep."

My husband, beautifully, chimed in. "She is suffering, you guys. There's no way."

Still, the doulas were hesitant. "Let's give her another day, all right? Her water hasn't broken."

They did have a point, so I finally agreed to wait and see.

Thursday passed, and we went through more of the off-and-on the whole day.

Then, finally, *finally*, on Friday, my water broke.

And out of sympathy, I guess, it started *pouring* outside.

If you weren't aware, there are never thunderstorms in L.A. That might have been the only thunderstorm I'd ever really seen while living there. It was intense.

I didn't care. "All right," I announced. "I'm done. This is it."

We packed up and headed to the hospital where our backup OB was practicing, which was not in Beverly Hills or the Holly-wood Hills or anywhere super luxurious. It was in Compton.

I didn't want a hospital. I'd had a plan.

We had to go through three security checkpoints in order to get in.

I didn't want a hospital. I'd had a plan.

They made us *wait* at security, despite the fact that I was screaming and obviously super pregnant.

I didn't want a hospital. I'd had a plan, and this—this *mess*— was not it. This was not 100 percent natural or beautiful and organic. This was the most un-spiritual-like thing that I could possibly imagine going through.

So, the intake is packed, there's a long line to get into this hospital, and the security guards are taking everything out of our packed bags to inspect, no matter how many times I tell them, "Hello, we're about to deliver a baby!"

They didn't care. "Hold on one second. We're going to call upstairs and—"

"There *is* no holding on!" I cried. "The baby is coming!"

We finally get up into the room—that hospital room, with its hospital bed, and hospital floor. That room I swore would never be my son's first surroundings.

Outside, it was pouring rain on Compton and thundering like the world was about to end.

Inside, I was screaming, and it was scary, and this was a hospital, and—

And it was the most beautiful thing on earth.

My doulas came in, and they brought crystals and candles and made it all special and earth-mama for me. Then the entire *ward* basically came in—I had a full audience of residents and doctors who just wanted to see this baby come out.

And then I push him out, this beautiful new life, and it was like we had planned it that way all along.

He was meant to be born in the hospital. I just didn't know it until I got there.

I had promised myself that I would never, ever put myself or my child in a place like that. Watching my parents go through their suffering, the awful smell, the dirty floor—I had promised myself that I wouldn't end up there.

But then I did end up there, and it happened to be the most beautiful experience of my life.

What could I do but embrace it? What could I feel besides overwhelming joy?

When we teach and talk about karma, we often say, "The things that we resist, persist." The fears that we resist or we avoid end up coming up again and again in our lives. Because that fear is meant to show us something. It's meant to teach us something, if we'll just pay attention.

In all your journeys forward, in all your trials and triumphs and striving for your dreams, don't forget the beauty of surrender. Don't forget to embrace the space that you find yourself in. Let yourself go, let yourself release, and in those moments, when you give birth to your fears, let yourself just *be*.

Now go fly forward.

Love,
Neeta

Resources

For a list of additional resources mentioned
throughout the book, including declaration worksheets,
guides, and free audios, as well as accompanying
printable downloads to begin deepening your journey
while also sharing with your communities, head to
thatsuckednowwhat.com/resources.

Acknowledgments

What an incredibly divine gift this entire process has been. I first would love to celebrate my co-pilot and #1 cheerleader always, Ajit Nawalkha. From the moment I shared the vision of this book with you, you have always been the illumination path lighting the way for me to shine. Thank you for holding our children and balancing the act as we knew it was going to be a fun ride with both littles immediately at the same time birthing this book. To my little Arie, thank you for being the best teacher in expanding my emotional capacity—challenging me to stretch and expand into areas I have not yet reached. I'm better because of it all. For Aiyla Rey, our queen who arrived at the same time as the nascent stages of this masterpiece—birthing both of you simultaneously was such a gift. You gave me the freedom to let go of any perfectionism and lean into wisdom and full support so I could trust my inner knowing and pour my heart out in voice notes and on paper. You activated that Shakti energy with SO much flow and ease.

To my brother, Vinay—thank you for the memories, the adventure, the highs and lows. We've come such a long way and I'm so grateful you've been there through all of the feels. To my dear Bhua and Uncle Glenn, my pseudo parents, my hard rocks, thank you for your gifts in shaping me for who I am—and how we got here, what a life we've built together!

To my dear agent, Steve! From the very beginning we had a truly deep connection. Thank you for always cheering me on, believing in me, and always desiring the best vision for this book—what a gift you are, and I couldn't have wanted anyone else by my side.

For the team at Meghan Stevenson—wow from the very beginning, the inception of this idea, and our discussions around it. Meghan, thank you for helping pull out the very essence of what this book was meant to shape and create, thank you for what you do for SO many authors—providing a solid foundation for other authors to fly forward—thank you, thank you!

Thank you to the entire team at Hay House, especially Anne Barthel—you knew how to shape and mold this book to have the voice that it needed to spread its wings.

To my dear colleagues who took the time to help brainstorm, Miki, Sahara—thank you, queens, without you there wouldn't be the edge it deserved to make it accessible to SO many. Let's embrace more sucky moments and rise from them like goddesses.

To my dear bestie Jason, for all the back and forth—you always knew how to make me laugh during the crazy bits! Now for my absolutely epic dream team: Sigute, Fran, Stacey, Jill, Christine, and Olivia—my heart is overflowing with gratitude for how much love you've shown this book from its inception, with every chapter, every outline, and every story. Thank you for giving it that same love as forever students, normalizing our shitty moments with a little more color and depth.

To my ladies who inspire me to rise greater, Jenni, Selena, Emily, and Vasavi, I SO adore each and every one of you, and am beyond lucky to have you around me as pillars of support, friendship, and no-BS, keeping it 100 percent real and authentic. Thanks for holding my hand at times and pushing this book beyond the edges it deserves. To all of my clients whose stories inspired many of the chapters of this book, thank you for creating ripple effects for healing and transformation.

Finally, last but certainly not least, thank you to my collaborator, master interviewer, right-hand sidekick, who many times was my brain while I nursed Aiyla during our heartstorming weekly calls, who helped organize my thoughts during late-night voxers around every morsel of this book—Blair. Without you, this book would not be here, without you going to the depths and visiting the duality of every emotion, every story, every fiber you emulated as yours—you have such a gift—thank you for embodying the essence in the craft of what was meant to flow. Like a beautifully synchronized orchestra, it was magic. You have sparked a fire within me, making it possible to add the spunk and sass along with the sweet serenity which has been the magic of this book. Thank you for pulling out the pieces like a true detective and being wicked patient with me during times of revision like a mad scientist—knowing that thousands of readers would benefit. My heart is forever grateful.

For my colleagues and friends near and far who asked, and ignited conversations around *The Brave Table* podcast, and who were so eager to have this book birthed into the wild, thank you for being great supporters, listeners, storytellers, and evangelists for the book—you know who you are.

Finally, to each of you readers, my followers—you are the true gift. Thank you for DM'ing me, submitting e-mails that were long and that you apologized for, while sharing your most vulnerable human moments—it's because of you I am inspired to do this work daily. Thank you and keep on being brave.

About the Author

Dr. Neeta Bhushan is a cosmetic dentist turned three-time international best-selling author and world-renowned emotional health advocate. She is also the founder of Global Grit Institute, a wellness education platform for optimizing well-being, and co-founder of Dharma Coaching Institute, a coaching organization training coaches to become the highest versions of themselves. Neeta has shared her thought leadership on grit and resilience on international stages and as the host of her top-rated podcast, *The Brave Table*.

After realizing how trapped she felt running the million-dollar dental practice she built, Neeta embarked on a journey that led her across 45 countries as she researched the intersection of human behavior, ancient wisdom, Eastern philosophy, and therapeutic psychology. That knowledge, along with other life experiences overcoming multiple adversities, which include being orphaned at a young age, surviving an abusive marriage, and extensive loss, contributed to the powerful message of resilience she shares in this book. Neeta is a mother of two and currently lives in Austin, Texas, with her husband and children.

www.neetabushan.com

Hay House Titles of Related Interest

YOU CAN HEAL YOUR LIFE, the movie, starring Louise Hay & Friends
(available as an online streaming video)
www.hayhouse.com/louise-movie

THE SHIFT, the movie,
starring Dr. Wayne W. Dyer
(available as an online streaming video)
www.hayhouse.com/the-shift-movie

*   *   *

BE YOUR FUTURE SELF NOW: The Science of Intentional Transformation,
by Dr. Benjamin Hardy

*THE DHARMA IN DIFFICULT TIMES: Finding Your Calling in Times of
Loss, Change, Struggle, and Doubt*, by Stephen Cope

*F THE SHOULDS, DO THE WANTS: Get Clear on Who You Are, What You
Want, and Why You Want It*, by Tricia Huffman

*HAPPY DAYS: The Guided Path from Trauma to Profound Freedom and Inner
Peace*, by Gabrielle Bernstein

All of the above are available at your local bookstore,
or may be ordered by contacting Hay House (see next page).

*   *   *

We hope you enjoyed this Hay House book. If you'd like to receive our online catalog featuring additional information on Hay House books and products, or if you'd like to find out more about the Hay Foundation, please contact:

Hay House, Inc., P.O. Box 5100, Carlsbad, CA 92018-5100
(760) 431-7695 or (800) 654-5126
(760) 431-6948 (fax) or (800) 650-5115 (fax)
www.hayhouse.com® • www.hayfoundation.org

———

Published in Australia by: Hay House Australia Pty. Ltd.,
18/36 Ralph St., Alexandria NSW 2015
Phone: 612-9669-4299 • *Fax:* 612-9669-4144
www.hayhouse.com.au

Published in the United Kingdom by: Hay House UK, Ltd.,
The Sixth Floor, Watson House, 54 Baker Street, London W1U 7BU
Phone: +44 (0)20 3927 7290 • *Fax:* +44 (0)20 3927 7291
www.hayhouse.co.uk

Published in India by: Hay House Publishers India,
Muskaan Complex, Plot No. 3, B-2, Vasant Kunj, New Delhi 110 070
Phone: 91-11-4176-1620 • *Fax:* 91-11-4176-1630
www.hayhouse.co.in

———

<u>Access New Knowledge.</u>
<u>Anytime. Anywhere.</u>

Learn and evolve at your own pace
with the world's leading experts.

www.hayhouseU.com

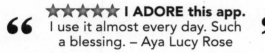

Hay House Podcasts
Bring Fresh, Free Inspiration Each Week!

Hay House proudly offers a selection of life-changing audio content via our most popular podcasts!

Hay House Meditations Podcast

Features your favorite Hay House authors guiding you through meditations designed to help you relax and rejuvenate. Take their words into your soul and cruise through the week!

Dr. Wayne W. Dyer Podcast

Discover the timeless wisdom of Dr. Wayne W. Dyer, world-renowned spiritual teacher and affectionately known as "the father of motivation." Each week brings some of the best selections from the 10-year span of Dr. Dyer's talk show on Hay House Radio.

Hay House Podcast

Enjoy a selection of insightful and inspiring lectures from Hay House Live events, listen to some of the best moments from previous Hay House Radio episodes, and tune in for exclusive interviews and behind-the-scenes audio segments featuring leading experts in the fields of alternative health, self-development, intuitive medicine, success, and more! Get motivated to live your best life possible by subscribing to the free Hay House Podcast.

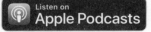

Find Hay House podcasts on iTunes, or visit www.HayHouse.com/podcasts for more info.